ESRI

THE ECONOMIC AND SOCIAL RESEARCH INSTITUTE

The Economic and Social Research Institute (ESRI) is a non-profit organisation which was founded in 1960 as The Economic Research Institute. The Institute is a private company, limited by guarantee, and enjoys full academic independence. It is governed by a Council consisting of 32 members who are representative of business, trade unions, government departments, state agencies, universities and other research institutes.

NCCA
National Council for Curriculum and Assessment
An Chomhairle Náisiúnta Curaclaim agus Measúnachta

The National Council for Curriculum and Assessment

The National Council for Curriculum and Assessment (NCCA) is the statutory body that advises the Minister for Education and Science on curriculum and assessment for early childhood, primary and post-primary education. The Council is a representative structure, the membership of which is determined by the Minister.

MOVING UP

The Experiences of First-Year Students in Post-Primary Education

Emer Smyth, Selina McCoy
and *Merike Darmody*

The Liffey Press
in association with
The Economic and Social Research Institute

Published by
The Liffey Press
Ashbrook House
10 Main Street
Raheny, Dublin 5, Ireland
www.theliffeypress.com

A catalogue record of this book is
available from the British Library.

ISBN 1-904148-51-4

This study was funded by the National Council
for Curriculum and Assessment (NCCA)

Printed in the Republic of Ireland by ColourBooks Ltd.

CONTENTS

LIST OF TABLES

LIST OF FIGURES

ACKNOWLEDGEMENTS

This study was commissioned by the National Council for Curriculum and Assessment (NCCA). We are particularly grateful to Anne Looney, John Hammond and Peter Johnson for their extremely helpful support and assistance during the course of the research. The study benefited from discussions of preliminary findings with the Junior Cycle Review Committee and the Council of the NCCA.

The study would not have been possible without the assistance of school principals, teachers, first year students and their parents. We would like to express our sincere gratitude for the time and effort invested by the case-study schools in the research process.

We are particularly grateful to Michael O'Leary, St Patrick's College, for his invaluable advice on the use of reading and mathematics tests. Helpful comments on earlier drafts of the study were given by our colleagues, Dorothy Watson, Tim Callan, Philip O'Connell and Brendan Whelan. We would like to thank Helen O'Gara of the Educational Research Centre for her efficiency in processing the student test scores. Pat Hopkins is to be thanked for her, as always, efficient production of copies of the many versions of the book.

Any remaining errors or omissions are the sole responsibility of the authors.

Chapter One

INTRODUCTION

The transition from primary to post-primary education has been recognised as a crucial stage in young people's schooling career. Young people's experiences of the transition process can influence their subsequent academic and social development and difficulties during the transfer from primary to post-primary school can contribute to later educational failure. The transition from primary to post-primary education has been the focus of a good deal of research internationally with studies focusing on students' social adjustment to their new school as well as changes in the learning environment (see, for example, Hargreaves and Galton, 2002; Eccles et al., 1993; Gutman and Midgley, 2000). In Ireland, research has begun to emerge on young people's experiences of the transition process (Ó Dalaigh and Aherne, 1990; Naughton, 2000; O'Brien, 2001). However, most existing research focuses on the psycho-social adjustment involved in making the transition from primary to post-primary school, with only a few studies addressing issues related to curriculum and learning in a systematic way (Galton et al., 1999; Lord and Harland, 2000). This study sets out to examine the experiences of first-year students in terms of both their adjustment to post-primary education and their perceptions of the curriculum and learning within junior cycle.

The following section places the study within the context of existing research on the transition from primary to post-primary education in Ireland and internationally. The objectives of the study are outlined in section two while the way in which the study was carried out is described in section three.

1.1 RESEARCH ON THE TRANSITION FROM PRIMARY TO POST-PRIMARY EDUCATION

This section outlines the existing research in relation to: student anxieties and expectations about moving to post-primary school; personal and social factors influencing the transition process, including parental support and student personality; organisational and institutional factors shaping the transition, including the move to a bigger school and a different approach to discipline; and academic factors affecting the transfer to post-primary school.

1.1.1 Pre-transition anxieties and expectations

Anticipating the move to post-primary school is found to cause a certain amount of anxiety for the majority of prospective first-year students. At the same time, most of the students are looking forward to moving into the "big school". In Ireland, O'Brien (2001) explored the issue of pre-transition anxieties and expectations using essays written by students in the sixth class of primary school. These essays suggested a tension between feeling excited about going to post-primary school and feeling anxious; a similar ambiguity was reported by Naughton (2000) and by Hargreaves and Galton (2002) in the British context. The main anxieties centred on fear of being bullied, changes in friendships and relations with teachers. Lucey and Reay (2000) and Naughton (2000) suggest that students' conceptions of post-primary school are greatly influenced by the horror stories and "urban myths" about "rites of passage" communicated to them by their peers. A number of organisational factors, including disciplinary procedures, timetables, more difficult work, increased homework, having several teachers and subjects, and changing classrooms were also found to contribute to pre-transfer anxieties (Naughton, 2000; O'Brien, 2001). Girls are found to express more anxiety than boys about transferring to the new school (Hargreaves and Galton, 2002; O'Brien, 2001). O'Brien (2001) reports that students in designated disadvantaged schools appear more reluctant to transfer to post-primary school and were worried about more difficult schoolwork in the new school. Concern about post-primary school was also expressed by those students who did not secure a place in the school of their choice.

In spite of anxieties about making the transition to post-primary school, research has found that only a minority of students experience serious difficulties once they have moved to the new school (O'Brien, 2001; Hargreaves and Galton, 2002). The kinds of students who experience the greatest difficulties are discussed in the following sections.

1.1.2. Personal and social factors influencing the transition

There are various personal and social factors that affect students' transition experiences and their adjustment to post-primary schooling. These factors include family background, student personality and self-confidence, the process of adolescent development, interaction with peer groups and teachers, bullying, and preparation for transfer (Franklin and Madge, 2001; Galton, Gray and Rudduck, 2003; Hirsch and Rapkin, 1987). The following sections discuss these factors in greater detail.

Family background

The relationship between socio-economic background and educational outcomes has been well documented internationally. Students from lower income and minority ethnic groups have been found to be potentially more "at risk" in making the transition to post-primary school (Gutman and Midgley, 2000). Over and above the effect of objective socio-economic characteristics, parental support has been found to be a crucial factor in facilitating young people's successful integration into post-primary education (Anderson et al., 2000). The nature of authority structures within the family also influences the transition process. In one US study, the opportunity to participate in family decision-making was predictive of better adjustment to junior high school while young people whose parents did not involve them in decision-making fared more poorly (Eccles et al., 1993). Similarly, Lord et al. (1994) find that adolescents' perceptions of their family environment influence their adjustment to junior high school. Young people who report a democratic family environment tend to have higher self-esteem and are more positive about their experiences of school. Successful adjustment to the new school was associated with parents' support of their child's autonomy, the quality of the affective relationship between the parent and adolescent, and parents' investment in providing opportunities for their children outside of the home (Lord et al., 1994).

Student personality and self-concept

A number of studies have indicated the consequences of the transition to post-primary education for students' view of themselves and their academic abilities. Wigfield et al. (1991) explored young people's specific self-concept in four domains (Maths, English, social activities and sports), along with a more global measure of self-esteem. They found that, in the United States, self-esteem scores declined across the transition to junior high school, but increased again subsequently. Self-concept in relation to specific performance domains (such as Maths and English) also diminished due to changes in the school and classroom environments to which students were exposed. However, while young people on average became more negative in their view of themselves during the transition process, some groups of students were relatively "protected" from this decline. Lord, Eccles and McCarthy (1994) argue that greater confidence in one's academic, social and athletic abilities in the sixth grade is associated with gains in one's self-esteem following the transition to junior high school. Sixth grade self-esteem and academic ability predicted both the extent to which adolescents reported liking junior high school and parents' rating of their children's adjustment to the transition. Students' perception of their social skills was the single best predictor of successful adjustment.

Gender differences are also apparent in the relationship between self-concept and adjustment to the new school. Girls are found to report more feelings of depression than boys over the transition process (Hirsch and Rapkin, 1987). Lord et al. (1994) discovered in their study that perceptions of one's own physical appearance was a more important predictor of increasing self-esteem for girls than for boys while self-consciousness about classroom performance was a more important predictor of declines in self-esteem for boys than for girls. Thus, for girls transition difficulties tend to relate to their social relationships while for boys difficulties tend to centre on academic issues. Girls and boys are found to respond to the new school environment in different ways: while boys become more competitive, attention- and status-seeking, girls tend to retreat into girls' only groups, avoiding contact and social comparisons with boys (Jackson and Warin, 2000).

It should be noted that aspects of young people's self-concept are not fixed and are responsive to the home and school environment. More positive self-ratings are associated with experiencing academic achievement, having positive interactions with teachers and receiving parental support (Lord et al., 1994; Ross and Broh, 2000; Smyth, 1999). In other words, students who have received support and encouragement at home and school tend to have more positive views of themselves and their abilities.

Adolescence

Adolescence is seen in western cultures as a bridge between childhood and adulthood (Naughton, 2000). Adolescence is a time of self-discovery, emerging independence, and physical and emotional growth and young people's experiences at the time, including in the educational sphere, can have life-long consequences (Gutman and Midgley, 2000). The biological and physiological changes associated with early adolescence coincide with the changes in the social and learning environment that characterise the transition to post-primary education. Eccles et al. (1993) suggest that the mismatch between the needs of developing adolescents and the restricted opportunities afforded them by their social environments, including their opportunities to participate in classroom decision-making, may contribute to transition difficulties.

Relationships with peers

The transition from primary to post-primary education means the disruption of friendship patterns if, as commonly occurs, students from the same primary school transfer to different post-primary schools. This is especially important as peer groups come to assume a more prominent role in the lives of adolescents (Gutman and Midgley, 2000). Lord et al. (1994) argue that early adolescence, which coincides with the transition from primary to post-primary schooling in many western countries, can also be characterised by an increased emphasis on physical appearance and social presentation. Confidence in one's competence in peer relationships and social skills is, therefore, particularly important for young adolescents. Crockett and Losoff (1984) found that the importance of friendship and peer groups increased over time and investment in social networks took up a considerable proportion of adolescents' free time.

In a new school setting students need to re-negotiate their friendships and social networks. This issue is often more salient for girls than for boys. On moving to secondary school, girls tend to stay in primary school-defined groups while boys mix in broader groups, for example, through communal games of football (Hargreaves and Galton, 2002). Interactions with friends may be beneficial to children's learning as they may feel more comfortable in the learning environment and less subject to competitive pressure (Demetriou et al., 2000). School policy to retain students in friendship dyads or groups appear, therefore, to reduce anxiety around the transition process. However, difficulties may arise if there is a tension between the student's learning goals and that of the group; a student within an anti-work peer group may find it difficult to resist the pressure of their peers (Demetriou et al., 2000). Moving into post-primary school also involves a change in status for students who move from being the older students in their primary school to being the youngest students in their new school. Being the youngest in the school and knowing very few classmates may cause a heightened concern about their status in relation to their peers (Eccles et al., 1993).

This change in status is often seen as making students more vulnerable to bullying by their peers. Fear of being bullied is a common focus of anxiety before students make the transition to post-primary school (O'Brien, 2001). However, this is not just an "urban myth" since bullying in terms of physical, verbal or indirect aggression is a feature of many school contexts (Ma et al., 2001). Bullying is seen as one way in which young adolescents manage peer and dominance relationships as they make the transition into new social groups. Thus, bullying may be used for displays of dominance whereby boys target other boys (Pellegrini and Long, 2002). Rates of bullying are generally found to decrease after the initial transition into post-primary schooling.

Relationships with teachers

A number of studies stress the importance of teacher support to students in the transition process (Hargreaves and Tickle, 1980; Gutman and Midgley, 2000). Eccles et al. (1993) suggest that a transition into a less supportive classroom will have a negative impact on adolescents' interest in the subject matter being taught in that classroom. The decline is especially problematic during early adolescence when children are in particular need of close relationships with adults outside their homes. However, relations between teachers and students at post-primary level are often quite different from those at primary level. Because of the increased number of students and the separation into different subjects, teachers are less likely to know students personally within secondary schools (Lord et al., 1994) and the relations between teachers and students often deteriorate after the transition (Eccles et al., 1993). Furthermore, teacher expectations may be lower for some groups of students, especially those from lower socio-economic backgrounds (Gutman and Midgley, 2000).

Preparation for transfer

While individual student characteristics may be predictive of successful adjustment to post-primary school, the way in which the transition process is handled by schools is also a key factor. Anderson et al. (2000) argue that adequate preparation is key to a successful transition. They maintain that there is a need for a planned, multi-faceted and long-term effort which involves parents, children and school staff. Hargreaves and Galton (2002) have found that the prevalence of structured programmes to facilitate the transition has increased since the 1970s in Britain. Such programmes may reduce student anxiety about making the transition (Berliner, 1993; Reyes et al., 1994). However, such initiatives are only likely to be successful if they engage with students' own concerns: "their value lies in bringing the largely imagined world of the secondary school into the 'known' experience of the Year 6 child" (Lucey and Reay, 2000, p. 202). Furthermore, transfer programmes have often been found to neglect issues to do with differences between primary and secondary school in curriculum, teaching methods and learning goals (Hargreaves and Galton, 2002).

1.1.3 Organisational and institutional issues in the transition from primary to post-primary education

Students encounter a range of, almost universal, organisational changes as they transfer from primary to post-primary schooling. These changes are largely reflective of the different organisational and administrative contexts of primary and post-primary schools, their differing educational aims and philosophies, and their differing physical and social environments. Among the main adjustments to be made by students are changes in the physical environment and school size, the number of teachers and subjects, the longer school day, the structured timetable, the way in which subjects are taught and the nature of rules and discipline. These changes correspond with the move from a child-centred primary school system to a post-primary system characterised by teacher and subject differentiation. As one study noted, the move is from a generalist environment, in terms of both the physical classroom environment and teacher background, into one with a more specialist subject focus (Ferguson and Fraser, 1999).

> The prospect of going to "big school" presents children with a dilemma central to the experience of "growing up"; that in order to gain freedom and autonomy from adult regulation one must be willing to relinquish some measure of the protection which that regulation affords (Lucey and Reay, 2000, p. 203).

Primary/Post-primary divide

Central to the distinction between primary and post-primary education in Ireland are the discrete organisational, administrative and training systems of the two sectors. The separateness of school buildings, fundamentally different pre-service education for teachers at both levels, separate teacher representative bodies, separate curriculum and assessment planning (OECD, 1991) are all contributors to the gulf that exists between the primary and post-primary sectors in Ireland (Naughton, 2000). In its 1991 Report, the OECD commented on the "often quite distant" relations between the sectors, with poor communication and flow of information. This contrasts with the greater emphasis on structured programmes to facilitate the transition in other educational systems (see, for example, Hargreaves and Galton, 2002, on the British context).

Similarly, the long-term traditional separation of the primary and post-primary sectors in Ireland is identified by Burke (1987) as being responsible for difficulties experienced by pupils in transferring from one level to the other. Burke argues that difficulties relate to the new subjects taken by students, more structured time-tabling, having more teachers, different teaching methods and differences in the underlying philosophy of the two sectors:

> One of the root causes of the transition problem is the fundamental differences that exist between the philosophy underlying the traditional approach to education, which is still the dominant philosophy of second-level education in Ireland, and the thinking behind the new approach at first level [child-centred, informal and progressive] (Burke, 1987, p. 6).

In a similar vein, O'Brien (2001) comments, in general there is "a gulf in the curriculum and the approach to learning between first and second levels" (p. 85). In particular, the distance between the culture of "care" in the primary school and the academic and exam-oriented culture of post-primary education was seen as a major obstacle to successful transfer. Furthermore, several commentators have referred to the impact of differences in the nature of pre-service training provided to teachers at primary and post-primary levels (Naughton, 2000; Burke, 1987). The need for co-ordination, or at least commonalities, in the training of primary and post-primary teachers is raised as a means of addressing these issues (Burke, 1987). These commentators refer to the situation as it related to the 1971 primary curriculum; it is possible that the difference in approaches between primary and post-primary schools may become even more marked when the 1999 revised primary curriculum, with its emphasis on the child as active learner, comes fully on stream.

Information flow between primary and post-primary schools

The issue of the nature and extent of information flow from the primary to the post-primary system and the extent to which such information is accessible and utilised has received scant attention in the literature, particularly in Ireland. In the UK, McCallum (2000) looked at the range of information transferred from primary to secondary schools: such information included meetings between heads of first year in second level and primary school students during the year prior to transfer; the use of transfer sheets filled in by the primary school teacher covering areas such as comments on attitude, behaviour, attendance, comments on social circumstances, statements of special needs and any talents or expertise; samples of the student's work, written narrative reports and record of achievement folders, as well as assessment test results. The research showed wide variability in terms of the accessibility of such material to secondary school staff; in some schools, all teachers had access while in others, access was restricted to heads of departments, tutors or those working with special needs students only. In addition, the extent to which such information was used in assigning students, ensuring curriculum continuity and meeting special needs varied widely; overall, a great deal of the information was not used, with a resulting lack of curriculum continuity for students. Some schools simply conducted their own assessment tests upon entry and failed to use any of the information received from the primary schools. Overall, the study found that there was little acceptance of other teachers' assessments of students.

Galton et al. (2000) similarly found that many secondary principals in Britain never looked at the transfer documents that were passed on from primary schools, maintaining that secondary teachers could more efficiently ascertain a child's ability in their specialist subject without reference to primary records, particularly since these were often regarded by secondary teachers as vague and sometimes misleading.

Physical environment/school size

A key aspect of the post-primary school which may represent a major area of change for the student is the physical environment of the school; its size, location, facilities and appearance. Naughton (2003) observes that, owing to their community-based function, primary schools tend to be smaller on average than post-primary schools. Economies of scale also demand that resources be concentrated in larger units at post-primary level. The smaller primary system is generally perceived as being more supportive and "intimate", while the larger post-primary setting is seen as more informal and less personal. Similarly, Burke (1987) noted that parents often perceived the larger size and organisation of the post-primary school as a factor that made it less personal and more formal. Some parents believed that it was easier for students to go unnoticed at post-primary level than was the case in primary school because of the greater number of teachers in contact with their child, as well as the larger size.

Many studies have observed the initial feelings of confusion and loss as students become familiar with the layout and structure of their new school (O'Brien, 2001; Jackson and Warin, 2000). However, most studies found students adapted quickly and without any serious difficulties to the larger post-primary school. The layout of the post-primary school, and, in particular corridors, stairs and signs, have been found to be important in facilitating this adjustment (Bryant, 1980 in Lucey and Reay, 2000).

Schools also vary widely in the nature and comprehensiveness of their facilities, both academic and sports-related, which research has shown to play an important role in the process of adjustment to the post-primary school, as well as to levels of engagement and ultimately educational success and attainment (Galton et al., 2003; McCoy, 2000; Smyth, 1999). Pupil participation in a range of "non-curricular" activities, such as music, drama and extra-curricular sports, was found to be particularly important in promoting retention within the educational system (McCoy, 2000). However, levels of resources available for the provision of such activities vary across schools, with schools which are less likely to be able to draw on additional "voluntary" funding from parents at a disadvantage.

Structure of the day

The transition to a more subject-centred curriculum also requires students to become familiar with highly structured timetables.[1] In particular, the use of a timetable requires that students become organised to a degree that was not necessary in the more student-centred primary setting. Most Irish studies (see, for example, O'Brien, 2001) have found that, while the timetable might be daunting for students initially in terms of finding rooms and being organised enough to have the correct books for their classes, the majority of students come to terms with the management of the timetable within the first few weeks.

---

[1] While timetables may be used at primary level, they are unlikely to be as structured as those used at post-primary level where students are required to change teachers and often location at set times.

Students typically must also adapt to a longer school day upon entering the post-primary school. This was identified as a particular problem for students attending schools in more remote rural areas. O'Brien (2001) found that parents of students in small rural schools had concerns for their children leaving the familial environment of their primary school and travelling sometimes on local transport, others on school buses, to their new post-primary schools. This necessitated longer days in order to travel on top of the already longer post-primary school day.

Rules and discipline

Some studies have also pointed to changes in the nature of rules and discipline as students move from the primary to post-primary system. In a recent Irish study, O'Brien (2001) found that half of the students in her study perceived the code of discipline in their post-primary school to be harsher with more rules to observe than at primary level. Rules relating to uniform and style were also seen by students as being monitored more strictly at post-primary level and were generally seen to be more restrictive than at primary level. In line with Drudy and Lynch (1993), post-primary schools are held to be characterised by a culture of control and a greater level of formality than transferring first-year students are accustomed to.

1.1.4 Academic factors affecting the transition from primary to post-primary school

Much of the international research on the transition from primary to post-primary education has focused on students' social adjustment to school life rather than on their experiences of learning (Galton, Morrison, Pell, 2000). However, for students, the transition means being confronted with many new academic subjects, having several teachers rather than one and, in many cases, experiencing different teaching methods.

A central issue emerging from existing research is the lack of curriculum continuity between the primary and post-primary levels. Observation of classroom practices in Britain in the 1970s indicated little continuity in terms of curriculum content or teaching methods. In subjects such as Maths, students were faced with new terminology and new ways of carrying out procedures (Galton et al., 2000). The introduction of the National Curriculum in Britain was found to change the nature of primary teaching with senior classes in primary schools becoming more like secondary schools had been in the 1970s (Hargreaves and Galton, 2002). However, a lack of continuity persisted between primary and secondary levels, with different content and language in some subjects, a repetition of familiar skills and knowledge in some cases and little attempt to find out what pupils had actually done at primary school (Hargreaves and Galton, 2002). In spite of improvements in transfer procedures between primary and secondary schools in Britain, curriculum and teaching methods have remained largely unchanged and induction programmes rarely discuss the new ways of learning and styles of teaching evident in secondary school (Hargreaves and Galton, 2002). Similarly, a study of curriculum in Northern Ireland indicated a variation in the knowledge and skills of pupils transferring from different primary schools, some pupils entering secondary level without the expected skills and some repetition of material previously covered by pupils (Harland et al., 2002). Low attainers were less likely than high attainers to feel their primary school had prepared them well for their secondary studies. A similar discontinuity between the primary and secondary levels has been documented in the North American and New Zealand contexts (Walsh, 1995; Ward, 2000).

Teaching methods were also found to differ between primary and post-primary levels with a shift from an emphasis on student involvement in discussion to one where students were expected to listen to the teacher (Stables, 1995). Compared with primary school, there is more emphasis on setting exercises based on the textbook or worksheets and few opportunities for group discussion or hands-on experimentation; there are more adult-dominated teacher-pupil exchanges with the emphasis on imparting information (Hargreaves and Galton, 2002). The transition has been characterised as a move from a pupil-centred environment to a more structured, teacher-dominated one (Ward, 2000). In the Irish context, it has been argued that, in spite of curriculum reform, little has changed in teaching methods within lower post-primary education with the emphasis on instruction rather than participation (Gleeson, 2000; Callan, 1997; NCCA, 1999; Naughton, 2003). The quality of teacher–

student interactions is also found to change over the transition with
teachers being seen by students as less helpful, friendly and understanding at post-primary level than at primary level (Ferguson and Fraser,
1999). Some students in Britain report greater differences between their
primary and secondary schools than others with attitudes among students
from attached primary schools being more positive while students from
smaller primary schools reported less positive interaction with secondary
teachers (Ferguson and Fraser, 1999).

Social rather than academic concerns often predominate in the minds
of students before transferring to post-primary school (Hargreaves and
Galton, 2002). However, many students in a New Zealand study were
found to be concerned with the difficulty of school-work and about the
amount of homework they would receive (Ward, 2000) and students in a
British study were "not looking forward" to Maths, homework and English (Hargreaves and Galton, 2002). The transition is found to be associated with different academic standards and exposure to a wider variety of
subject areas taught by different teachers (Walsh, 1995).

Lack of curriculum continuity along with changes in teaching methods have been seen to have implications for student academic progress in
the first year of secondary school. A study from the 1970s in Britain indicated that over forty per cent of students failed to make progress in
English, Maths and reading comprehension following transfer (Galton
and Willcocks, 1983). However, this analysis was based on fewer than a
hundred pupils and the differences in scores were relatively small. It is
probably more appropriate to say that students have been found to experience an *interruption* in progress rather than a *decline* in overall performance. A dip in progress was also apparent among students in the
1990s, even though the introduction of the National Curriculum in Britain had been intended to improve curriculum continuity across the two
levels (Hargreaves and Galton, 2002).

A decline in grades (and school attendance) following the transition
to high school has also been documented in the American context (Reyes
et al., 1994; Crockett et al., 1989; Simmons and Blyth, 1987). This decline has been attributed to differences between the school sectors in relation to educational demands, teacher attitudes and classroom organisation (Eccles et al., 1993). Declines in student performance over the tran-

sition period have been found to be more marked among low income and minority students (Simmons et al., 1991).

Although post-primary school presents academic challenges for students, many students enjoy the new subjects and can cope with their school-work (Harland et al., 2002; O'Brien, 2001). In the early years of post-primary school, students tend to prefer subjects in which they can work with their friends, can make something or engage in discussion (Keys and Fernandes, 1993). Students' views of academic subjects in post-primary school are also found to depend on their relationship with the subject teacher (Measor and Woods, 1984).

Attitudes to school are found to change over the course of the transition process. Student self-esteem, view of their own abilities (academic self-concept) and perceived social ability may decline during the transition process as they are faced with a more academically competitive environment (Wigfield et al., 1991). British research indicates a decline in general self-image but little change in academic self-image (Hargreaves and Galton, 2002). Other studies place these trends in the context of longer term changes in attitudes to school life. By the end of first year, students are found to enjoy school less and be less motivated in relation to their school-work (Galton et al., 2000). The decline in enjoyment of school is most evident among higher ability students, although this group is more confident about their ability to cope with school-work at secondary level (Hargreaves and Galton, 2002). In a study in Northern Ireland, pupils' levels of enjoyment and interest are found to decline in years 9 and 10 (Harland et al., 2002). Keys and Fernandes (1993) also indicate that older cohorts of students are less likely to report liking school or liking teachers, are less interested in their lessons, and have less favourable perceptions of their school's reputation.

In making the transition to post-primary school, many students are placed for the first time in classes grouped on the basis of ability.[2] There has been considerable academic debate about the impact of ability grouping on a range of student outcomes (Harlen and Malcolm, 1997; Ireson and Hallam, 2001) with some studies indicating no effect of grouping on

---

[2] Students in primary school are often divided into within-class groups on the basis of ability, however (see Devine, 1993).

performance (see, for example, Slavin, 1990) and others emphasising the negative effect on those assigned to lower stream classes (see, for example, Oakes, 1985). Within the Irish context, students allocated to lower classes within streamed schools are found to underperform academically, all else being equal (Smyth, 1999). Lynch and Lodge (2002) indicate the negative labelling associated with lower sets or bands with students more likely to consider themselves "outsiders" within the school. Furthermore, lower classes are found to spend a lower proportion of time on task and experience a higher level of negative teacher-student interaction than higher classes.

In the Irish context, there has been no systematic study of the way in which school policy and practice influence student adjustment and learning over the course of the transition from primary to post-primary education. Naughton (2003) stresses the difficulties arising from lack of curriculum continuity and the persistence of traditional pedagogical practices. He finds that post-primary teachers tend to be unfamiliar with the assessment approaches, the curriculum content and the methods of instruction used in sixth class. In spite of concerns on the part of students before moving to post-primary education, O'Brien (2001) finds that students are generally positive about first year after transfer, although they feel their workload has increased. Morgan (in NCCA, 1999) found that school principals considered transition difficulties to be related to literacy and numeracy problems, the increased number of subjects taken and lack of family support. The junior cycle curriculum was seen to be suitable for average and high ability students but it was seen as less suitable for educationally disadvantaged and "at risk" students.

1.2 OBJECTIVES OF THE STUDY

This study sets out to address the gaps in Irish research on how post-primary schools can influence the integration and learning of their students in first year. It seeks to examine the experience of first-year students, in particular their encounter with the curriculum and the psychosocial adjustment involved in transferring from primary to post-primary school.

The central research questions to be addressed in the study are:

1. How do schools vary in the way in which they seek to integrate first-year students into the school?

2. To what extent are different kinds of integration policies associated with greater psycho-social adjustment and initial academic perform-ance among first-year students?

3. How do schools differ in the way in which they organise the curricu-lum for first-year students?

4. How does curricular provision influence the ease of integration into post-primary schooling?

In order to answer these questions, previous research on the transition process was used to derive the following hypotheses:

- It is expected that first-year students will settle in more quickly and experience fewer transition difficulties in schools with more devel-oped programmes designed to integrate students into the school.

- First-year students will make greater academic progress in schools with more highly developed integration policies.

- Exposure to more subjects in the form of a taster programme is hy-pothesised to lead to greater transition difficulties, especially for stu-dents with lower prior ability levels.

The way in which the study was carried out is discussed in the following section.

1.3 RESEARCH METHODOLOGY

Many studies of the transition process focus on tracking a group of stu-dents identified in the final year of primary education into post-primary school (see Hargreaves and Galton, 2002 on the British context; O'Brien, 2001 on the Irish context). However, the concern in this study is with the impact of (variation in) the way in which post-primary schools manage the transfer and learning process on student experiences of first year. Such a study requires that we capture the important dimensions of varia-tion among post-primary schools (for example, the prevalence of induction programmes, the use of ability grouping and the timing of subject choice) while, at the same time, having sufficient student numbers in each school to allow us to explore variation among groups of students in terms of gender, social background and prior ability. Given the extent of active school choice among students and their parents in Ireland (see Hannan et al., 1996), students from any given primary school are likely to transfer to a large number of post-primary schools with very different approaches to subject choice, ability grouping and student integration. Following students from the primary school could, therefore, result in having only a small number of students from the targeted primary school in any given post-primary school. As a result of these potential difficulties, the study examines the transition process from the perspective of the post-primary school. This approach inevitably results in a loss of information on student experiences before the transfer to post-primary education. It should also be noted that the findings will reflect the views of post-primary management and teachers on the transition process. A study of views among primary teachers may highlight different issues. In spite of these potential limitations, the approach taken does provide us with rich data on the quality of, and variation in, student experiences over the course of first year and allows us to identify aspects of policy and practice which facilitate student integration into post-primary education.

The study was carried out in four main phases which involved gathering information from a number of different sources, including principals, teachers, students and parents.

1.3.1 Survey of school principals

In order to explore the way in which post-primary schools manage the transition process, a postal survey of all post-primary school principals was carried out in early 2002. The questionnaire covered issues relating to the transition from primary to post-primary schooling, support structures for first-year students, approaches to subject choice and ability grouping along with perceptions of the junior cycle curriculum. (The questionnaire is available from the ESRI and NCCA websites.) There was a high response rate (78 per cent) to the survey, with a total number of 567 principals participating in the survey. Data from the postal survey allowed us to relate the pattern of variation in first-year provision to school characteristics, including school size, gender mix and whether the school is designated disadvantaged (see Chapter Two).

Figure 1.1 shows the position of the selected schools in relation to the three dimensions specified; pseudonyms are used to identify the schools. As mentioned above, the schools were identified on the basis of information within the postal questionnaires sent to school principals. The information on the school's approach to student integration related, by necessity, to the *number* of interventions in place rather than the *quality* of such programmes. When more detailed information was gathered from the case-study schools, it was evident that three of the schools (Dixon St, Wattle St and Wynyard Rd) had a stronger emphasis on student integration than was apparent from the postal survey responses. These schools can therefore be regarded as closer to the "stronger emphasis" schools in terms of their policy and practice. This issue is further discussed in Chapter Three below. The profile of the selected schools in terms of size, sector and social mix is outlined in Figure 1.2. The twelve schools came from a wide geographical spread.

Figure 1.1: Theoretical sample of case-study schools

Subject Choice		Student Integration	
		Less Emphasis	*Stronger Emphasis*
Early	Mixed ability	Barrack St Wattle St	Dawson St
	Streamed/banded	Park St Hay St	Dawes Point
Later (taster)	Mixed ability	Wynyard Rd	Fig Lane Belmore St
	Streamed/banded	Dixon St	Lang St Wentworth Place

Note: Pseudonyms are used to identify the schools.

A review of the relevant literature (see above) indicated that three aspects of school practice were likely to be crucial in shaping students' experiences of the transition process: the school's approach to integrating first-year students into the school, the school's approach to subject choice and the approach to ability grouping. On the basis of information collected through the postal survey of principals across all post-primary schools, a "theoretical sample" of case-study schools was selected in terms of these three main dimensions. This theoretical sample was designed to directly test the impact of school practice on students' experiences within first year. As well as taking account of the main dimensions of school practice being investigated, efforts were made to achieve a mix of schools in terms of sector, gender mix, disadvantaged status and region.

Figure 1.2: Profile of case-study schools

School	Size	Sector	Social Mix
Dawson St	Medium	Community/ comprehensive	Mixed
Lang St	Small	Vocational	Working-class; disadvantaged
Barrack St	Small	Girls' secondary	Working-class; disadvantaged
Dixon St	Large	Vocational	Working-class; disadvantaged
Park St	Large	Boys' secondary	Mixed
Hay St	Small	Vocational	Working-class
Fig Lane	Large	Coeducational secondary (fee-paying)	Middle-class
Wentworth Place	Large	Boys' secondary	Mixed
Wynyard Road	Small	Girls' secondary	Mixed
Dawes Point	Small	Boys' secondary	Working-class; disadvantaged
Belmore St	Large	Girls' secondary	Mixed
Wattle St	Small	Boys' secondary	Mixed; disadvantaged

1.3.2 Interviews with key personnel and teachers dealing with first-year students

Within each of the twelve case-study schools, in-depth interviews were conducted with key personnel dealing with first-year students. The personnel included school principals, deputy principals, guidance counsellors, year heads for first year, first-year class tutors, home–school liaison co-ordinators, learning support and resource teachers, and other key personnel, such as counsellors and chaplains. These interviews focused on:

- Policy and practice in relation to student transition into post-primary education;

- Support structures for first-year students;

- Perceptions of the needs of first-year students;

- Organisational issues regarding first-year students, including ability grouping and subject choice;

- Parental involvement within the school.

Interviews with a total of 103 key personnel were conducted by two members of the project team in May 2002. These interviews were recorded and transcribed. The transcripts were coded using the QSR N6 software package to systematically identify the main themes emerging from the interviews.

Structured interviews were also conducted with teachers teaching first-years in the twelve case-study schools. A total of 226 teachers were interviewed, making up 93 per cent of all first-year teachers in these schools. The interviews focused on their approach to teaching first-year students, perceptions of the junior cycle curriculum, receipt of information on in-coming students and perceptions of first-year students.

1.3.3 Interviews with students

In September 2002, self-completion questionnaires were administered to incoming first-year students in the case-study schools. The questionnaires focused on student experiences of the transition process, their perceptions of their new school and their views on the curriculum. (A copy of this questionnaire is available from the ESRI and NCCA websites.) Questionnaires were completed by a total of 916 students, making up 91.5 per cent of all first-year students in the twelve schools. Drumcondra Level 6 reading and computation tests were also administered to first-year students to provide a baseline for assessing academic progress over first year.

In order to more fully explore students' own experiences of the transition process, group interviews were conducted by two members of the project team with first-year students in October 2002. One of the case-study schools discontinued their involvement in the project and so was not included in the group interviews, the second wave of the student survey or the interviews with parents. Within the remaining eleven schools, a group of six students from each class was selected at random by the project team from the list of first-year students in the school and students were interviewed within their class groups. A total of 38 group interviews were conducted in the eleven schools, including a total of over two hundred students. These interviews focused on students' expectations of post-primary school, their feelings about making the transition, their views on their new school and aspects of first year they would like to change. These interviews were recorded and transcribed; transcripts were analysed using the QSR N6 package.

In order to monitor changes in students' views over the course of first year, self-completion questionnaires were administered to first-year students in the eleven schools in May 2003. Drumcondra Level 6 tests in reading and computation were once again administered to the student group. Questionnaires were completed by 750 of the original students surveyed, making up 81 per cent of the total first-year intake in the eleven schools. There is some evidence that the attrition rate, that is, the proportion of students surveyed in September who did not complete a questionnaire in May, was higher for students from non-national backgrounds, most likely indicating greater mobility among this group. Furthermore, the attrition rate was higher for those in bottom classes in streamed schools than for those in other class types. The data collected in May were therefore reweighted to take account of attrition by class type and across the different schools. The second round of questionnaires focused on how students had settled into post-primary education and collected more detailed information on their experiences of the different subject areas over the course of first year. (A copy of the questionnaire used in May of first year is available from the ESRI and NCCA websites.)

1.3.4 Interviews with parents

Interviews with parents of first-year students were conducted in order to explore their perceptions of the transition process. The method of approaching parents varied across schools with some schools facilitating direct contact with parents while others acted as intermediaries in approaching parents for interview. As with many other studies, it was difficult to secure a high response among parents (see, for example, O'Brien, 2001). A total of 81 parents were interviewed over the phone. Because of the differences in the extent to which different groups of parents were willing to be interviewed for the study, this group of parents cannot be taken as representative of all parents of first-year students as it is likely to over-represent those who are more actively involved in school life. However, the interviews do provide a useful insight into parental perspectives on the transition process and can be used to contextualise students' own reported experiences.

In sum, a comprehensive range of information was collected on the transition process from a number of different sources. Exploring issues from the perspectives of a range of stakeholders, including students, school management, subject teachers and parents, yields a more complete picture of policy and practice within post-primary schools. A combination of quantitative and qualitative techniques allowed us to explore students' own experiences of the transition process while at the same time placing their accounts within the context of generalisable findings on policy and practice across post-primary schools. The selection of a theoretical sample within which detailed case-studies were conducted allowed us to examine the relationship between key dimensions of how the transition process is managed at the school level and student adjustment to post-primary education. Given the comprehensive nature of the information collected for this study, it is possible to highlight factors which facilitate young people's academic and social adjustment to post-primary education.

1.4 OUTLINE OF THE BOOK

The primary emphasis in this study is on students' own experiences of the transition process. However, it is crucial to place their experiences within the context of policy and practice across different schools. Chapter Two presents findings from the postal survey of school principals to analyse policy and practice regarding the transition process across a range of post-primary schools. Student integration and support structures for first-year students in the twelve case-study schools are discussed in Chapter Three. In Chapter Four, interviews with key personnel and first-year teachers are used to explore curricular provision and learning structures in these schools. Chapters Three and Four therefore provide a context for the information on student perspectives presented in Chapters Five, Six and Seven. Students' own experiences of the transition process are explored in Chapter Five, drawing on the completed questionnaires along with in-depth group interviews with students. Students' views of the first-year curriculum are described in Chapter Six. Chapter Seven looks at changes over the course of first year in students' adjustment to post-primary education, their attitudes to school and their performance in reading and mathematics. Parental perspectives on the transition process are analysed in Chapter Eight. The main findings of the study and the implications for policy are discussed in Chapter Nine.

Chapter Two

SCHOOL INTEGRATION AND FIRST-YEAR CURRICULUM IN POST-PRIMARY SCHOOLS

2.1 INTRODUCTION

This chapter presents the main findings of a postal survey of school principals carried out in early 2002. The questionnaire covered issues relating to the transition from primary to post-primary schooling, support structures for first-year students, approaches to subject choice and ability grouping along with perceptions of the junior cycle curriculum. The total sample size was 567 schools, a response rate of 78 per cent. The data have been reweighted to reflect the profile of school size and type in the population as a whole.[1]

2.2 NATURE OF FIRST-YEAR INTAKE

2.2.1 Changes in first-year intake

Almost half of the participating schools had experienced some decline in their student intake over the previous five years with just one-fifth of schools increasing their student numbers (see Figure 2.1). Declining intake was attributed to local demographic trends and increased competition from existing schools. Such declining intake can result in the loss of one or more teachers from a school. This may have implications for curriculum provision in the school (depending on the subject expertise of the "lost" teacher(s)).

---

[1] The proportion of designated disadvantaged schools within the sample (30 per cent) is also similar to that within the total population of post-primary schools.

Figure 2.1: Change in student intake levels

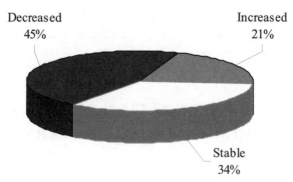

Decreased
45%

Increased
21%

Stable
34%

Student intake is found to have decreased in both urban and other areas.[2] The proportion of schools that reported their student intake as relatively stable does not differ significantly between urban and non-urban schools.

Vocational schools were the most likely to experience a decrease in student intake (51 per cent), slightly higher than the figure for girls' secondary schools (48 per cent) and boys' secondary schools (46 per cent). Coeducational secondary schools were least likely to experience a decrease (30 per cent) and were most likely to gain students: over a quarter of coeducational secondary schools experienced an increase in their student population. The decline in student intake was more pronounced in disadvantaged than in non-disadvantaged schools (see Figure 2.2).

The vast majority (85 per cent) of post-primary schools usually accept all students who apply to the school. Fee-paying schools, larger schools and those in urban areas are more likely to be over-subscribed than other school types. In contrast, vocational schools and designated disadvantaged schools are very unlikely to be over-subscribed. Figure 2.3 presents the criteria described by over-subscribed schools as being very important in deciding which students to accept (schools can mention multiple reasons). The majority of these schools consider it very important to have an older sibling of the new student in the same school. Just under half of selective schools based entry on attending an attached or feeder primary school and living locally. Other factors mentioned included a "first come first served" approach and religious denomination.

---

[2] Of schools participating in the survey, about 30 per cent were from urban areas (defined as being in Dublin, Cork, Galway, Limerick or Waterford).

Figure 2.2: Intake numbers by disadvantaged status

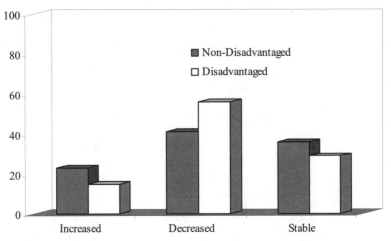

Figure 2.3: Relevance of criteria in accepting students

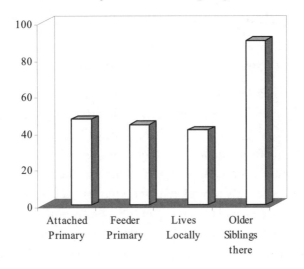

2.2.2 Competition between schools

Principals were asked about the extent of competition between local schools and the degree of "negative selection" (or "cream-off") experienced by their school. Forty-four per cent of schools described themselves as suffering "somewhat" or "a great deal" from this type of selection where the more academically able students tended to go to other schools. Vocational schools reported experiencing more negative selection than the other school types (see Figure 2.4).

Figure 2.4: Experience of negative selection (somewhat/a great deal)

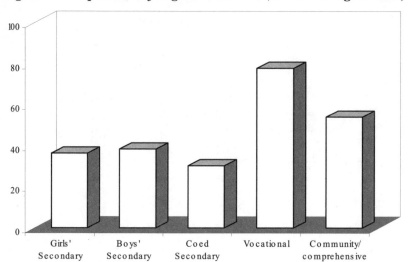

2.2.3 Prevalence of literacy and numeracy problems

Principals were also asked about the prevalence of literacy and numeracy problems among their first-year intake. The largest group (45 per cent) reported that 6-15 per cent of students had such literacy and numeracy problems as to adversely impact on their educational development or classroom discipline. As might be expected, the prevalence of numeracy difficulties is significantly correlated with the prevalence of literacy problems. Vocational schools tend to report a significantly higher prevalence of literacy and numeracy problems than other school types, as do designated disadvantaged schools (see Tables 2.1 and 2.2). As might be expected, there is a direct relationship between experience of negative selection (or school cream-off) and reported levels of literacy and numeracy problems among students.

Table 2.1: Serious literacy problems by school type

School Type	Serious Literacy Problems				
	<5%	*6–15%*	*16–30%*	*31–45%*	*>45%*
Girls' Secondary %	36	40	15	6	2
Boys' Secondary %	25	49	18	3	5
Coed Secondary %	23	58	14	4	1
Vocational %	5	35	30	17	13
Community/ Comprehensive %	5	60	22	9	5

Table 2.2: Serious numeracy problems by school type

School Type	Serious Numeracy Problems				
	<5%	*6–15%*	*16–30%*	*31–45%*	*>45%*
Girls' Secondary %	33	44	15	7	2
Boys' Secondary %	27	44	20	4	4
Coed Secondary %	24	54	15	5	1
Vocational %	6	35	31	16	12
Community/ Comprehensive %	6	55	27	9	3

In terms of geographical location, schools in Dublin are more likely to report students having higher and lower literacy and numeracy difficulties, while those in other areas are more likely to report average levels (see Tables 2.3 and 2.4). This indicates greater levels of polarisation among Dublin schools, capturing both highly selective schools and those suffering high "cream-off", while schools outside Dublin are more likely to comprise a more academically mixed intake.

Table 2.3: Proportion of first-year students with literacy problems in Dublin and other areas

Proportion with Literacy Problems	Dublin	Other Areas
< 5 %	27.3	15.8
6–15 %	34.1	48.7
16–30 %	14.4	22.6
31–45 %	9.1	8.7
Over 45 %	14.4	4.0

Table 2.4: Proportion of first-year students with numeracy problems in Dublin and other areas

Proportion with Numeracy Problems	Dublin	Other Areas
< 5 %	26.0	16.5
6–15 %	37.4	46.6
16–30 %	12.2	25.4
31–45 %	13.0	7.8
Over 45 %	11.5	3.3

2.2.4 Additional support for students with literacy and numeracy difficulties

Learning support and resource teachers are an important support for students with learning difficulties. According to the survey, the majority of post-primary schools employ one or more learning support teachers. All community and comprehensive schools employ at least one learning support teacher followed closely by vocational and co-educational secondary schools. Ninety-five per cent of designated disadvantaged schools have learning support teachers compared with 87 per cent of non-disadvantaged schools. Community/comprehensive schools are also the most likely to employ at least one resource teacher (see Figure 2.5); boys' and coeducational secondary schools are less likely than other school types to employ resource teachers. The numbers of full-time learning support teachers vary between 1 and 5 and part-time from 1 to 7. As to resource teachers, the numbers vary between 1 and 4 for full-time, and 1 to 7 for part-time, teachers. The majority of these teachers are dedicated to one school rather than shared between schools.

Figure 2.5: Employment of resource teachers by school type

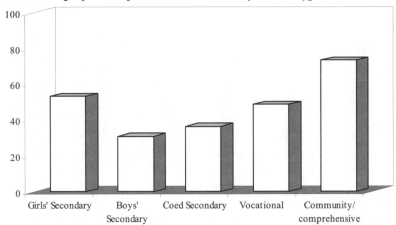

Schools with designated disadvantaged status are more likely to employ resource teachers than schools that do not fall into this category; 69 per cent of the disadvantaged schools report having one or more resource teachers compared with 38 per cent of non-disadvantaged schools. As might be expected, learning support and resource teachers are more likely to be employed in schools where the reported literacy difficulties are higher (see Figure 2.6 for resource teachers).[3]

Schools use a variety of approaches to providing learning support to students, including: a special education unit within the school, separate classes, withdrawal for certain class periods, additional teaching resources within certain classes and addressing students' needs within regular classes. Figure 2.7 below demonstrates the most common approaches taken. The approach used most often is to withdraw students from certain classes. This is followed in frequency by additional teaching resources being used within certain classes and addressing students' needs within regular classes.

---

[3] The pattern is the same regarding reported numeracy difficulties.

Figure 2.6: Employment of resource teachers by perceived literacy problems

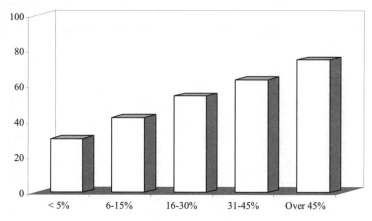

Figure 2.7: Extra support for students with literacy and numeracy difficulties

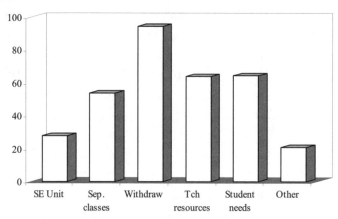

As can be seen from Figure 2.8, school principals are fairly equally divided in terms of levels of satisfaction and dissatisfaction with learning support structures. As might be expected, schools without learning support and/or resource teachers report higher dissatisfaction levels than other schools.

Figure 2.8: Level of satisfaction with learning support structures for first-year students

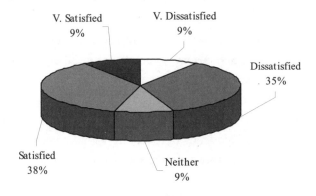

2.3 INFORMATION ON STUDENTS

Thirty per cent of schools have an attached primary school with the remainder drawing on students from one or more feeder primary schools. The vast majority (89 per cent) of schools without attached primary schools report having a stable number of core feeder primary schools. Most post-primary schools have between four and seven feeder primary schools.

2.3.1 Information received from primary school about in-coming first-year students

School principals were asked whether they received information on all, most, some, a few or no students from their (main) feeder primary school. Information received from primary schools can be divided into the following main categories: written report on academic performance; written report on behaviour; written report on physical needs of the student; verbal communication on academic performance; verbal communication on behaviour; verbal communication on physical needs. Only a minority of schools receive information on all in-coming students: in the majority of schools there does not appear to be a formal arrangement regarding the information received on in-coming students. This may also relate to data protection issues and the implications of transferring data on students for confidentiality. In terms of what use is made of information that is transferred and who it is made available to, Chapter Three examines the accessibility and distribution of data in schools.

According to Figure 2.9, schools are more likely to receive information on in-coming students via verbal than written communication. However, only a minority of schools (32-37 per cent) receive verbal information on all students. Schools are somewhat more likely to receive information on students' academic performance than on other student characteristics. Schools with attached primary schools are somewhat more likely than others to receive written reports on in-coming students. However, there is no difference in the frequency of receiving verbal communication between schools with attached primary schools and those without.

Figure 2.9: Type of information received on all students

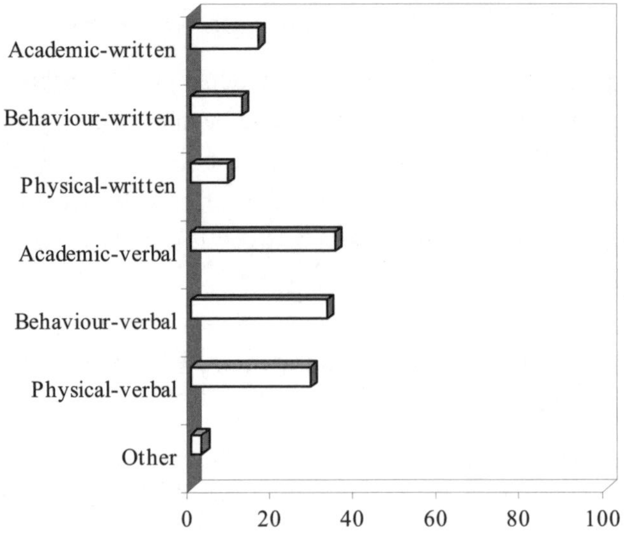

2.3.2 Level of satisfaction with the information received

Figure 2.10 indicates the extent to which post-primary school principals are satisfied with the information provided to them by primary schools in the following areas: academic performance; coverage of curriculum; student behaviour; family circumstances; and special educational needs. Overall more than half of school principals are satisfied with the information they receive. The lowest level of satisfaction relates to information on coverage of the curriculum. As might be expected, satisfaction is directly related to the amount of information received from primary schools. Chapter Four returns to these issues and examines the extent to which post-primary teachers feel they are familiar with the curriculum at primary level. In addition, Chapter Six examines whether the low levels of information on curriculum coverage result in a greater level of repetition of subject matter in first year.

Figure 2.10: Satisfaction by type of information (% v. satisfied/satisfied)

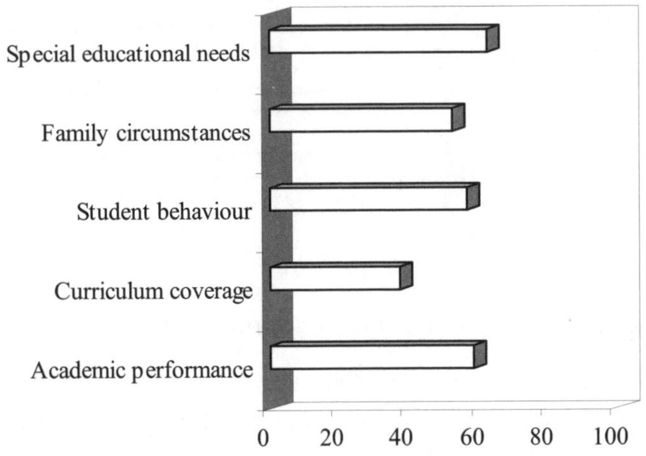

2.4 CONTACT WITH STUDENTS AND PARENTS BEFORE ENTRY TO THE SCHOOL

2.4.1 Types of pre-entry contact

The following types of contact are used with students and parents before students enter first year within the school: information session for prospective students; information session for parents; visits to feeder primary schools; visits to parents/students by Home-School-Community Liaison Officer; information brochure sent to parents/students; letter sent to parents/students; open day/evening. With the exception of visits to parents, the vast majority of schools incorporate open days/evenings, information to parents and students, letters and brochures as part of their pre-entry contact with students and their parents (see Figure 2.11). Other means of contact mentioned in the survey include special induction programmes, interviews and school newsletters.

Figure 2.11: Types of pre-entry contact

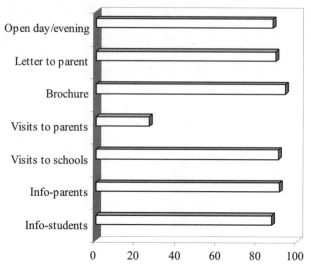

2.4.2 Usage of ability tests on students coming into first year

Schools use a variety of pre- and post-entry tests. The majority of schools use various standardised tests (such as Drumcondra tests, Sigma-T, Micra-T, Gapadol, NFER-Nelson, Shonnell, and Richmond). A considerable proportion of schools (42 per cent), however, have opted for their own tests in Mathematics, English, Irish and other subjects. In total, twenty-six different types of tests were mentioned by school principals.

Around half of schools use pre-entry tests, over a quarter use post-entry tests, eighteen per cent of schools test students both before and after school entry while a small number (6 per cent) of schools do not use ability tests. Table 2.5 shows a summary of testing approaches used by school type. There is no significant variation in the timing of testing by school type, though community/comprehensive schools are somewhat more likely than the other school types to test students before entry. There is no significant variation by disadvantaged status in the use of ability testing.

Table 2.5: Testing of students by school type

	Pre-entry	Post-entry	Both	No tests
Girls' secondary %	43.2	26.1	22.7	8.0
Boys' secondary %	33.8	31.0	26.8	8.5
Coed secondary %	28.0	36.0	26.0	10.0
Vocational %	28.0	32.2	28.8	11.0
Community/comprehensive %	48.8	19.5	24.4	7.3

The most important reason given for carrying out ability entry tests is the identification of students who may require learning support, followed in frequency by providing baseline data for on-going monitoring of students' achievement and allocating students to base classes (see Figure 2.12).

Figure 2.12: Reasons given for using ability grouping (% v. important/ important)

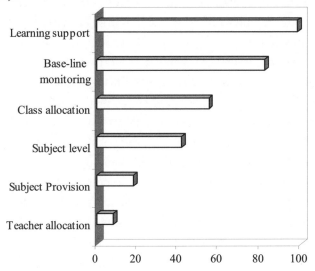

2.5 ABILITY GROUPING

Schools vary in the way in which they allocate students to *base* classes. They may employ streaming whereby students of similar assessed ability are grouped into classes, ranked from "higher" to "lower". They may use banding, a somewhat looser form of streaming, where pupils are divided into broad ability bands (for example, two higher and two lower classes) but classes within these bands are mixed ability. Alternatively, students may be placed in mixed ability base classes; this can be based on random (e.g. alphabetical) allocation or, more rarely, schools may use ability test scores to achieve a mix across classes.

The majority (70 per cent) of schools surveyed used mixed ability base classes in first year with 16 per cent using banding and 14 per cent streaming (see Figure 2.13). The pattern used for Junior Certificate classes was broadly similar with only a few schools changing from a mixed ability approach after first year. The pattern indicates an increase in the use of mixed ability base classes since the 1990s (see Smyth, 1999). Ability-based differentiation (that is, the use of either banding or streaming) in first year is more prevalent in schools with more than 200 students. Its prevalence also varies by school type, being most common in vocational and community/comprehensive schools and least common in coeducational and girls' secondary schools. Such differentiation is also more common in disadvantaged than non-disadvantaged schools (52 per cent compared with 21 per cent). Interestingly, the use of ability-based differentiation increases with the proportion of students with literacy difficulties; 13 per cent of schools with fewer than 5 per cent with such difficulties use streaming/banding compared with two-thirds of those where more than 45 per cent of students have literacy difficulties.

While the adoption of ability-based differentiation may well be a response to relatively high levels of literacy and numeracy difficulties in a school, previous studies have illustrated the potentially negative impact of such streaming, particularly for those students allocated to the lowest streams (see Smyth, 1999; Hannan and Boyle, 1987), with streaming having a polarising impact on student academic performance.

Figure 2.13: Ability grouping for first year and Junior Cert year

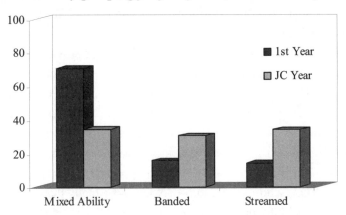

The use of mixed ability base classes does not necessarily imply mixed ability teaching across all subjects. In first year, 17 per cent of schools who have mixed ability classes use setting for one or more subjects. Setting involves time-tabling higher and lower classes at the same time within particular subjects so that students may move levels depending on their ability in a specific subject. The use of setting for one or more subjects increases by Junior Certificate year taking place in 86 per cent of schools with mixed ability base classes. Setting is more prevalent in Mathematics, Irish and English than in other subjects. Setting is typically employed in these three subjects for curriculum reasons and is facilitated by the greater numbers of students taking these subjects (see Smyth, 1999 for further discussion).

2.6 APPROACHES TO INTEGRATION

2.6.1 General approach

Schools use a variety of approaches in helping first-year students to adapt to post-primary education. Figure 2.14 demonstrates some of the approaches used. The two most widely used approaches are a class tutor system and an induction day, which are in operation in the vast majority of schools. Over half of the schools used a student mentoring system or a study skills programme. Over a quarter of schools had language courses to help non-national students to integrate into the school. Almost a third of schools mentioned other approaches, including a year-head system, sports and other social activities, meetings with parents and specific induction activities (such as summer camps).

Holding an induction day or having a class tutor system does not vary significantly by school type since the vast majority of schools use these approaches. However, very small schools (that is, those with fewer than 200 students) are less likely to have an induction day or class tutor system. A student mentor system is more prevalent in girls' secondary and community/comprehensive schools than in other school types. Again smaller schools are less likely to employ such an approach to student integration. Girls' secondary schools are also somewhat more likely than other schools to have a study skills programme for in-coming first-year students. There are no significant differences between disadvantaged and non-disadvantaged schools in the approach used to help integrate first-year students into the school.

Figure 2.14: Approach to integration of first-year students

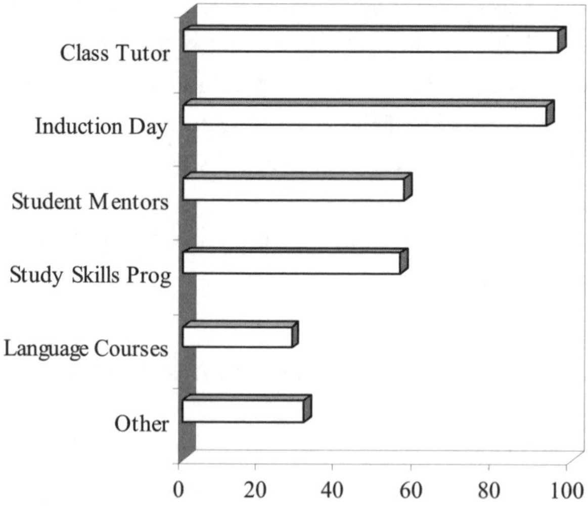

Further analysis was conducted to explore whether some schools are characterised by a strong emphasis on student integration. Twenty-nine per cent of schools used four or five different methods of settling first-year students into the school.[4] Having a strong emphasis on student integration was more prevalent among larger schools; 40 per cent of very large schools (over 600 students) compared with only 12 per cent of very small schools (under 200 students) had such an emphasis. This may relate to there being a greater need for stronger integration policies in larger schools simply for logistical reasons. A strong emphasis on student integration was also more evident in girls' secondary schools than in other school types. There was no difference between disadvantaged and non-disadvantaged schools in their emphasis on student integration. Urban schools are more likely than rural schools to have a strong emphasis on integration but this pattern is due to their greater average size rather than their location per se.

2.6.2 Most important approach to integration

The majority of school principals across all school sectors considered the single most important method of integrating students to be the class tutor system (Table 2.6). The induction day was seen as the next most important approach to student integration. The class tutor system was regarded as the most important factor by both disadvantaged and non-disadvantaged schools.

Table 2.6: Single most important approach to integration by school type

	Induction Day	Class Tutor	Mentors	Study skills prog.	Other
Girls' secondary %	24.3	63.1	8.7	1.0	2.9
Boys' secondary %	28.4	55.7	11.4	1.1	3.4
Coed secondary %	22.4	63.2	7.9	1.3	5.3
Vocational %	28.3	61.6	2.9	0.0	7.2
Community/ comprehensive %	38.9	48.1	7.4	1.9	3.7

---

[4] Language courses for non-nationals were not included in this analysis as provision reflects not just school policy but the prevalence of non-national students among the first-year intake.

2.7 USE OF PASTORAL CARE AND SIMILAR PROGRAMMES

2.7.1 The nature of support structures

The vast majority of schools use pastoral care or other personal/social development programmes as a support for first-year students. Such support programmes are common across all school types, but especially prevalent in community/comprehensive and girls' secondary schools. The prevalence of pastoral care programmes increases with school size; 91 per cent of very large schools have such programmes compared with 62 per cent of very small schools. It should be noted, however, that in the context of a small school informal relations between teachers and students may substitute for formal provision.

In the majority of schools, such programmes catered for all students in the school. However, in over one-third of schools programmes were targeted at first-year students or junior cycle students only.

The nature of the pastoral care system varied across schools. In over half of schools, it involved a class tutor system. In a quarter of schools it involved a year-head system or the SPHE programme. Other features included the existence of a pastoral care team (15 per cent of schools), the guidance counsellor (13 per cent) or school chaplain (11 per cent).

2.7.2 Satisfaction with support systems in place for first-year students

The majority of post-primary principals reported being broadly satisfied with support systems for first-year students in their school (see Figure 2.15). As might be expected, principals in schools without formal pastoral care programmes reported greater dissatisfaction levels (29 per cent compared with 13 per cent of those in schools with formal programmes). Principals were asked what other supports they would like to see in place for first-year students. The most frequently mentioned supports were learning support (20 per cent of schools), psychological support (18 per cent) and a home-school liaison co-ordinator (18 per cent). Other supports mentioned included a resource teacher and smaller class sizes.

Figure 2.15: Satisfaction with first-year support structures

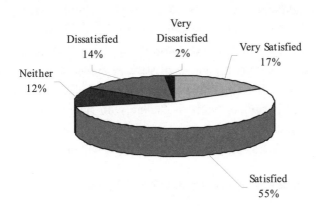

2.7.3 Specific support systems used for Travellers and non-nationals

Schools were asked whether they had any specific support structures in place for non-national students and for students from Travelling families. Thirty per cent of schools had supports for non-nationals while 34 per cent had supports for Travellers. The main support for non-national students was extra English classes (52 per cent of schools); other supports included other additional tuition (15 per cent) and extra teaching resources. The main supports for Travellers were additional tuition (28 per cent) and extra teaching resources (25 per cent).

2.8 TRANSITION DIFFICULTIES

2.8.1 The prevalence of transition difficulties

Principals were asked what proportion of first-year students in their school tend to experience sustained difficulties (that is, beyond the first term) in making the transition into post-primary education in relation to: academic progress, social interaction with peers, behaviour in class and absenteeism.[5] Table 2.7 indicates the average prevalence of reported problems. It is clear that the greatest difficulties are reported in relation to academic progress followed by behaviour in class.

---

[5] It should be stressed that this information relates to the *perceptions* of principals. Student information from the case-study schools will allow us to explore the extent to which students appear to experience transition difficulties (see Chapter Seven).

Vocational schools tend to report significantly more problems than other school types. In addition, designated disadvantaged schools report greater problems than non-disadvantaged schools. On further analysis, the higher prevalence of problems found among vocational and disadvantaged schools is found to relate to their greater intake of students with literacy/numeracy problems (see Table 2.8). The prevalence of reported difficulties in academic progress and behaviour tends to decline with school size. Interestingly, there is no significant difference in reported transition difficulties between schools with a linked primary school and those without.

Table 2.7: Prevalence of reported transition difficulties

	Academic Progress	Social Interaction	Behaviour in Class	Absentee-ism
Girls' secondary	9.2	4.6	5.5	5.2
Boys' secondary	9.8	4.5	6.7	5.0
Coed secondary	9.2	4.7	6.9	4.6
Vocational	14.0	7.3	10.4	9.1
Community/ comprehensive	9.4	4.3	7.6	6.5

Table 2.8: Transition difficulties by literacy problems in first year

Serious Literacy Problems	Academic Progress	Social Interaction	Behaviour in Class	Absentee-ism
<5 %	6.5	3.9	4.0	2.7
6–15 %	7.4	4.2	5.4	4.5
16–30 %	14.5	6.6	10.1	8.2
31–45 %	16.4	8.3	13.8	10.9
Over 45 %	27.4	10.9	17.3	18.4

Average reported difficulties tend to be somewhat lower in schools with pastoral care programmes and/or those with a strong emphasis on integration, although the differences are not statistically significant. In overall terms, the quality of such programmes is likely to be more significant than the presence of such programmes per se.

Table 2.9: Factors identified as contributing to difficulties (%)

Factors	A Great Deal	Quite a Lot	A Little	Not a Factor
Lack of family support	17.6	29.3	34.8	12.5
Literacy problems	17.2	41.7	32.6	3.3
Numeracy problems	16.3	41.7	32.6	3.7
Taking more subjects	14.9	42.0	27.6	9.1
Moving to larger school	9.1	28.8	41.7	13.6
New peer group	9.0	35.2	40.9	8.2
Homework	8.7	40.9	37.9	6.7
Different teaching styles	8.7	29.0	43.9	11.7
Having several teachers	8.0	21.2	43.8	20.2
Length of the school day	7.7	22.8	38.5	24.7
Travel time to school	5.3	16.0	36.5	35.4
Inadequate preparation for transfer	4.7	14.1	48.7	24.8
Schoolwork too challenging	4.4	33.6	47.0	8.6
Bullying	2.6	12.8	66.5	12.1
Participation in extra-curricular activities	1.9	8.1	32.9	49.7
Schoolwork not challenging enough	0.5	2.9	35.4	52.2

2.8.2 Factors contributing to sustained difficulties in the transition process

Principals were asked to specify the importance of factors contributing to difficulties in the transition process from a list of possible factors. Table 2.9 above indicates that factors seen as contributing "a great deal" to such difficulties included lack of family support, literacy and numeracy difficulties, and the greater number of subjects taken by students. The level of the schoolwork (schoolwork being too challenging or not challenging enough), bullying by other students and participation in extracurricular activities were seen as not contributing a great deal to transition difficulties. Overall principals were more likely to identify non-school factors as contributing to difficulties. It should again be noted that these responses relate to principals' perceptions. The case-study information may reveal that students see other factors as contributing to their difficulties in making the transition (see Chapter Seven).

2.9 SUBJECT PROVISION AND SUBJECT CHOICE FOR FIRST-YEAR STUDENTS

2.9.1 Subject provision for first-year students

Schools are found to vary in the number of subjects they provide to first-year students (see Figure 2.16). The most common pattern is the provision of 17 or 18 subjects, although the number provided ranges from 11 to 23 across schools.

Figure 2.16: Number of subjects provided to first-year students

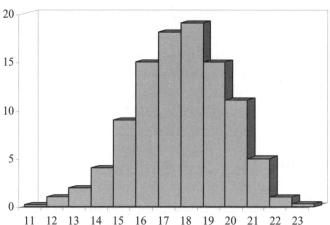

The number of subjects provided varies significantly by school type, with the highest level of provision found in the community/comprehensive sector and the lowest level in boys' secondary schools. Subject provision is also found to vary significantly by school size, with the average number of subjects ranging from 15.7 in very small schools (those with fewer than 200 students) to 18.5 in large schools (those with more than 600 students).

The nature of subject provision in schools is quite dynamic; one-fifth of schools had dropped one or more subjects from the first-year curriculum in the previous five years while 60 per cent of schools had added one or more subjects (over and above the addition of CSPE). Dropping a subject was more common in schools with a declining intake; over one quarter of such schools had dropped a subject compared with one-tenth of schools with an increasing intake of students.

The subjects most frequently dropped were German (24 per cent of schools who dropped a subject), Technology, Music and History. The most frequently added subjects were Social, Personal and Health Education (SPHE), Computer Studies, Music and Religious Education.

2.9.2 Factors influencing curriculum provision

The factors having the greatest influence on curricular provision were seen as the desire to give students a broad experience of the junior cycle, requirements of the Department of Education and Science, staff availability and school ethos (see Figure 2.17). Over a quarter of the schools mentioned the ability profile of students as a very significant factor, although the gender mix of students was seen as significant by only a minority (14 per cent) of principals. Over a third of schools mentioned student preferences as a significant factor in shaping the curriculum while over a tenth suggested that parental preferences played an important role. It is unclear from the data in what way students and parents influence subject provision; it may be by explicit demands but it is more likely to reflect subjects being dropped from the curriculum due to a reduction in take-up.

There is little systematic variation in the factors seen as influencing subject provision across school sectors, size of school or disadvantaged status. There is, however, a slight tendency for larger schools to mention school ethos as a very significant factor, perhaps reflecting greater logistical constraints on smaller schools; 62 per cent of very large schools mention this as an important influence compared with 48 per cent of very small schools. In addition, disadvantaged schools are more likely to mention the ability level of students as a significant factor; 40 per cent of disadvantaged schools suggest it is a very significant factor compared with 22 per cent of their non-disadvantaged counterparts. As might be expected, coeducational schools are more likely to mention the gender of students as a factor than those in single-sex schools. In addition, community/ comprehensive schools, girls' secondary schools and larger schools are more likely to mention student preferences as a significant factor.

Figure 2.17: Factors having a "very significant" influence on subject provision

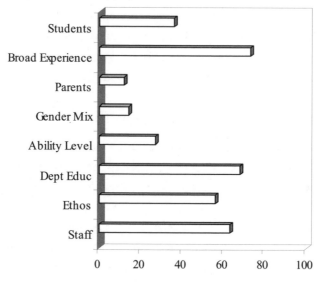

2.9.3 Perceptions of the Junior Cycle Curriculum

School principals were asked whether they agreed or disagreed with a number of statements relating to the junior cycle curriculum and provision for first-year students in their school (see Figure 2.18).

The vast majority (96 per cent) of principals felt that there was a good range of subjects on offer in their school. A significant minority (42 per cent) of principals felt that first-year students in their school take too many subjects. Interestingly, the pattern of responses did not vary by the actual number of subjects taken by first-year students. Overall, the majority (over 70 per cent) felt that subject sampling was a good idea. As might be expected, support for subject sampling was greater in schools where students tried out subjects for part or all of first year before making their choice (see below).

Four-fifths of respondents felt that the junior cycle "curriculum is suitable for the majority of first-year students in the school". Principals in disadvantaged schools were more likely to disagree with this statement than principals in other schools, although the proportions involved were small (14 per cent). In addition, those in schools with a relatively high proportion (over 45 per cent) of students with literacy problems were more likely to disagree with this statement. Even though principals generally felt the curriculum to be suitable for the majority of students, 57 per cent considered course content to be too challenging for a significant minority of first-year students. Principals in disadvantaged schools were more likely to agree with this statement as were those in schools with higher proportions of students with literacy problems.

Figure 2.18: Perceptions of the Junior Cycle curriculum

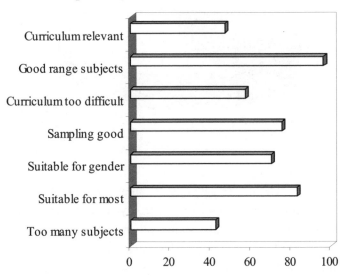

Fewer than half of school principals felt that the curriculum was relevant to students' everyday lives. There is no systematic variation in these responses by school type, disadvantaged status or student intake. In general, the curriculum was seen by principals as equally suitable for boys and girls. As might be expected, principals in single-sex schools were less likely to have an opinion on this statement.

2.9.4 Approach to subject choice

Schools were found to differ in the way in which they make subjects available to their students (see Figure 2.19). Over half (57 per cent) of schools allowed students to make a choice of subjects at the end of first year[6] with a further 18 per cent of schools allowing students to take part in a "taster" programme (lasting less than a year) before choosing their subjects. In a fifth of schools, students choose their subjects before or immediately on entry to the school while students are allowed no choice of subjects in a small minority of schools.

Figure 2.19: Timing of subject choice

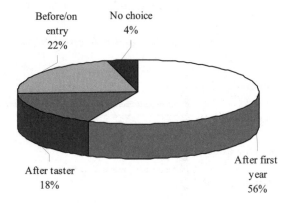

Girls' secondary schools are more likely than the other school types to postpone subject choice until the end of first year; over three-quarters do so compared with around half of the other school types. Very small schools are more likely than other schools either to have no choice at all or to postpone choice until the end of first year. There are no significant differences between disadvantaged and non-disadvantaged schools in their approach to subject choice. The approach to subject choice is re-lated to the approach to ability grouping. In one-third of schools where streaming/banding is used in first-year, students are required to choose

---

[6] This also included schools that provided a wider exposure to subjects in first year than in subsequent years.

their subject before/on entry or have no choice at all; this is the case for 23 per cent of schools using mixed ability base classes.

Schools vary in the number of subjects taken by students in the first term of first year, in part because of their differing approaches to subject choice. Students typically take thirteen or fourteen subjects in the first term, although the number taken ranges from 10 to 21 (see Figure 2.20). There is no significant variation in the number of subjects taken by school size. However, students in vocational and boys' secondary schools tend to take fewer subjects while those in girls' secondary and community/comprehensive schools tend to take more subjects. Students in disadvantaged schools tend to take fewer subjects in first year than those in non-disadvantaged schools. In addition, students tend to take fewer subjects in schools where more than 30 per cent of the cohort has literacy problems. These figures reflect the average pattern across schools. However, in thirty per cent of schools some students take fewer subjects than others; in around one third of these schools, this is due to the base class within which students are located.

Due to differences between schools in their approach to subject choice, the number of subjects taken in the first term of first year may be greater than the number taken in Junior Certificate year. Figure 2.21 shows the number of subjects taken in the exam year, including non-exam subjects. Students typically take 12 to 14 subjects at this stage although the number taken varies from 9 or fewer to more than 16. Students in boys' secondary and vocational schools tend to take fewer subjects, although the differences across school types are less marked than in first year. Furthermore, those in disadvantaged schools and those in schools with a relatively high intake of students with literacy problems tend to take fewer subjects at the Junior Certificate level.

Figure 2.20: Number of subjects taken in first term of first year

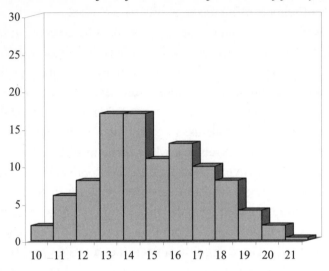

Figure 2.21: Number of subjects taken in Junior Cert year

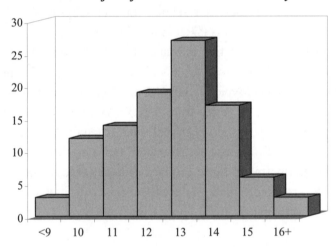

Because of the overlap between disadvantaged status and the prevalence of literacy problems, it can be difficult to disentangle the effects. Figure 2.22 shows the average number of subjects at Junior Certificate level taken by disadvantaged status and whether more than 30 per cent of the student in-take has literacy problems. It appears that the highest average number of subjects is taken by those in schools without significant literacy problems, whether they are designated disadvantaged or not. Students in schools with literacy problems take fewer subjects overall but within this group, those in disadvantaged schools take fewer than those in non-disadvantaged schools (11.5 compared with 12 on average). It thus appears that student intake both in terms of disadvantage and literacy difficulties influences school policy regarding the number of subjects taken at Junior Certificate level.

Figure 2.22: Average number of subjects in Junior Cert year by disadvantaged status and student intake

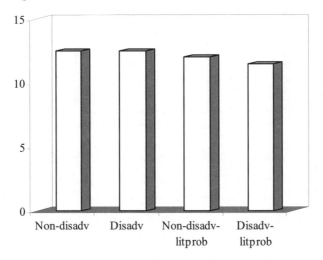

2.9.5 Time allocation to subjects

As well as differing in the number of subjects taken by students, schools can differ in the time spent on certain subjects in the first and Junior Certificate years. Schools were asked about the number and length of class periods allocated per week to Irish, English, Mathematics, Science, a foreign language and Physical Education. The greatest amount of time in first year is allocated to Mathematics, English and Irish (169 to 180 minutes), a similar amount of time is devoted to Science as to a foreign language (147 to 149 minutes) while the least amount of time is devoted to PE (see Figure 2.23).

Figure 2.23: Average number of minutes allocated weekly to certain subjects in first year

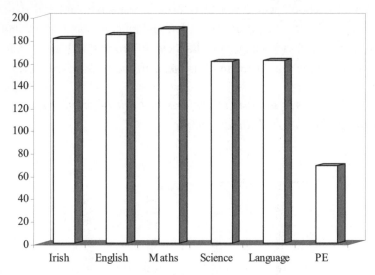

As might be expected, schools which allow students to select subjects after sampling them (either for all or part of first year) tend to spend less time on the selected subjects in first year, with the exception of PE. This occurs because of the greater number of subjects taken in first year. Vocational schools and girls' secondary schools tend to spend somewhat less time on Irish, English and Mathematics than other school types; the pattern for girls' schools is related to their tendency to postpone choice of subjects. In terms of PE, boys' and coed secondary schools spend somewhat more time on the subject than other schools. There is no significant variation in the time allocated to the specified subjects by school size or disadvantaged status. However, there is a slight tendency for schools with a relatively high proportion of students with literacy problems to allocate more time to English.

There appears to be a greater amount of time allocated to Irish, English, Mathematics, Science and foreign languages in Junior Certificate year than in first year, reflecting the reduction in the number of subjects taken between first and Junior Certificate year (see above). Interestingly, less time is allocated to PE in Junior Certificate year than in first year (see Figure 2.24). At Junior Certificate level, vocational schools allocate somewhat less time to Irish and Mathematics than other school types. A greater amount of time is allocated to PE in boys' secondary schools than in girls' or vocational schools. At Junior Certificate level, there is a slight tendency for disadvantaged schools to allocate less time than non-disadvantaged schools to Irish and Mathematics. Furthermore, the amount of time spent on Irish appears to decline with the literacy level of the intake. At Junior Certificate level, the amount of time spent on Irish, English, Mathematics or PE does not vary by the number of subjects taken. However, students spend somewhat less time on Science and foreign languages in schools where they take more subjects.

Figure 2.24: Average weekly time allocated to selected subjects in Junior Cert year

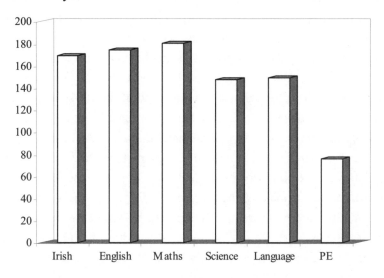

2.10 CONCLUSIONS

The nature of student intake to post-primary schools has changed markedly in recent years. Just under half of schools have experienced a decline in the number of incoming first years because of demographic trends and increased competition between local schools. This competition has contributed to the concentration of students with literacy and numeracy problems in a minority of schools, principally vocational and designated disadvantaged schools.

There appears to be an inadequate flow of information between primary and post-primary schools. Only a minority of school principals receive information on all their in-coming students and almost half are dissatisfied with the amount of information they receive. Where information is given to post-primary schools, it tends to be verbal rather than written. However, the vast majority of schools obtain information on the ability levels of students by conducting tests either before or after their entry to the school. This issue of information flow to post-primary schools and extent to which such information is accessible to teachers and other staff members is examined further in Chapter Three.

There is a good deal of contact between schools and students/parents before entry to the school, usually taking the form of school visits, open days and the dissemination of written material. The induction day and class tutor system are seen as the main ways in which students are integrated into the school. Girls' secondary schools along with larger schools tend to have more developed measures to assist student integration. In addition, the majority of schools have a pastoral care system for first-year (and other) students. In general, school principals are satisfied with the support structures for first-year students in their school (the views of teachers and students are examined in Chapters Three and Five, respectively). However, a minority of students are seen as experiencing sustained difficulties in making the transition into post-primary education. Such difficulties are more frequently reported by schools with a concentration of students with literacy/numeracy difficulties, mainly vocational and designated disadvantaged schools. Lack of family support, literacy/numeracy problems and the number of subjects are seen as the main factors contributing to potential difficulties in the transition process. Support structures for students appear to play a part in reducing the incidence of such difficulties but information from the case-study schools will be used to explore the quality of such provision and its impact on students (see Chapter Seven). In general, principals appear to focus on non-school factors as hindering the transition for their students, perhaps not always recognising the significant organisational changes students face at transition.

Schools are found to vary in the extent of subject provision for first-year students, the approach to, and timing of, subject choice, and in the way in which students are allocated to base classes. There has been a marked increase since the mid-1990s in the proportion of schools which allocate students to mixed ability base classes in first and Junior Certificate years. Where it exists, ability-based differentiation is more prevalent in vocational, community/comprehensive and disadvantaged schools along with schools with a concentration of students with literacy/ numeracy difficulties. In addition, the majority of schools tend to postpone ability-based differentiation in specific subjects (such as Irish, English and Mathematics) until second or third year.

Almost three-quarters of schools now provide students with some exposure to a variety of subjects before they make their choice for the Junior Certificate. First-year students receive exposure to fewer subjects in vocational schools, boys' secondary schools, designated disadvantaged schools and those with a concentration of students with literacy/ numeracy difficulties. This pattern is also evident within the Junior Certificate year, although the differences between school types are less marked than in first year.

This chapter has outlined policy and practice across post-primary schools in relation to student integration and curriculum provision for first-year students. Information from this postal survey was used to select twelve case-study schools, varying across the key dimensions of the approach to transition, including the emphasis on student integration, the approach to ability grouping and the timing of subject choice (see Chapter One). The remainder of this study explores the transition process within these case-study schools, allowing us to explore the nature of the transition in a variety of school settings and from the perspectives of school management, teachers, students and parents.

Chapter Three

STUDENT INTEGRATION AND SUPPORT STRUCTURES IN THE CASE-STUDY SCHOOLS

3.1 INTRODUCTION

The role of school integration and support structures in assisting the transfer of students from primary to post-primary school is explored in this chapter. As in Chapter Four, it draws on interviews held with the "key personnel" in the twelve case-study schools, that is: the School Principal, Deputy Principal, Home–School–Community Liaison Co-ordinator (HSLC), Guidance Counsellor, Stay in School Initiative Co-ordinator, 8-15 Programme Co-ordinator, Year Head, Class Tutor(s), Learning Support Teacher(s) and Resource Teacher(s), where applicable. It also presents information gathered from questionnaires administered to 226 subject teachers of first-year students in these schools. Information provided by the school personnel in direct contact with the first-year students gives us a valuable insight into the difficulties these students may encounter in transferring from primary to post-primary school and complements the information gained from students presented in Chapters Five, Six and Seven.

Among the issues addressed in the present chapter are the types of integration "packages" on offer to students in the twelve case-study schools, the perceived adequacy of these supports, the prevalence of sustained transition difficulties among students and the factors held to contribute to such difficulties.

3.2 APPROACH TO STUDENT INTEGRATION

Based on the information obtained from the school staff, the twelve case-study schools seem to share many similar characteristics regarding the procedures in place addressing the transition from primary to post-primary school. Among the approaches taken are providing an open day/night for students and their parents; an induction programme involving various activities and games or an induction day where more information is given to the new students than at the open day; visits to and from primary school(s); school assembly; and an introductory talk by the Principal, Class Tutor or Year Head.

However, the extent and "quality" of these induction practices vary greatly between the schools. In some schools, an extensive induction programme has been designed lasting for a number of days and involving various activities. Often in these cases the programme's design and coordination is linked to a post of responsibility. In other cases, the Class Tutor and Year Head are considered to be the most important supports and sources of information for the new students, with little additional support on offer to students. A number of schools participating in the study also use student mentors in helping students to adjust to the new school setting. The student mentors are usually the "first port of call" if a first-year student experiences problems in the school. These student mentors are volunteers from older year groups in the post-primary school, often drawn from fifth or sixth year.

Drawing on an overall examination of integration practices in the twelve schools, schools can be loosely classified as having stronger or weaker integration programmes (Table 3.1). Those with stronger and more comprehensive integration programmes are Dawson Street, Dixon Street, Fig Lane, Wentworth Place, Lang Street, Dawes Point, Belmore Street, Wynyard Road and Wattle Street. Conversely, Barrack Street, Park Street and Hay Street appear to have somewhat less extensive integration programmes.

Table 3.1: School profiles[1]

	School Type	Level of Integration[2]	Integration Programme/ Open Day	Student Mentors	Other
Dawson Street	Community/ comp.	Stronger	Induction day and open night	Yes	Study skills programme
Dixon Street*	Vocational	Stronger	Induction programme (3 days) and open night	Yes	Lunch time clubs, information meetings, school sale uniform days, transition initiative for special education.
Fig Lane	Fee-paying co-educational	Stronger	Induction programme and open day	Yes	Staggered start of school year, 1st and 6th years for the first week; summer camp for students
Wentworth Place	Boys' secondary	Stronger	Induction day, parents' night, and open day	Yes	Visits to primary schools
Wynyard Road	Girls' secondary	Stronger	Induction programme and open nights	No	Induction programme co-ordinator
Lang Street*	Vocational	Stronger	Induction day and open day	No	Collaboration between staff in primary and post primary schools; involvement of Home-School Liaison Co-ordinator (HSLC), Resource and Learning Support

[1] Marked with (*) are the "designated disadvantaged" schools.

[2] Stronger and weaker integration refers to level/amount of support provided for first year students.

	School Type	Level of Integration[2]	Integration Programme/ Open Day	Student Mentors	Other
Dawes Point*	Boys' secondary	Stronger	Visit to secondary school (HSLC) and open day	Yes	Stay in School Retention Initiative (SSRI) activities
Belmore Street	Girls' secondary	Stronger	Induction days (2) and open day	Yes	Study skills programme; youth counsellor
Wattle Street*	Boys' secondary	Stronger	Open day	No	Home School Liaison Co-ordinator (HSLC) – students know this person already from primary school; study skills programme
Barrack Street*	Girls' secondary	Weaker	Induction day and parents' night	Yes	Home School Liaison Co-ordinator (HSLC), class teachers, pastoral care class, visits to primary school
Park Street	Boys' secondary	Weaker	Induction day (2 days) and open night for parents	No	—
Hay Street	Vocational	Weaker	Open night	No	—

[2] Stronger and weaker integration refers to level/amount of support provided for first year students.

The following section explores in greater depth the different school practices utilised in the twelve case-study schools in addressing the transition from primary to post-primary school. This is followed by an examination of the extent to which students are perceived to experience sustained difficulties in the transition to post-primary education, and the factors held to contribute to such difficulties.

3.2.1 Pre-entry contact

Schools can attempt to facilitate student adjustment to post-primary education by having contact with students before they come to the school and/or by putting in place programmes to integrate students once they have arrived in the new school. The interviews conducted with key personnel indicated that many case-study schools address the issue of student adjustment by building up contacts with students while they are still in primary school. In many cases, some of the school staff and/or older students from the post-primary school visit the prospective new students in their sixth class of primary school and give a talk about what they can expect in the "Big School". The visit to the primary school in these cases is seen as part of the transition programme, the aim of which is to help the students to adjust to the post-primary school. Students' own views of such contacts are discussed in Chapter Five.

The most frequently used form of pre-entry contact was to organise an open day or night in which prospective students and/or their parents could visit the post-primary school. All of the case-study schools operated an open day/night, in some cases organised in conjunction with assessment tests. During an open day most schools organise a tour of the school for the new students and provide them with relevant information about the post-primary school:

> The day they came in here to do their entrance exam — it starts really then. They did that last month. We would have brought them around and shown them the facilities (Deputy Principal, Park Street School).

An open day (or an open night) provides information about the post-primary school to both the students and their parents. Whether both the students and their parents are invited to attend these information sessions together varies by school. An open night tends to be focused more towards the parents. Information provided during the session covers issues such as an introduction to the school and the programmes offered; school rules and regulations; subjects offered by the school. A tour of the school is also organised in most cases:

> . . . the opening nights where people come and are allowed to visit the school and the school's programme is presented to anybody who wishes to come. . . . It would be January or even before it. So the parents get an introduction to the school and the programmes we offer (Induction Programme Co-ordinator, Wynyard Road School).

> We invite in parents to an open night and on that open night a number of teachers would help me in going through everything that we have to offer here in the school — from the rules, the regulations to all the various subjects and so on and we bring the parents on a tour of the school. . . . We don't bring in the students and I go through what I call about 20 or 23 questions. The frequently asked questions that parents have about streaming, about going down town, about uniform, whatever else — all the various questions that the parents have (Principal, Park Street School).

> On the open day we would have all the school open and we would have displays in classrooms and we would have displays in the gym of gymnastics and that kind of thing, we'd have the computer rooms where the children would be able to do a little program. We've teachers doing things there and the art room would be doing pottery and that kind of thing. They'd be able to do something and we'd have a lot of our own students in showing them around (Principal, Belmore Street School).

In the majority of the case-study schools, information nights are organised for the parents where they have the opportunity to talk to the school staff. The parents are also told what is expected of their child in the post-primary school:

> We also have an open night . . . [we] speak to the parents and let them know what it would be like for the students . . . and what would be expected of their children . . . during the month of August their parents normally would meet with the principal (Year Head, Dawes Point School).

These occasions were seen as giving parents a chance to meet some of the teachers, be informed of school rules and regulations and ask questions. Parents' perspectives on contact with the post-primary school are discussed in more detail in Chapter Eight.

An extensive use of open day practices is also reported in a study carried out in Britain by Franklin and Madge (2001). In their study they discovered that 89 per cent of the students they interviewed had, before moving into post-primary school, visited the school beforehand and the rest stated that they would have liked to do so. The present study confirms these findings with such practices operating in the majority of Irish schools (see Chapter Two for the national picture), with such open days/nights generally being attended by students and their parents with the aim of familiarising them with the new school setting, as well as with the rules and regulations.

As well as the open day, some of the case-study schools organised visits by groups of students to the school where they are given a chance to look around and meet with some of the school staff. The transition programme in these cases is seen as a gradual, step-by-step process:

> . . . so that is their gradual transition and by Christmas generally they are well settled in. I think we offer them a fairly good transition programme in a non-big structured way (Guidance Counsellor, Barrack Street School).

Belmore Street, Barrack Street and Wentworth Place schools tended to host school visits more than the other case-study schools.

Some schools introduce the subject teachers to the prospective students before the school year actually starts. The students may also have a chance to attend "sample classes" in an attempt to make them feel more at ease in the new school:

> The idea is that at the end of that week some of the edge will be taken off the transition [. . .] so that they will have a sense of the place, they will have a sense of at least some of the teachers (8-15 Programme, Dixon Street School).

> It would be yes, the programme. [. . .] Transfer from primary to post-primary. That consists of a one-hour session, which is facilitated by the youth worker and the support teacher. That is followed up by a

whole day session from 9.30 to 2.30 with the whole class broken
down into small groups of six. And they explore the concerns they
have going into post-primary school. Issues like bullying or reading
a time table, how to organise yourself for the day. Those kinds of
things. So every 6th class student gets that (8-15 Programme Co-
ordinator, Lang Street).

Class Tutors and Home–School–Community Liaison Teachers are, in
some schools, actively involved in the transition programme, which involves visits to the post-primary school in order to familiarise students
with the new surroundings. In some cases this "introduction" to the post-
primary school is carried out well before the new school year starts:

It would be the Home School Liaison Teacher who would bring
them over, organise to bring them over from the primary school and
they would come in here and I just talk to them for a few minutes,
maybe show them a few little experiments to give them a little interest in science before they come here, that they might look forward to
it . . . [it] would be about October it would be a year nearly before
they'd come in here (Class Tutor, Dawes Point School).

In common with the study carried out in Britain by Galton, Gray and
Ruddock (2003), the present study highlights the importance of maintaining good collaboration between the staff of primary and post-primary
schools in order to effectively co-ordinate the transition of students from
the primary to the post-primary school:

The whole induction process is collaboration again between the staff
of the school here and the staff of the Primary School at sixth class
level. They would be the main operators in this transition and our
teachers here would work hand-in-hand with the teachers over there.
In the early days it would be the primary teachers in sixth class, the
principal of the Primary Schools and myself and the Deputy Principal. [. . .]. By the time we come to the entrance assessment there is a
senior post holder to deal with those children (Principal, Lang Street
School).

It was evident from the interviews with "key personnel" that second
level schools with feeder primary schools have closer links between the
two school settings compared to, for example, Fig Lane school that

draws pupils from a large catchment area. In some cases Home–School Liaison Co-ordinators reported close collaboration with feeder primary schools:

> There's a home school person in each [feeder school] and we work as a team and it's considered that the whole process of education is integrated right through for early, pre-school, Early Start up to Leaving Cert., that we look at it in an integrated way. We plan our activities, our term's activities together, we share resources in terms of finance, in terms of maybe a service or expertise, so we meet regularly. We meet once a week as what we call a family cluster [. . .]. There's a formal meeting every week but there's a lot of incidental meetings as well plus contact on the phone (HSLC, Dixon Street).

> It would be [a good relationship] because one of the things, we had a programme here . . . [that] was partially a transition programme in that it took the children at 6th class level and it went right through to Junior Cert. and the principal of the primary school and the home school liaison co-ordinators in the primary schools were on the committee so there's been quite a close link with the national school (Principal, Dixon Street).

> [The relationship] would be very good. Over the years we would have developed a very strong relationship with all our feeder Primary Schools, in some cases stronger than others because they are closer to us, but as principal and deputy principal likewise, we would be constantly in and out of the Primary Schools, we would be known there by everybody, by the children and the teachers there and they in turn would be known to us and would come to our school regularly as well. In fact we would provide them with some facilities, like the use of the PE hall and so on (Principal, Lang Street).

However, in some cases the link between the two school settings is not very strong:

> Not a great deal [of contact] really. In that connection, between these schools there is very, very little contact. I would know some of the school principals and I suppose I would know most of them. When I would visit they would talk to me about some individual students, but generally speaking very, very little. Sometimes we look for additional information from them but not too often — only in particular

cases or where there are problems that seem to be arising. Some schools send in reports (Principal, Park Street).

Rarely would we meet them [primary school teachers] as a group. There would want to be something very special on for that to happen. Individually we would meet some of them around. Most people would know some of them, but I would have to say myself that there are teachers over there, particularly over the last four or five years, that I wouldn't know, so there is not much contact at all (Principal, Wattle Street).

3.2.2 Induction programmes and practices

In most cases, the main induction practices operate when the students are already in the post-primary school and a range of programmes are implemented to assist the "new arrivals". The nature and comprehensiveness of such programmes varies between the schools. Some schools have an elaborate induction programme in place that often commences before the school officially starts while the programmes on offer in other schools are largely confined to the help of Class Tutors and Year Heads. One such school with a more comprehensive induction programme is Wynyard Road where a teacher holds a post of responsibility as co-ordinator of the transition programme. This teacher also has responsibility for designing the programme. In this school, the induction programme lasts 3.5 days and involves many activities, including swimming, assembly, time set-aside with their class teachers and other social activities.

The schools generally acknowledge the difficulties students can face in making the transition and try to monitor their experience. In Dixon Street School students are given an opportunity to reflect on their transition and settling in experiences in the first Social, Physical and Health Education (SPHE) class:

> They have all these little games and so on and then at the end of their first SPHE class we evaluate how they have settled in, in their new school . . . they just have to share how they are getting on and writing a comment on things they find easy or difficult and then it's written up on the board what they're going to work at to help one another and that sort of thing . . . what their initial responses to the school

were and now after a week are they more comfortable in their sur-roundings (Deputy Principal, Dixon Street School).

3.2.3 Role of Year Head and Class Tutor

The most direct contact that the first-year students have is with their Class Tutor and Year Head; such a Tutor or Year Head generally takes a central place in the integration of new students in all of the case-study schools. The main role of a Class Tutor is to look after the interests of their students and to address issues such as the general rules of the school, including uniform, and organising book lists. The tutor also deals with bullying, and other problems that the students under his or her care may experience:

> Each class is allocated a tutor, so they would go through the rules in their diaries, give them out the [school] diary and you know there is all the rules about uniform, and smoking, expect good attendance . . . [they] would fill out sheets, that would tell a little bit about, you know family background, maybe where they come in the family or school, previous primary school, home number, address, all that. The tutors would have all that information in case they wanted to contact family (Year Head, Wentworth Place School).

> The tutor support would probably be the biggest one that they [first-year students] have at the moment. The child would have an assigned tutor (8-15 Programme Co-ordinator, Dixon Street School).

> There are always a number of students who will have some prob-lems. It is up to us all but in particular it is up to the Class Tutor and The Year Head to have a focus and to be alert, particularly during the first two or three weeks (Principal, Wentworth Place School).

The Year Head's main role is generally to monitor students' academic progress and discipline. Compared to the Class Tutors, they generally have less contact with the first-year students. One Year Head commented on their role as:

> Looking after all the First Years really. I have all their files. I update their files. If they have been in trouble with teachers and discipline problems I deal with that. We have a system of yellow forms and red forms for lots of serious offences and if they get three yellow forms

they get a red form and I'm usually expected to talk to them and explain to them what they have been doing wrong and give out to them
really, and keep an eye on their academic progress and usually if
they have problems they come to me about them (Year Head, Dixon
Street School).

In addition to the formal responsibility of the year head and class tutors,
many subject teachers played an informal role in providing support and
assistance to first-year students. One-third of the teachers surveyed (ex-
cluding tutors and year heads) considered themselves very involved in
dealing with personal problems among first-year students; almost an equal
proportion did not consider themselves to be at all involved in this area.
There is little variation in teacher involvement across schools or the characteristics of teachers such as gender, age or years in the school (with the
exception of greater levels of involvement among teachers in the school
for more than 10 years), suggesting that there is no one type of teacher that
first-year students are likely to relate to easily; rather such ease of contact
is perhaps more likely to relate to a teacher's personality.

3.2.4 Other support structures for first-year students

The majority of case-study schools have established peer support or student mentor structures (Prefects, "Amigos", Mentors, "Buddies") whose
assistance is often used in the transition process of the first-year students.
The staff in most of the case-study schools feel that, while experiencing
problems and/or difficulties in adjusting to the new school setting, the
first-year students may find it easier to relate to another student, at least
initially, rather than to a teacher:

They [the mentors] go down at the big break and they also go down
between classes and they [students] know they can approach them if
they have any problems and we feel that sometimes they might approach them more easily than they would approach a teacher if there
was any question of bullying or anything like that. Usually they get
friendly with these girls and they help them over any difficulties. We
find that a good system (Principal, Barrack Street School).

The student mentors are sometimes responsible for giving information
on the school layout and rules to the new students; they talk to the first

years about bullying and difficulties they may encounter in the post-primary school and generally look out for the new students:

> So they are allocated a senior prefect, sixth year, and they come in on that day [open day] and they show them round, they bring them all around the school and they tell them all about different things, where the shops are, the toilets and they talk to them about bullying and they try to build a relationship (Year Head, Wentworth Place School).

Sometimes the student mentors are asked to target specifically the students who may need extra help and attention:

> You have to watch out for people who tend to get lost, loners, people who get bullied, people who are not very forthcoming and might just fall through the cracks in many ways (Deputy Principal, Fig Lane School).

In Dixon Street School, student mentors are involved in a comprehensive programme where they visit the prospective first-year students in the primary school and organise a school tour for them:

> We have fifth years and they are called the Amigos, they are a peer mentoring group and they actually work with me in the games club which is nice, so the first years have kind of peer role models — older students. They work with the kids in the primary school and when the primary school comes up, they know a lot of the sixth years, which is nice. They know the oldest kids in the school (8-15 Programme, Dixon Street School).

The importance of selecting student mentors on a voluntary basis was often stressed by school personnel. It was felt that when such a support is provided on voluntary basis, it is more effective as the older students have chosen to participate in it, rather than having been asked to do it:

> The prefect would have been through the school and he would have volunteered for this job — not a person who would have been chosen — so they would have the school's interests at heart (Principal, Wentworth Place School).

3.2.5 Teachers' perceptions of integration supports

In order to explore teachers' awareness and perceptions of integration supports and programmes for first-year students, first-year students' subject teachers were asked about the main types of approaches their school used in attempting to ensure the successful transition of their students into post-primary school.

As shown in Table 3.2, the main approach mentioned by teachers related to the use of a class tutor or form teacher system (cited by 41 per cent of teachers). Student mentor systems were also frequently mentioned (36 per cent). The organisation of an induction day or programme was also cited by over a third of teachers. Finally, the provision of extra-curricular activities was also seen as an important area in facilitating the successful integration of students (mentioned by nearly one-in-five teachers).

Table 3.2: Main approaches mentioned by teachers used to help students settle into post-primary school

Rank Order	Approach Used	% of Teachers
1	Class Tutor/Form Teacher	40.7
2	Student Mentor/links with Senior Students	35.8
3	Induction Programme	19.0
4	Induction Day	18.1
5	Extra-curricular Activities	18.0
6	Year Head	14.2
7	Home–School–Community Liaison Co-ordinator	8.0
8	Teacher Talk to Students Informally	7.5
9	Meeting with Parents	7.1
10	Pastoral Care	6.2

Note: Total adds to more than 100 as teachers were asked to give main approach(es).

Teachers in Dawson Street and Wentworth Place were more likely to cite the class tutor/year head approach (Figure 3.1), while student mentors were more frequently mentioned in Fig Lane and Belmore Place (Figure

3.2). The provision of an induction day/programme to foster student integration was more frequently cited in Wynyard Road and Lang Street (Figure 3.3). Finally, the relative weight attached to extra-curricular activities varied widely: a considerable proportion of teachers in Park Street, Dixon Street and Dawes Point identified extra-curricular activities as an approach while teachers in Barrack Street and Wentworth Place failed to cite such activities as factors in facilitating student transition and integration (Figure 3.4).

Figure 3.1: Tutor/Year Head

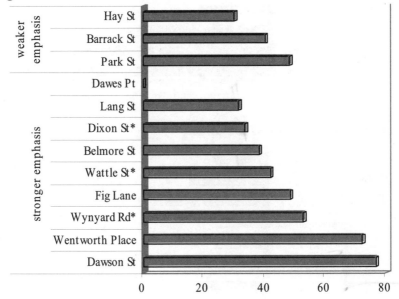

Figure 3.2: Student mentors

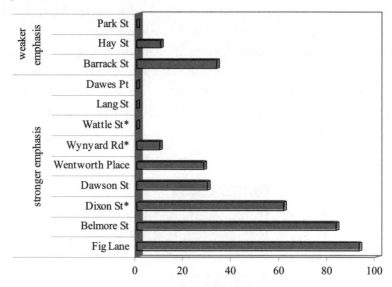

Figure 3.3: Induction Day/Programme

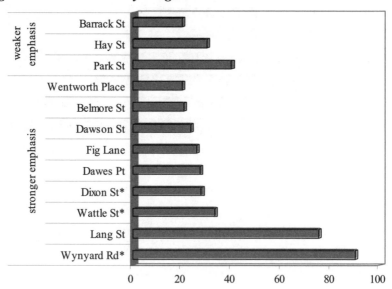

Note: * Schools initially classified as "low integration" which were found to have more developed integration policies.

Figure 3.4: Extra-curricular activities

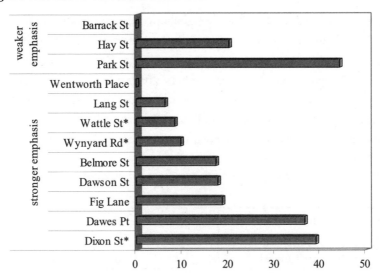

The analysis of the teachers' survey demonstrates that there is little evidence of other "innovative" approaches used by the case-study schools regarding the transition from primary to post-primary school. Outside of the above-mentioned approaches (Tutors, Year Heads, Mentors, Induction Programmes and extra-curricular activities), the following approaches were also central in the teacher responses in a number of schools:

- Dixon Street: Meeting with the parents and primary-post-primary co-ordination

- Wentworth Place: The role of Pastoral Care

- Dawes Point: Home–School–Community Liaison Co-ordinator and the SSRI/Breakfast Club

- Belmore Street: HSCL Co-ordinator.

However, the interviews with the "key" personnel revealed that the way in which the main support structures are used and activities involved varies greatly between schools.

3.2.6 Information received by teachers on in-coming students

Chapter Two highlighted some dissatisfaction among post-primary principals with the information flow between primary and post-primary schools regarding in-coming first-year students. The present study also explored the extent to which the teachers involved in teaching first-year students are provided with relevant information on first-year students. One third of teachers surveyed indicated that they had received no information on first-year students prior to their entry (Table 3.3).

Table 3.3: Information provided to teachers on students coming into first year

Rank Order	Information	% Teachers	Main Schools Mentioning
1	Home Background	22.1	Fig Lane; Barrack St; Hay St
2	Health/medical issues	15.9	Wynyard Rd; Fig Lane
3	Learning Difficulties	15.9	Fig Lane; Dawson St; Dixon St
4	Assessment test results	14.2	Hay St; Wynyard Rd; Wattle St
5	Academic progress within primary	11.9	Dawes Pt; Fig Lane; Wynyard Rd
	No Information	34.2	Wentworth Pl (84%); Park St (68%)

Where information was provided to teachers, the main issues covered related to students' home background. Academic information was also prominent, chiefly relating to learning difficulties, assessment test results and academic progress:

> [. . .] maybe if they have behavioural problems, maybe if they have certain weaknesses in certain subject areas — that kind of general information (Deputy Principal, Barrack Street).

The presence of health, medical or psychological problems was also cited. It can be argued that having such information available would help teachers to target students who might need more support in making the transition. Sometimes parental permission is necessary to obtain information about a student:

> No, I think we get all the information we need and in the case of children who have been assessed we actually get, their assessment is released, psychological assessment, the information on that is released by the primary school to us with the parents' permission (Principal, Dixon Street).

It was evident from the interviews with the school staff that not everybody has access to information about in-coming students:

> The form teachers — if there were a particular difficulty, yes, we would pass it on to the subject teachers. But if it is of a very personal and private nature and something that parents don't want, then we don't pass it on to the teachers, unless they give us permission to do so. Usually the form teacher would have it so she would be aware that in fact there are difficulties and then would maybe mind the first-year student to ensure that they cope with some of the difficulties in the first term particularly (Deputy Principal, Barrack Street).

> Well, some of the information would be available say to the guidance counsellor, maybe the chaplain. The information then is used to place the students into classes and if there was anything relevant to a particular class teacher, it would be passed on to him (Principal, Dixon Street).

In some schools the link between primary and post-primary schools seemed to be relatively close which facilitated the information flow between the two school settings. Information is often exchanged in an informal way:

> It [the relationship with the feeder primary school] would be pretty close now. They would feel free to ring us up and things like that and they do it about particular students — they might say ". . . I'm recommending this girl to go down to you next year." She might be from a lone parent family or something else like that "and the reason we are sending her down there is because we want you to look after her" — that type of thing, a good flow of information — you know (Principal, Wynyard Road).

> I have a very close involvement with the home school co-ordinator
> there. We share funding and courses and information and support. I
> spend time in her school and she spends time here. We meet regu-
> larly and I get to know a lot of the parents before they even come
> here (HSCLO, Lang Street).

> The information is sufficient because of the relationship we have
> formed with the primary school. And any information that we lack is
> always available if we go back (8-15 Programme Co-ordinator, Lang
> Street).

However, in some cases it was evident that the school staff would like to
have more information available about the in-coming first-year students:

> I do think that we don't get a profile on the students coming in and
> that would save a lot of time and bother if we were to get that. There
> should be more liaisons; I should have a profile of every student
> coming into the school. We've a lot of great examples of cases and
> we didn't get it and as a result, a lot of time was wasted (SSRI, Hay
> Street).

Some teachers reported that the information is not available and they
would need to phone the old school if they have queries about particular
children. Background information about a new student was considered
important:

> Well, you'd like to know their home situation, about their parents
> and little things like that, you know. So you don't, as you say, put
> your foot in it, saying you know, can I contact your parents where
> there might be a one-parent family or something like that. Because
> they do get offended very easily. So that would be one area (Class
> Tutor, Park Street).

In sum, the level of co-operation between the primary and post-primary
sectors, the type and quantity of information provided and access to this
information varies by schools. In some cases having linked primary
school(s) helps to improve the information flow, at least between certain
members of school staff like Home–School–Community Liaison Co-
ordinators. Access to information also varies by school and depends on
the type of information. Sensitive information is generally given only to
a limited number of school staff.

3.3 PERCEIVED ADEQUACY OF TRANSITION SUPPORT SYSTEMS

The vast majority (almost 90 per cent) of subject teachers in the case-study schools see the current supports as adequate with the exception of Park Street (a boys' secondary school) where over a third of teachers see the supports as inadequate. Inadequate support may lead to sustained difficulties being experienced by students and subsequent early school leaving. These and similar issues will be discussed in Section 3.4.

In identifying any additional support required to ensure a more successful transition and fewer transition difficulties, the role of (additional) learning support is most frequently cited (by one-quarter of teachers) (Table 3.4). The home-school-community liaison scheme, counselling or psychological support, extra-curricular activities and smaller class sizes are also mentioned. There is evidence that some personnel in the case-study schools feel they do not have sufficient resources to address the needs of students who would be most in need of help.

Table 3.4: Main supports teachers would like to see for first years (which are not available currently)

Rank Order	Support	% Teachers	Main Schools Mentioning
1	More learning support/remedial	23.0	Wattle St; Fig Lane; Hay St
2	Home–School–Community Liaison Scheme	7.5	Park St
3	Counselling/psychological support	6.6	Wattle St; Barrack St
4	Extra-curricular activities	5.8	Dawes Point
5	Smaller class sizes	5.3	Dawson St
6	Time for teacher-student interaction	4.4	Dixon St
7	Student mentoring	4.4	Wentworth Pl
	No extra support needed	18.1	Belmore St; Barrack St; Dawson St

3.4 PERCEIVED PREVALENCE OF SUSTAINED
TRANSITION DIFFICULTIES

Key personnel within the case-study schools tended to report that the numbers of students who experience sustained difficulties, that is difficulties that last beyond the first term, tend to be relatively small. Problems that last beyond the first year are considered rare. Most students are seen to settle into the post-primary school within a month. Overall, subject teachers of the first-year students estimate that approximately one-in-ten students experience sustained difficulties in making the transition to post-primary school (Figure 3.5). The figure is almost double that in Dixon Street (a designated disadvantaged school), while significantly fewer students are considered to be experiencing such difficulties in Belmore Street, Wynyard Road, Lang Street, Fig Lane and Wentworth Place (5–6 per cent).

Figure 3.5: Perceived prevalence of sustained transition difficulties

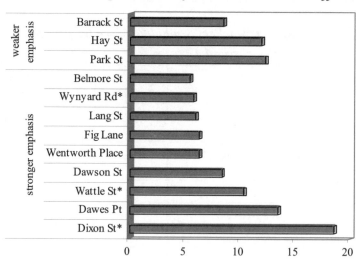

Note: * Schools initially classified as "low integration" which were found to have more developed integration policies.

3.5 FACTORS CONTRIBUTING TO SUSTAINED DIFFICULTIES

In the interviews, "key members" of the school personnel reflected on the settling-in experiences of first-year students and the factors contributing to sustained difficulties where they arose. Bullying was identified as one of the most serious issues affecting adjustment to a new school:

> Some of them would find it easy enough in the second term but the issues around the bullying and that sort of stuff could go into the second term and that is an issue that needs to be addressed very quickly. You need to be aware of that and again the role of the form teacher there is absolutely crucial (Deputy Principal, Dixon Street School).

Difficulties in settling into the new school are also seen as relating to a child's personality and behavioural difficulties. Having initiatives and support in place for students in general, and targeting these students in particular, is seen to be of utmost importance:

> You are looking at different issues really. You are looking at behavioural problems which would be one of the main reasons that the child wouldn't settle in — involved in anti-social behaviour outside of school which obviously carried over into school — and an inability to relate to the teachers and an inability to relate to classmates. . . . Those children will have those problems next year (8-15 Programme, Dixon Street School).

There is a certain commonality across schools in staff perceptions of the difficulties students experience during the transition from primary to post-primary school. These difficulties can be broadly divided into three categories: a) organisational factors, b) self- and peer- related factors, and c) academic factors.

The majority of subject teachers (two-thirds) cited problems related to personal factors such as home background and personality issues, which corresponds to the information provided by the interviews with "key personnel". Factors pertaining to the organisation of the school/ class were cited by 40 per cent of teachers, while academic issues were mentioned by 37 per cent of teachers (see Figure 3.6a and Table 3.5).

Figure 3.6a: Teachers' views on factors contributing to students'
experiences of sustained transition difficulties

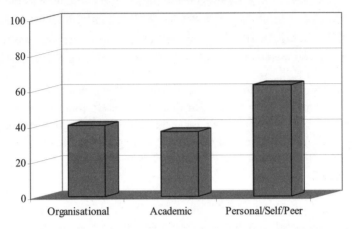

Table 3.5: Main reasons mentioned by teachers for students'
experiencing sustained difficulties in the transition to post-primary
education

Rank Order	Reason/Factor in Difficulty	% of Teachers
1	Home background	24.3
2	Move to larger school	19.9
3	New peer group/loss of primary school peer group	18.6
4	Number of teachers	17.3
5	Lack of academic ability	17.2
6	Personality: anxious, lack of confidence, shy	14.2
7	Immaturity	10.6
8	Structure of school day	10.6
9	Number of subjects	10.2
10	Lack of family support	8.0

Note: Total adds to more than 100, as teachers were able to give multiple reasons

The relative weight attached to these various factors showed some variation between schools. As illustrated in Figure 3.6b, problems arising
from the organisational structure and set-up of the post-primary school

were particularly strong in Dixon Street (mentioned by 83 per cent of teachers in this school). Issues relating to academic/ability difficulties were mentioned more frequently among teachers in Wentworth Place, Fig Lane and Wattle Street (Figure 3.6c). Finally, teachers in Wattle Street, Lang Street and Belmore Street more frequently identified factors relating to personality and peers as contributing to transition difficulties among their students (Figure 3.6d).

Figure 3.6b: Organisational factors as contributing to students' experiences of sustained transition difficulties

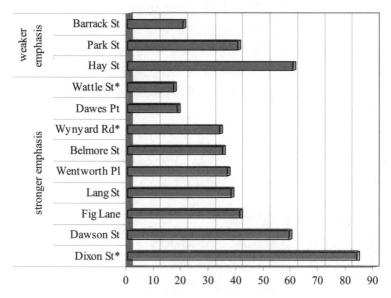

Figure 3.6c: Academic factors as contributing to students' experiences of sustained transition difficulties

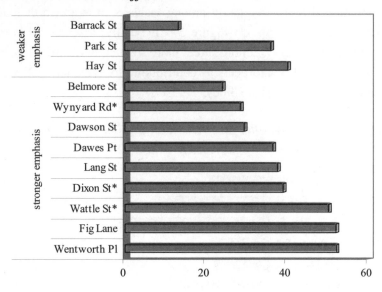

Figure 3.6d: Personal/peer factors as contributing to students' experiences of sustained transition difficulties

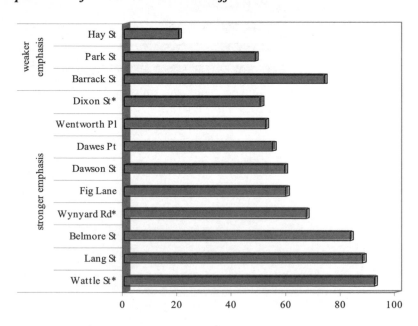

3.5.1 Organisational Factors

School personnel interviewed about the organisational factors which contribute to difficulties among first years identified the following issues: developing a relationship with a number of different teachers, moving from one classroom to another, coming from a small (rural) school into a vast post-primary school, reading the timetable, organising their books and other similar issues:

> Well I suppose the [. . .] teachers and the different demands being made by different teachers. Everybody has their own way of approaching things. They would have great difficulties around that. They were only used to one teacher and now suddenly they have a variety of different teachers (Deputy Principal, Barrack Street School).

> Some of them have come from very small primary schools and again that takes a little while (Deputy Principal, Dixon Street School).

> Obvious ones would be the whole confusion around timetable and the number of teachers (Wynyard Road School).

Problems can also occur due to the differences between the primary and post-primary systems in Ireland (Burke, 1987), as discussed in Chapter One: in primary schools there may be more movement in the class and group work, whereas in post-primary schools students are often expected to sit with their books, listening and working quietly:

> The two systems are very different and there is a kind of conflict there in the way that things are done (Principal, Park Street School).

It was evident from the interviews that initial confusion was to be anticipated and the majority of students were seen to need time to get used to the new system. However, some students were seen as thriving with the move from class to class and being excited about the change and their new subjects. Most of the students were seen to settle in within the first week or so. There are also factors such as the workload, weight of books, dealing with lockers, different approaches towards students' participation in class, getting to know the rules, getting to respond to the demands of post-primary schools which were identified as contributing to difficulties in settling in.

3.5.2 Self- and peer-related factors

Among the other factors influencing students' experience of transition from primary to post-primary are those associated with their sense of self and negotiating their status among their peers. Bullying and the related experiences of anxiety and isolation were seen as a serious obstacle to the process of settling into the new system. The changing status of students, finding themselves the youngest students in the new school, is a further issue often referred to by key personnel.

Bullying, anxiety and isolation

Confirming the findings of Naughton (2000) and O'Brien (2001), the study identified bullying as a serious issue, mentioned by the majority of school staff interviewed. The problem was acknowledged in all twelve case-study schools and all schools have reported setting up strong anti-bullying policies. Some schools have support structures in place for the victims of bullying and lectures are organised in some schools for parents and students to alert them to the signs. Deliberate taunting of other students was mentioned as occurring in most of the schools, although all the schools had strict policies on such behaviour. A number of schools mentioned the "slagging" of first-year students by older students who, in many cases, may not realise that this might cause upset among first-year students. Students also experience anxiety due to rumours they hear about the school (from siblings or friends) and the "first year initiation". These are some of the key personnel's views on bullying:

> Quite a bit of that bullying came with them from the Primary School. It had been going on in the Primary School and it came up here and it is hard to root out even though the two form teachers have been working on it in a big way. Hopefully we will have it rooted out but it is a problem though (Principal, Barrack Street School).

> Bullying is a huge thing — huge. And isolation. And then of course there is the pull into the anti-social behaviour, the modelling of the older students — you see it happening a lot. I think that the issues that

the kids face are the same as kids moving into any other school face — anxiety (8-15 Programme Co-ordinator, Dixon Street School).

Some teachers considered bullying more serious with girls as it is less visible:

In terms of boisterousness or bullying or anything it can actually be worse with the girls if it takes place, it's more vicious and it can be more insidious, they can just exclude people (HSCL Co-ordinator, Dixon Street School).

Bullying can also take the form of mobile phone text messages; as this is less visible, it is believed that it is more difficult to address this issue:

One thing that worries me is text bullying, that really would worry me a lot because you cannot actually see it, you know what we would see would be kind of name-calling or pushing or taking something belonging to them, this type of thing or hiding a copy and getting them into difficulty, that type of bullying (Guidance Counsellor, Park Street School).

But the most common thing for me would be bullying, where they are being hassled or harassed in various ways, and they . . . stop coming to school as a result, and you know, [they are] pretty upset about that and very often may not have told their parents (Guidance Counsellor, Wentworth Place School).

Students who are immature are seen as experiencing more anxiety in post-primary school, which can make the settling-in process longer than usual:

There's one particular guy now in that class for tutoring that I have and I think he's finding it very difficult to adjust. He's probably immature and I'll say that [it] probably will take him all of first year before, he's very prone to crying and he's very prone [to] . . . come looking for attention and that sort of thing, So you know you'll always have that with some of them. Some are much more streetwise (Class Tutor, Park Street School).

In all twelve case-study schools the key personnel identified bullying as a serious issue that can have long term consequences for the victim if it continues unaddressed. Quieter students, and those who are less mature or in some way different, are seen as more likely to experience bullying and as a result can experience greater difficulty in settling into the new school setting.

Students' change of status and sense of self

During the transition from primary to post-primary school students go through a "change of status" — they become the youngest in the school, an important change from being the eldest students in the primary school:

> The biggest thing is, and we all know this, coming from the primary school, they're the sixth class kids, they're the big kids in the school, suddenly they're coming here and they're the first years. So they're not the kings of the castle anymore (Chaplain, Dixon Street School).

Some of the school staff interviewed considered the personality of the child as an important factor in settling in; more confident and outgoing students were seen to settle in quicker than shy, timid students. Being involved in sports or other team activities was also seen to have a positive effect on the settling-in process:

> There was one particular guy who just wasn't settling into it and he was a quiet kind of guy and certainly wouldn't have been aggressive and he would have been a gentle personality and he found it extremely tough. . . . He was very sensitive. He just didn't like the rugby because it wasn't his game at all. . . . He was finding it hard coming into the school and wasn't getting involved and as a result was beginning to be on his own (Guidance Counsellor, Fig Lane).

Friendships are also considered important in the transition process. Many students have moved from their primary school to the post-primary school with one or several friends who may be in their class. A number of the case-study schools attempted to facilitate this by putting them in the same class, if possible. In most case-study schools, some of the first-year students had an older brother or sister already in the school, which was also seen to help in settling in:

> Each year I would say maybe at least one third have brothers and sisters here . . . so a third of them know the place very well and because

> we have got such a broad extra-curricular range of activities, they are in here a lot, they would know their way around (Guidance Counsellor, Fig Lane School).

A number of students in the schools do not know anybody and need to make new friends. The impact of falling in and out of friendships can have serious effects on students, especially girls, which confirms the findings of the study by O'Brien (2001):

> The first days they are really lost sometimes, even with helping them and they get into terrible panic and also if a friend leaves them in the first month or two . . . they have great expectations of friendship . . . [and] their best friend might have found a new friend in a month and they can be very hurt and devastated and they don't know how to have patience and how to just be able to say hello to a few people and be fairly friendly with them, they want to have best friends straight away . . . it really is a big thing (Principal, Belmore Street School).

It was also argued that introverted and quiet students are likely to find it harder to establish themselves in a new group. Further, this is considered to be more difficult if students have learning difficulties:

> I think the personality is central. . . . generally, you would find that the more confident character will find the transition easier, I think. Maybe that is external, but the livelier student and the more confident student seems to be the one that settles into it quicker and will establish themselves in the group a lot quicker, whereas the more introverted student or quieter student will take more time and might feel that they are a bit on the outside (Guidance Counsellor, Fig Lane School).

> I presume shy kids have a little bit more difficulty. Kids who have been bullied before are nervous. Some kids, a small minority of kids who have reading and learning difficulties obviously have more difficulty, because quite frankly I think it is expecting the impossible (Guidance Counsellor, Fig Lane School).

Academic factors

Although the teachers mostly mentioned non-academic difficulties in relation to settling in, namely students' character and bullying, there were some staff who identified academic factors as well:

> They must deal with homework from five or six subjects in a night — that kind of thing. The first day that the form teacher has them, she explains to them how to use their homework journal and they keep on explaining that [. . .] but some of them find it more difficult than others, but the majority don't (Principal, Barrack Street).

> [The students] don't have the same problem with homework as they used to and since Christmas I've received very little complaints whereas before it you'd hear a lot of complaints (Class Tutor, Park Street).

> We have two ways of tackling [difficulties]. We have a remedial teacher in the school who would pick up on known people with literacy or numeracy problems and give them assistance and we have another system then whereby the special programmes like JCSP and so on, have built into them sections which will improve literacy and improve numeracy by way of games or by way of special projects [. . .] We feel that if a child is innumerate or illiterate then you won't make much progress with any other subject (Principal, Lang Street).

Dealing with the amount of homework and students' academic ability were perceived by school personnel as factors potentially hindering the adjustment process.

3.6 SUMMARY AND CONCLUSIONS

This chapter draw on the perceptions of key personnel in the twelve case-study schools as well as subject teachers of the first-year students in relation to the transition to post-primary school. The results illustrate that the factors influencing the transition process from primary to post-primary school are complex. All students are seen to experience some disruption and discontinuity coming from the primary school system.

The school personnel from all twelve case-study schools reported that the new students had problems initially with getting used to the size of the school which in many cases was considerably bigger than their primary school. This resulted in students getting lost trying to find their way to subject classrooms. Some of the schools had anticipated this and had, hence, devised various play-related activities (such as a treasure hunt) to familiarise the students with the new building even before the school officially started. The use of maps and older students to assist the new arrivals was also mentioned.

Another novelty for the first-year students, as seen by the teachers, was the number of subject teachers they encountered. Being used to having just one teacher in the primary school, the first-year students had to get used to the variety of teaching styles and demands of their new teachers.

Starting post-primary school coincides with early adolescence and constitutes a time when students may be particularly vulnerable regarding relationships and their sense of self. Although the schools try to facilitate the transition process by putting some friends together in a class, this is not always possible and results in the child having to negotiate his or her place in a new group of children. The ease of this process was seen as depending largely on the child's personality and maturity.

Closely related to the child's personality, bullying was identified as a major issue in the adjustment experience. The seriousness of the issue was stressed by all twelve case-study schools who all reported having a strict anti-bullying policy in place. Bullying is also related to "first year initiations" whereby within the first weeks older students "test out" the new arrivals.

The problems that occur during the process of transition are seen to be generally short-lived and the majority of the students settle in quickly after getting used to the new structures and demands of post-primary schooling. However, a minority of students are perceived as experiencing sustained difficulties in settling in (on average one-in-ten, according to the subject teachers). For them, even the open days and induction programmes designed by schools are not always sufficient. Sustained difficulties are seen as linked with issues such as bullying, immaturity, learning difficulties, and the personality of the students.

Chapter Four

CURRICULAR PROVISION AND LEARNING STRUCTURES IN THE CASE-STUDY SCHOOLS

4.1 INTRODUCTION

Academic factors and school practices can contribute to, or alleviate, adjustment difficulties during the transfer from primary to post-primary school. Students can experience discontinuity of the curriculum due to the differences between the primary and post-primary systems (Burke, 1987). Difficulties may occur, for example, with the introduction of new subjects that were not covered at primary school, the changing demands of subjects, an increased number of subjects, the impact of ability grouping practices in the post-primary school, as well as changing homework demands.

However, schools vary widely in their practices regarding the number of subjects available for students, the timing of subject choice and ability grouping practices (see Chapter Two). Table 4.1 gives an overview of such practices in the twelve case-study schools. Half of the schools adopted mixed ability base classes with their first-year students, with the remaining half utilising some form of ability grouping. The number of subjects taken by first years varied widely across the schools: ranging from 12 to 18 subjects. These differences largely reflect variations in the timing of subject choice and the availability of subject "taster" programmes for first-year students. These and other curricular issues are discussed during the course of this chapter, culminating in a profile of the main aspects of curricular provision in the twelve schools and some of the ways schools vary in the nature and perceptions of curricular provision.

Table 4.1: School profiles

School Name	School Type	Subjects Taken 1st Term of 1st yr	Timing of Subject Choice	Ability Grouping
Fig Lane	Fee-paying coed	17	Taster programme, pick at the end of 1st year	Mixed ability
Wynyard Road	Girls' sec school	18	Pick at the end of 1st yr	Mixed ability
Lang Street*	Vocational	17	Pick at the end of 1st year	Streamed
Belmore Street	Girls' sec school	16	Pick at the end of 1st year	Mixed ability
Wentworth Place	Boys' sec school	15	Taster programme	Banded
Dixon Street*	Vocational	13	Taster programme	Streamed
Dawes Point*	Boys' sec school	12	Pick before entry	Streamed
Wattle Street*	Boys' sec school	12	Pick before entry	Mixed ability
Dawson Street	Comm/comp	13	Pick before entry	Mixed ability
Barrack Street*	Girls' sec school	12	Pick before entry	Mixed ability
Park Street	Boys' sec school	12	Pick before entry, more restrictive choice	Streamed
Hay Street	Vocational	14	Pick before entry, more restrictive choice	Streamed

* Designated disadvantaged schools

The chapter takes the following format. Section two discusses school-level perceptions of the Junior Certificate curriculum and subjects offered. This is followed by an examination of the main approaches to subject choice in the schools. Section four details school practices in terms of ability grouping. The extent and nature of learning support and its perceived adequacy are discussed in section five. The approach used in teaching first-year students and how this may differ to other year groups is discussed in section six. Section seven discusses how the twelve schools vary across this range of curricular areas. A summary and conclusions section completes the chapter.

The chapter draws solely on the perceptions and experiences of school personnel, chiefly teachers, and does not incorporate the views and experiences of students themselves, who are the focus of Chapters Five to Seven. Interviews with a total of 103 key personnel were conducted in May 2002. In addition, structured interviews were conducted with 226 teachers teaching first-year students in the case study schools. This Chapter is based on analyses of these two sets of interviews.

4.2 PERCEPTIONS OF CURRICULUM

Teachers' views of the curriculum for first-year students were assessed in a number of areas: these included subject difficulty, suitability for lower ability students, time pressures and continuity with the primary curriculum. While less than one-in-seven teachers considered their subject too difficult for average ability students, this varied widely across schools, reflecting the varied intake of the schools (Figure 4.1). Most notably, teachers in Hay Street and Dixon Street were considerably more likely to rate their subject as too difficult (both schools with relatively low literacy levels among first-year students), while Dawes Point, Belmore Street and Fig Lane teachers were less likely to have such a view, not surprising given that the latter two schools have somewhat stronger literacy scores.

In terms of suitability of the curriculum for lower ability students, no clear pattern emerges according to intake characteristics; in fact, teachers in Park Street, Wattle Street and Wynyard Road were less likely to consider their subject as suitable for lower ability students, even though these schools have a higher ability intake (Figure 4.3).

Almost 40 per cent of teachers consider it difficult to cover the Junior Cycle curriculum in the time available (Figure 4.2). Teachers in Wynyard Road were considerably more likely to agree with this statement, while their counterparts in Fig Lane were less likely to perceive such difficulties. Surprisingly, both schools have somewhat higher first-year literacy scores.

Figure 4.1: Percentage viewing their subject as too difficult for average ability students (by school)

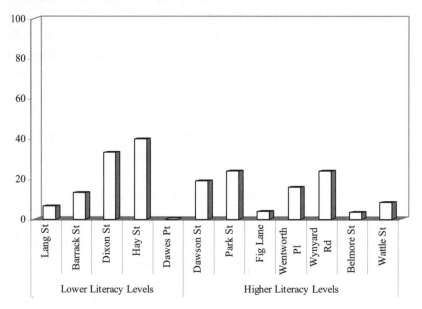

Figure 4.2: Percentage who consider it difficult to cover the Junior Certificate curriculum in the time available (by school)

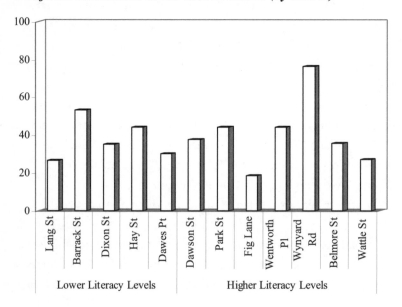

Figure 4.3: Percentage viewing the curriculum as suitable for lower ability students (by school)

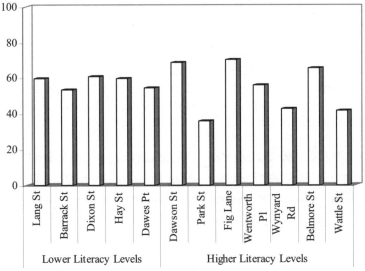

4.2.1 Overall perceptions of the curriculum

Comparing responses across all areas, it appears concern with the suitability of the curriculum for lower ability students (44 per cent) and perceived difficulties in covering the curriculum in the time available (40 per cent) emerge as the main issues concerning teachers (Figure 4.4). Teachers appear somewhat less concerned about their subject being too difficult for average ability students (15 per cent), the curriculum being out-of-date (one-in-seven) or the subject being marked too harshly in the Junior Certificate exam (one-in-ten).

The issue of suitability for lower ability students was also frequently mentioned in the in-depth interviews with key personnel. The issue of difficulty in reading textbooks was particularly prominent, as one principal commented regarding the Junior Cycle curriculum:

> It is suitable for a majority. There are a minority who have learning difficulties and whether another type of course would be more suitable for them is questionable. . . . Anybody who remains in school here, I would say 99.9 will get a Junior Cert of some kind, with effort, but their biggest difficulty really with doing a subject, if you

haven't a good reading age or if you have a low reading age, it affects subjects [. . .] the books are too difficult for them and that has never really been solved (Principal, Barrack Street School).

Similarly, the SSRI[1] co-ordinator in Lang Street asserts:

I think it's [the curriculum is] unsuitable for lower stream students. I think it's too broad, it has too much detail in it, it's irrelevant to what they know. It's difficult, . . . the textbooks they have, my lower stream students would not be able to read them. [There is] very difficult language in them.

Figure 4.4: Percentage considering their subject too difficult for average ability students; difficult to cover in the time available; suitable for lower ability students (disagree); out-of-date and marked too harshly

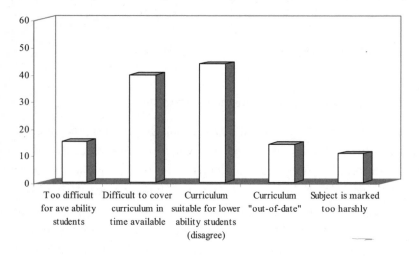

While the resource teacher in Dixon Street states:

I think for those really, really weak students it's not suitable and that would not just be in English, there's an awful lot of subjects that I

[1] The Stay in School Retention Initiative (SSRI) is aimed at keeping students in school up to the completion of Leaving Certificate. It was launched in 1999. The initiative is based on a written retention plan between the school and the Department of Education and Science, with the requirement that the school as driver of the initiative operates on a multi-agency basis and establishes cross-community links. It includes measures such as tracking of absences with follow-up action; additional teaching hours for at risk students; after hours initiatives; individual support with literacy and numeracy.

don't think are suitable. I don't know, I think to an extent that really, really basic level is not looked at at all and the same with the text-books, there's a Junior Cert textbook there, that's for a fifteen-year-old, third year, what do you use in first year? There are books and they're so babyish at some parts and as well as that there are parts that are too complicated. I never use text books with my weaker classes, they're not suitable, I adapt, take things out, make my own work sheets, I never use a text book, I've given them one so they don't feel left out, they have a text book which I looked at a couple of the stories in, it's not appropriate at all.

4.2.2 Perceptions by subject area

Subjects have been grouped (see Appendix Table 4.1) to examine variations in teachers' perceptions of the curriculum in different subject areas. In terms of perceptions of difficulty, marking severity and suitability for lower ability students, considerable cross-subject variation is apparent. Mathematics, Science and Business Studies were more likely to be seen as too difficult for average ability students (Figure 4.5), while teachers of languages and Irish were least likely to perceive their subject as suitable for lower ability students (Figure 4.7). Teachers of languages and practical subjects[2] were most likely to consider their subject to be marked too harshly in the Junior Certificate exam (Figure 4.9).

Teachers of humanities, business and language subjects were more likely to consider it difficult to cover the curriculum in the time available (Figure 4.6). Finally, Irish teachers were remarkably more likely to consider the curriculum as "out-of-date" (Figure 4.8).

---

[2] For these purposes, the practical subjects were taken to include Materials Technology (Wood), Technical Graphics, Metalwork, Home Economics and Technology (see Appendix A4.1).

Figure 4.5: Percentage viewing their subject as too difficult for average ability students (by subject)

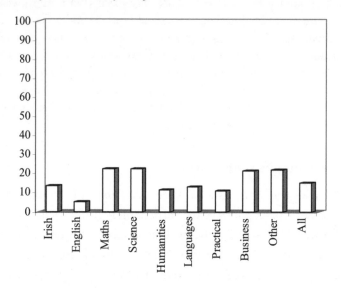

Figure 4.6: Percentage who consider it difficult to cover the Junior Certificate curriculum in time available (by subject)

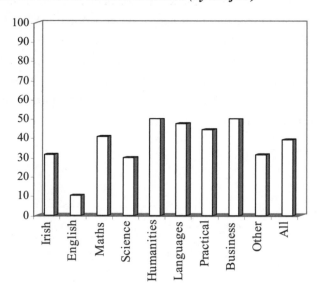

Figure 4.7: Percentage viewing the curriculum as suitable for lower ability students (by subject)

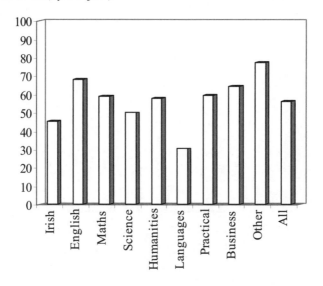

Figure 4.8: Percentage who consider many aspects of the curriculum out-of-date (by subject)

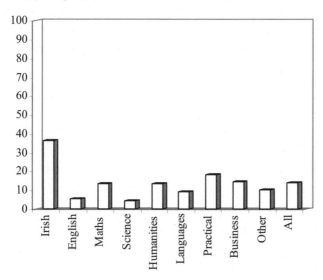

Figure 4.9: Percentage considering their subject marked too harshly in Junior Certificate exam

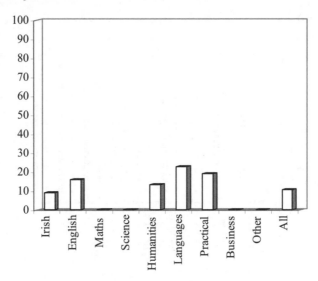

4.2.3 Perceptions of subject provision in own school

The vast majority (over 95 per cent) of teachers maintain that there is a good range of subjects provided for first years in their school; with little variation across schools or subject areas. In terms of number of subjects, 44 per cent of teachers contend that first-year students take too many subjects in first year in their school. However, as Figure 4.10 below illustrates, the prevalence of this view varies widely across schools, with some differentiation according to the number of subjects students take. Highest levels of concern about excessive numbers of subjects emerge in Wynyard Road (which has the highest number of subjects for first-year students), followed by Wentworth Place and Hay Street. Such concerns are less pervasive in Barrack and Wattle Street (schools which have among the lowest subject demands on students with 12 subjects). Overall, however, there is a lot of variation in perceptions of subject overload for each level of subject requirement.

Figure 4.10: Percentage of teachers who feel first-year students take too many subjects in their school and actual no. of subjects taken

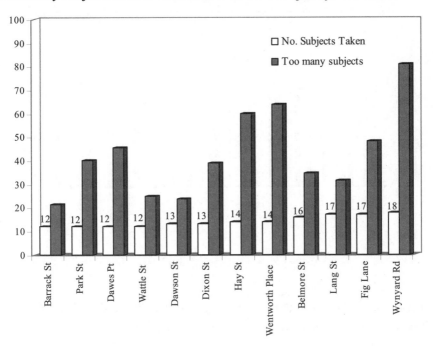

4.2.4 Curriculum continuity

Less than a third of teachers consider the primary school syllabus as a good foundation for taking their subject in first year, with no clear pattern across schools (Figure 4.11). Park Street and Belmore Street teachers were considerably less likely to have such views of the primary school curriculum. History, English and Mathematics teachers were more likely to consider the primary school syllabus as a good foundation, while those in Irish and, most notably, Geography were less likely to have such opinions (Figure 4.12).

Figure 4.11: Percentage viewing the primary school syllabus as good foundation for taking their subject in first year (by school)

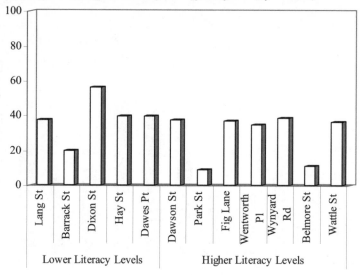

Figure 4.12: Percentage viewing the primary school syllabus as good foundation for taking their subject in first year (by subject)

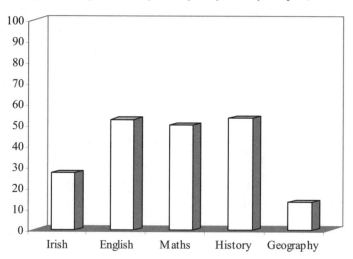

Only half of all post-primary teachers surveyed consider themselves familiar with the nature of the primary curriculum. However, as shown in Figures 4.13 and 4.14, there is some variation across schools and subject areas. Again Mathematics is prominent: familiarity with the primary school curriculum is greatest among Mathematics teachers. Responses of teachers in History and Geography suggest they are least familiar with the primary curriculum in these areas.

Figure 4.13: Proportion of teachers who feel they are familiar with the nature of the primary curriculum by subject

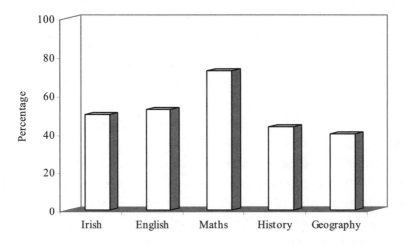

Figure 4.14: Proportion of teachers who feel they are familiar with the nature of the primary curriculum by school

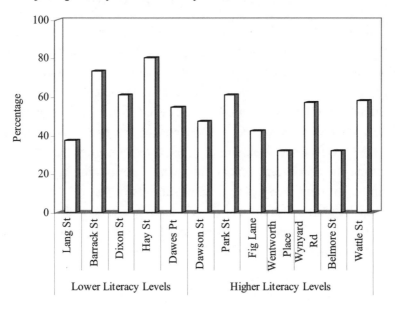

Teachers also display considerable variation across schools in their familiarity with the primary curriculum. Teachers in Hay Street (80 per cent) and Barrack Street (73 per cent) report high levels of familiarity, while their counterparts in Wentworth Place, Belmore Street and Lang Street are significantly less confident that they are familiar with the primary curriculum with only one-third expressing familiarity.

4.2.5 Involvement in curriculum and choice of books/materials

Previous work (Smyth, 1999) has shown wide variation in the division of labour in schools and the extent to which teachers are involved in the important management functions of schools, such as deciding the structure of classes, the subjects offered, the nature of subject packaging and subject choice. Within the case-study schools the vast majority of teachers consider themselves the main person or very involved in decisions regarding both parts of the curriculum to be taught (81 per cent) and the textbooks/materials to be used (78 per cent) for first-year students. Levels of perceived involvement in curriculum selection are somewhat lower among teachers in Dixon Street and Hay Street, while involvement in textbook/material choice is perceived to be lower in Fig Lane and Lang Street.

4.3 APPROACH TO SUBJECT CHOICE

As shown in Chapter Two, schools use different approaches to subject choice in Junior Cycle, some requiring students to choose their subjects before entry to the post-primary school while others allow students a period to try out the new subjects before they are required to choose: such variations are reflected in our twelve case-study schools.[3] In a number of schools students pick subjects at the end of the first year (e.g. Lang Street, Wynyard Road, Belmore Street) or after a shorter period of time (Christmas in Wentworth Place), following a period during which they get an opportunity to try out different subjects (a "taster" programme). Conversely, in other schools, such as Wattle Street, Dawson Street, Barrack Street, Park Street, Hay Street and Dawes Point, students choose their subjects before entry to the school in September.

---

[3] See Table 4.1: School Profiles.

The possibility of changing subjects or selecting different subjects at a later point in time thus varies somewhat. While in some schools students are rarely allowed to change subjects once chosen, in others students can try out a range of subjects, a "taster" programme, before they have to select their Junior Certificate subjects:

> Once they've chosen in first year there tends to be continuity right up to the three years. . . . So it's a three-year programme that they really start on (Deputy Principal, Hay Street).

While students may be presented with a choice of subjects, in some cases such choices open to students are quite restrictive:

> They [the subjects] are more or less picked for them and parents are told then on the open night. The only choices they have would be in the languages (Principal, Park Street).

Students attending Dixon Street, Fig Lane and Wynyard Road have the opportunity to try all subjects for a certain period of time after which they make their choice based on preference and ability. This "trial" period can last from eight weeks to a year. In the majority of the case-study schools offering such taster programmes, they lasted the full year. However, while such taster programmes were generally appreciated and recognised as beneficial to students, one principal argued against a long period of subject "tasting", arguing that students found it difficult to stay focused throughout this period on such a large number of subjects:

> There is going to be an in-built sampling from September to Christmas. Some schools give a year sampling and we think that is nearly too long. There is a danger then of loss of focus and a loss of responsibility. People wouldn't take ownership of their subject (Principal, Wentworth Place).

In the same vein, the Deputy Principal in Barrack Street observed that:

> What would happen is they [students] are inclined to do the best bits of different subjects.

Overall a majority of principals who offered taster programmes and the majority of students (see Chapter Six) expressed a preference for having a taster programme.

Having to choose subjects before coming into the school can cause difficulties for students as there may be no opportunity for them to obtain information from school staff on why they might choose one subject over another. The role of parents in advising their children on their choice of subjects is also particularly recognised in a number of schools. In several schools (Fig Lane, for example), parents receive information from the school regarding the choices available and are encouraged to contact the school if necessary.

School personnel identify a range of factors which they believe influence subject choice at this stage of a student's educational career. One such factor is the informal relations between students and teachers and, in particular, "a good student-teacher relationship". As observed by the Deputy Principal in Hay Street: "If they have a teacher they don't particularly like or that, they will tend to drop it". This is supported by the findings of Galton, Gray, Ruddock (2003) in their research into school transitions in the British context.

The twelve schools adopt different approaches in terms of the advice made available to students regarding subject choice. In a number of schools (such as Barrack Street), students choose their subjects before entry to the school, thereby relying on informal sources of advice, such as their family and friends, rather than advice from school personnel. In other schools, a subject teacher or a class teacher (Dixon St, Wattle Street) or Tutor and Year Head (Lang Street) advise students regarding the subjects to choose:

> I would say the subject teachers would give that, there wouldn't be any input from the guidance counsellor. . . . There isn't any guidance as such at that level, except that . . . if a teacher thought that a pupil was totally unsuitable for a certain subject the teacher would have some input into that (Principal, Dixon Street School).

In other cases (Fig Lane, Wentworth Place, Wynyard Road), the guidance counsellor advises the first-year students regarding subject choice. The principal and deputy principal were also identified as having an input into subject choice in some schools (Wentworth Place). The extent of the guidance counsellor's involvement in advising first-year students in subject choice was found to vary by school:

Yes, they are taken by careers people, [the Counsellor] who has a specific interest in first year and they would sort of on the basis of whatever assessment they would have made throughout the year would advise them and they would also have a look at their results and performance and of course coming into it would also be the pupil's own preference (Deputy Principal, Fig Lane School).

However, the interviews indicated that only one school, Fig Lane, employed a counsellor with specific responsibility to advise first-year students on their subject choice. In general, there appears to be a limited input from guidance counsellors at the junior cycle stage, unless either students or their parents seek advice:

Sometimes students would come in or parents would call me and say oh look he has a choice between whatever and whatever, what do you reckon and I think at that stage it really is not critical. . . . I don't want them to feel like a big fuss over this, the point is to get it right and do something enjoyable for the next two years and really make it count that way (Guidance Counsellor, Wentworth Place School).

Yet the need for adequate guidance, perhaps taking the form of an interview for first-year students, was highlighted by the Fig Lane Counsellor:

In an ideal situation all first years should get an interview. But unfortunately they are at the bottom of the ladder in the sense that we can't. . . . An ideal situation would be that each first year has an interview of 15 minutes, just to go through the reasons for their choice, pointing out things in relation to their choices (Guidance Counsellor, Fig Lane School).

In terms of subject availability and restrictions on subject choice, some schools, for example Fig Lane and Wattle Street, make all subjects available to all first-year students. In other schools restrictions are made, often on the basis of ability: for example, students who have learning difficulties in Park Street and Dawes Point are not offered foreign languages:

Those who had learning difficulties, very severe learning difficulties, for example, if they were dyslexic or if they had language difficulties that they weren't able to cope with English or Irish never mind a foreign language, . . . we actually offer them Home Economics in general (Guidance Counsellor, Park Street).

In summary, the timing and flexibility of subject choice varies considerably across the schools. While a number of schools offer lengthy periods during which students can try a range or all possible subjects (Fig Lane, Wentworth Place, Belmore St, Wynyard Road, Lang Street), in other schools students are required to choose their subjects prior to entry, often with little advice from school personnel (Dawson Street, Barrack Street, Park Street, Hay Street, Dawes Point and Wattle Street). Those schools offering taster programmes also seem more likely to offer specific subject advice or counselling sessions to their students, often at the point of subject choice. Fig Lane is particularly noteworthy in making all subjects available to all students and offering a specific counsellor to advise students on the subjects they might select.

4.4 APPROACH TO ABILITY GROUPING

School personnel have somewhat mixed views on the role and impact of ability grouping in Junior Cycle. It is felt, by some, that in a mixed ability environment students are more confident and have higher self-esteem. Weaker students can be taken out of the class for extra help where necessary.

> The advantage [of mixed ability] is that they're not feeling isolated, sometimes I find, when I was in the special school last year, and found that pupils that are socially fine would tend to label themselves if they were put into a grade that would seem to be remedial (Learning Support, Barrack Street School).

The availability of the Junior Certificate School Programme[4] was considered to be beneficial for some students, especially those having literacy and numeracy difficulties. However, it is not available in all schools.

> I would love to see that Junior Cert Schools Programme in here but we can't get [it] . . . I think that would benefit a lot . . . we don't have the resources for them. . . . it makes no sense, because we have that

---

[4] The Junior Certificate School Programme (JCSP) is a national programme sponsored by the Department of Education and Science and National Council for Curriculum and Assessment. It is currently operating in 150 schools and is targeted at young people who may leave school early.

> support in Leaving Cert Applied and Leaving Cert but we've nothing [in] Junior [cycle] (Guidance Counsellor, Dawson Street School).

It was also noted that segregating weaker students by putting them into inflexible groups by ability can undermine their self-esteem. Setting was seen as one way of solving the issue, with students being able to opt for subjects at different levels as they are timetabled together. It was also seen as a means of correcting for any initially incorrect placements. One deputy principal articulated the impact of streaming on self-esteem:

> [Those in the lower stream class] felt that they were different, they were all in the one class and it was obvious that they were doing a different curriculum from the rest and I really felt that whatever self-esteem or confidence we could have given them, it took that away from them — by putting them into the special class (Deputy Principal, Barrack Street School).

> It is difficult to know which is the better thing really, but I think in first year sometimes big mistakes can be made about placing them. . . . They may get an inferiority complex from day one if they are put into very strict inflexible groups and you can't judge anyone. People change. Some people develop in first year and show ability that may not have come [in with]. [You are] better off to let them see how they develop (Principal, Barrack Street School).

From a teaching point of view, however, it was felt that it is much easier to teach students when they are all at the same ability level. It was argued that it takes more time and effort to teach mixed ability groups. Some considered mixed ability groupings to be more beneficial to more able students.

> I think any sort of course work would just take twice as long because you'd have to stop and go back and maybe have one group working at a faster pace than the others and I just think from that point of view, it's easier [streaming]. I think it works better all around (Class Tutor, Park Street School).

> The advantages of the putting them all in together is that obviously the weaker ones don't feel that they [are] classified as being the weak ones. The disadvantage is that it can lead to the good ones being held back a bit because there is more disruption, the teacher has

to work more slowly . . . I think it's actually harder to teach, it's harder to teach them. But there are pros and cons for both systems (Class Tutor, Park Street School).

The discussion so far has related to the ability grouping of *base* classes. However, even in highly streamed schools, some optional subjects may be taught in mixed ability groups. Furthermore, students from mixed ability base classes may be grouped by ability for certain subjects, such as Mathematics (setting). The twelve schools varied widely in the type of pupil differentiation practices utilised within subject classes: the prevalence of mixed ability teaching with first-year students was found to vary by school and according to subject area, although there was no clear pattern according to the ability level of the student intake. As shown in Table 4.2, teachers in two schools report mixed ability teaching with all their classes (Fig Lane and Wattle Street). Conversely, only one-in-eight teachers in Dixon Street and Park Street are similarly teaching mixed-ability class groups. High levels of streamed teaching are also apparent in Wentworth Place, Dawes Point and Lang Street, respectively. In schools with streamed classes, teachers in Wentworth Place are most likely to report teaching above average ability students (53 per cent), those in Dawes Point more frequently report average ability classes, while teachers in Dixon Street and Lang Street are highest in reporting below average ability class groups.

The prevalence of ability grouping is considerably higher in the core subjects (Irish, 52 per cent, English, 53 per cent and, particularly, Mathematics, 74 per cent), while levels are lowest in practical subjects (presumably partly relating to logistical constraints given the smaller numbers of students taking these subjects). Approximately 60 per cent of teachers report teaching mixed ability classes in the science, humanities and languages areas.

Table 4.2: Types of ability group taught by teachers

School	Not Grouped	Grouped		
		Above Ave	*Average*	*Below Ave*
Lower Literacy Levels				
Lang St	31.3	18.8	43.8	46.7
Barrack St	86.7	0.0	0.0	13.3
Dixon St	12.5	25.0	50.0	50.0
Hay St	70.0	0.0	0.0	20.0
Dawes Pt	18.2	9.1	63.6	40.0
Higher Literacy Levels				
Dawson St	76.5	11.8	5.9	5.9
Park St	12.5	29.2	50.0	41.7
Fig Lane	100	0.0	0.0	0.0
Wentworth Pl	15.8	52.6	31.6	35.0
Wynyard Rd	50.0	10.0	20.0	21.1
Belmore St	96.6	0.0	3.4	0.0
Wattle St	100.0	0.0	0.0	0.0
Total	59.6	13.0	20.3	19.9

Note: Types of ability group taught can sum to more than a hundred as question refers to all first year classes taught.

Some variations are apparent according to teacher characteristics and status. Teachers employed in a part-time or job-sharing capacity are less likely to be assigned above average ability classes (no part-time teachers are teaching such groups, relative to 16 per cent of full-time teachers).

In summary, the twelve case-study schools vary in the type and prevalence of pupil differentiation practices. While Dixon Street, Park Street, Lang Street, Wentworth Place and Dawes Point have high levels of ability grouping, the other schools are more likely to adopt mixed ability grouping. Concerns over the potential negative impact of streaming appear somewhat greater among personnel in Barrack Street.

4.5 LEARNING SUPPORT:
APPROACH AND PERCEIVED ADEQUACY

As discussed in Chapter Two, schools vary in their selection and entry practices and in their student intake and composition. Reflecting such variations, schools vary in their (perceptions of the) prevalence of serious literacy and numeracy problems. Most notably, teachers in Dixon Street and Hay Street are more likely to perceive such difficulties.

Table 4.3: Teacher's perceptions of serious literacy and numeracy problems and adequacy of learning support provision

School	Literacy Problems > 20%	Numeracy Problems >20%	% Viewing Learning Support as Inadequate
Lang St	33.3	15.4	12.5
Barrack St	38.5	44.4	6.7
Dixon St	88.9	88.2	22.2
Hay St	77.8	77.8	10.0
Dawes Pt	40.0	44.4	9.1
Dawson St	12.5	21.4	0.0
Fig Lane	11.5	6.3	22.2
Wentworth Pl	0.0	0.0	20.0
Wynyard Rd	17.6	21.4	19.0
Belmore St	16.0	5.3	0.0
Wattle St	8.3	14.3	66.7
Total	26.4	27.4	20.0

The number of students receiving learning support in first year in these schools varies widely (see Chapter Six). As expected, where students are streamed, more students require learning support in the lower stream than in the other streams. The level of engagement of a learning support teacher with the students varies by school. In Barrack Street, for example, the students are seen twice a day by a learning support teacher. Learning support is available up to the end of junior cycle year, and often up to the end of senior cycle. Mostly, learning support is provided in Mathematics and English. In addition to actual learning difficulties, the

Fig Lane learning support teacher identified students' difficulties in organising their schoolwork as one of the areas she also addressed.

In all twelve case-study schools students are identified for extra help/learning support (LS) on the basis of the report from primary school, as well as the results of the pre- or post-entry assessment test. The Park Street principal also mentioned parents as an important source of information. Generally, students' reading ages are tested and those whose reading age is below a specified level are then usually withdrawn from certain classes to get extra help at a suitable pace in a small group.

While most students have no misgivings about being taken out of the class for extra help, some schools did note difficulties with a few students: there could be "difficulties with a few of them but a very small minority" (LS teacher, Barrack Street). Similarly, the LS teacher in Wentworth Place contends:

> It varies from kid to kid, at the beginning, it's always a bit hard on them, because they feel a bit singled out. . . . I have had kids who have not come to terms with it and who have always been conscious about it or been slagged about it but I would say for 95 per cent of the kids, the arrangement works OK. And it very much depends as well on the capacity of the child to kind of withstand whatever jibes are coming their way, some children would not be able to do that and it is a problem.

Learning support provision and the perceived adequacy thereof also displays wide inter-school variation. While overall one-in-five teachers consider the level of learning support provided in their school to be inadequate, teachers in Wattle Street (two-thirds) and Park Street (half) were considerably more likely to consider such provision inadequate. Teachers in the languages, English and business areas were also more likely to consider learning support inadequate (Figure 4.15).

Figure 4.15: Percentage viewing learning support as inadequate by subject area

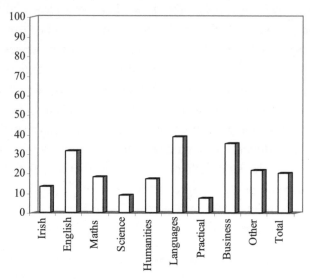

Satisfaction with learning support in the case-study schools depended somewhat on the resources available. The majority of key personnel in the case-study schools voiced the need to have more resources for learning support (although only a minority of subject teachers held this view). The growth of non-national students in Ireland was seen to have created an extra demand on the existing resources:

> We have non-nationals coming in even in First Year. . . . Some would have very little English. . . . At that time it was more or less volunteers that took them and helped them but now we are allowed hours (Principal, Barrack Street).

Other problems identified by the school personnel include a difficulty in finding qualified personnel for the posts and the limited number of hours available for dealing with students experiencing learning difficulties:

> We were having difficulty recruiting people for these posts so what we did was we started training them ourselves . . . so what we're doing now is we're identifying people who have an empathy with weaker kids and we are getting them on to the courses that are being run in the college of education . . . so we've put four people through those courses so far (Principal, Dixon Street School).

> Shortage of teachers I suppose as well, with a qualification or the willingness to do it, you know. . . . so trying to get the manpower or womanpower to do it is another problem (HSCL, SSRI, Hay Street School).

In all cases teachers commented on the positive impact of learning support services: "They probably do better in the exam (Junior Certificate) that they would otherwise" (LS teacher, Fig Lane).

> It's raised some of their confidence . . . other teachers have commented on their reading skills. At the very start of the year, these pupils refused point-blank to read out in class (LS, Barrack Street)..

> When I see students who are still here in fifth and sixth year who come from a support class, that's how I measure [success] (LS, Dixon Street).

> Some kids, it [extra help] made them identify with the school . . . they are very loyal to the school now, . . . [they] were manic when they came into the first year (LS, Dixon Street).

Most learning support teachers interviewed found that they get recognition from their colleagues and that there is a good interaction between the LS teacher and subject teachers. However, Dixon Street LS referred to a lack of understanding of the LS teachers' role in the school:

> Some teachers think there is very little learning support happening . . . their perception of learning support is extra support to them, either through team teaching or through withdrawal . . . but my picture of learning support is much broader.

In summary, owing to varying student intake, the twelve case-study schools varied widely in the levels of literacy and numeracy difficulties among first-year students and the perceived need for learning support. Teachers in Wattle Street and Park Street were most critical of levels of learning support provided in their school. Finally, learning support teachers in Dixon Street voiced some concerns over the perceived level of understanding among other staff members of the role of learning support.

4.6 TEACHING FIRST YEARS:
APPROACH USED AND ASSESSMENT

Previous research has examined the differences in teaching methods employed at primary and post-primary levels. Some of the differences in teaching between primary and post-primary systems in Ireland were alluded to by school personnel during interviews. Such differences are reflected in the methods taught to teachers in universities:

> The national school teachers are taught different methods. Now it's coming through and you can actually notice it now in secondary schools, the methods that they would have learned now are totally different than the way I would be teaching them . . . there's a little bit of a clash there sometimes (Class Tutor, Fig Lane School).

Most of the teachers interviewed reported that their approach to teaching first-year students is different from that of teaching other post-primary year groups. Whether they try to link what the student already knows to the curriculum in post-primary, however, seems to vary more across teachers:

> I suppose [I teach] in a more simple way, try to tie it in somewhat what they have done in Primary School and try to follow it from there (Year Head, Dixon Street).

> I start from the start, . . . anything really that can be the groundwork for next year (Class Tutor, Park Street).

> I do a lot of repetition, a lot of games, a lot of things that are actually childish enough for them to be interested in while still learn something. Because in primary school, everything is about games, so I think the transition is nicer if it's actually still the same (Class Tutor, Wynyard Road).

The majority of the teachers interviewed said that they use a different approach when teaching different ability groups. The Class Tutor in Park Street, for example, referred to a shorter attention span with lower ability students:

> With the weaker ones you'd have got twenty minutes . . . [you] won't keep their attention for forty minutes.

A teacher of Irish in Wentworth Place conducts higher ability classes more through Irish: "Those who are weaker . . . you tend to break a lot into English, just to explain things, to get things across to them". In many cases teachers indicated that they expect more of higher ability groups.

In total, two-thirds of teachers maintain that they adopt a different style of teaching with first-year students than with second or third year classes. While almost all teachers in Hay Street (90 per cent) maintain that they adopt a different style or approach with first years, just half the teachers in Wattle Street are similarly flexible in their approach.

The importance of not having expectations of the first-year students that are too high was stressed by the guidance counsellor in Fig Lane:

> The danger with First Years when you come back in September is you presume knowledge or that you presume that they would know more or are capable of more than they actually are and you just have to be conscious of that, particularly at the start of the first year. Just to slow down, and I would really emphasise explanations and go back over stuff as best as I can, and as often as is required (Guidance Counsellor, Fig Lane).

Many teachers try to employ different methods/activities to engage students in the subject. Among the methods mentioned by the teachers of different subjects were: demonstration and practical work involving experiments, project work, discussions, using a visitor or speaker, and exploratory work. In general, the aim is to provide greater variety in first year with a view to fostering a student's interest in the subject. However, a teacher in Wynyard Road found that:

> I don't know whether they would prefer [more open/flexible methods] but when it comes to exams, I think they would feel more secure — they would feel "that is in my copy, that is that and I know that". Whereas they might not trust that they have learned it.

It is also argued that teaching students at post-primary level is easier if teachers in the primary schools have prepared students for entry into the post-primary school, not surprising considering the "gap" existing between the two systems. However, no information was collected on primary school transition practices so it is not possible to examine this within the context of this study.

> Some schools . . . in sixth year gear towards secondary school so some of the students come in from particular national schools that have geared themselves towards it and they're actually very good . . . whereas other students if they haven't, if the teachers are just doing the normal syllabus, they're not as on top of things (Class Tutor, Fig Lane School).

Parents and students sometimes have certain expectations regarding a student's results. However, a student's grades may drop as they move into post-primary school as they have to contend with a wider range of subjects, new teaching styles and changing expectations (see Chapter One for a review of literature on these issues), differences which were considered substantial, as one teacher commented:

> The student might have been getting A's all along in national school and is now expecting that in first year and when they realise then that they're gone down to a C they can't understand it . . . there is a jump there and their parents can't understand that, all of a sudden they're doing things that are more difficult, they're doing it at a faster pace . . . [they should] make it more of a gradual leap rather than a huge jump in first year (Class Tutor No. 2, Fig Lane School).

4.6.1 Homework

In total three-quarters of teachers regularly prescribe homework to their first-year classes, with somewhat lower levels reported among teachers in Dawson Street, Belmore Street and Barrack Street. The vast majority report using class tests with first-year classes, with fewer teachers in Lang Street and Dixon Street making use of tests (Table 4.4).

Teachers who regularly prescribe homework are also more likely to use tests: while only half of those who never or almost never prescribe homework also indicate they use class tests, over 90 per cent of those who give homework in most or all lessons similarly use testing.

There is some variation in the frequency with which homework is given according to different subject areas. While approximately 90 per cent of teachers in Irish, English and Business Studies give homework in most or all classes, teachers in practical subjects (40 per cent most/every lesson), Science (62 per cent) and humanities (71 per cent) give homework less frequently. Likewise, the use of tests is somewhat lower in the practical subjects (three-quarters using tests), humanities (81 per cent) and business (86 per cent), compared to 95-100 per cent employing tests in languages, Mathematics, Irish and English.

Table 4.4: Different teaching style with first-year students; regularly give homework; use classroom tests

School	Use Different Style	Give Homework Always/Most of Time	Use Tests
Dawson St	58.8	64.7	88.2
Lang St	73.3	68.8	62.5
Barrack St	73.3	66.6	80.0
Dixon St	61.1	77.8	66.7
Park St	60.0	84.0	88.0
Hay St	90.0	90.0	100.0
Fig Lane	70.4	88.8	92.6
Wentworth Pl	60.0	76.0	92.0
Wynyard Rd	85.7	71.4	85.7
Dawes Pt	81.8	90.9	72.7
Belmore St	62.1	65.5	86.2
Wattle St	54.5	83.4	75.0
Total	67.3	76.5	83.6

4.6.2 Teaching style

Teachers can adopt different approaches to teaching: at one extreme is the more traditional teacher-directed "chalk and talk style", at the other a more student-centred approach involving greater interaction and negotiation of the content and methods of teaching. The nature and style of teaching shows considerable variation across the schools: in terms of reliance on Junior Certificate syllabus material, reliance on textbooks, use of computer and video/audio aids, use of group-work and the extent to which learning is student-directed or teacher led. Some evidence of gender and age variation between teachers is apparent, as well as variation across schools.

Syllabus and basic skills

The vast majority of teachers cover material from the Junior Certificate syllabus in most or every first-year lesson, while about half contend that they reinforce basic skills in most/every lesson (Figure 4.16).

Figure 4.16: Frequency with which teachers reinforce basic skills and cover material from Junior Certificate Syllabus

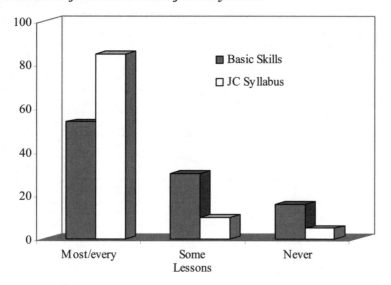

Interaction

One-fifth of teachers indicate that they never ask students questions in class, while 15 per cent say that students never ask questions in their class. Just 13 per cent of teachers indicate that they regularly question students or students ask questions in most/every class. There is some evidence that asking students questions in class is less frequent among those who have been teaching in the school for a longer period (Figure 4.17).

Figure 4.17: Frequency of asking students and students asking questions in class by mean years teaching in school

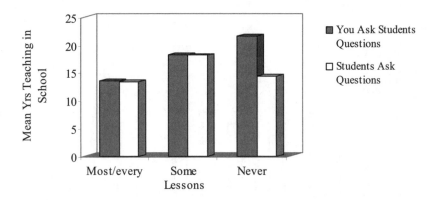

Again the extent to which students are given the opportunity (or take the opportunity) to suggest topics to be covered in class is very low, with such low levels remarkably constant across schools (Figure 4.18).

Figure 4.18: Frequency with which students suggest topics/subjects to be covered

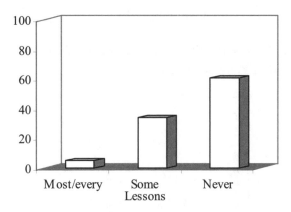

The adoption of traditional teaching and learning styles appears to show some variation across the twelve schools studied (Figure 4.19). While 40 per cent of teachers indicate that students regularly copy notes from the board, the adoption of such traditional methods is considerably lower in Wentworth Place (12 per cent) and higher in Dawes Point (60 per cent) and Lang Street (56 per cent).

Figure 4.19: Proportion of teachers who say students copy notes from the board in most/every class by school

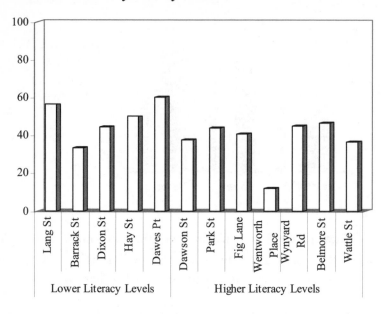

There is some evidence that reliance on teaching from the board is higher in Irish and languages areas (Figure 4.20).

Figure 4.20: Proportion of teachers who say students copy notes from the board in most/every class by subject

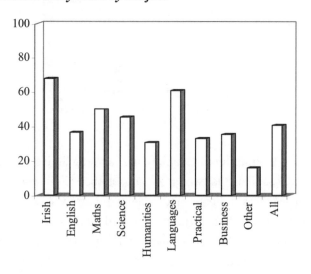

Group-work

Just over half of teachers indicate that they teach students individually using their textbook or worksheets for most/every lesson. Less than one-in-six teachers regularly choose to group students into pairs or larger groups. There is no pattern according to school intake with teachers in Barrack Street (lower literacy levels), Fig Lane and Wynyard Road (higher literacy levels) more likely to employ group work. Such group-work is more prevalent in the practical, business and language subject areas.

Other resources

The use of computer facilities is most prevalent in the business, science and practical subjects, while video and audio equipment is more frequently used in languages, Irish and Science. There is no clear pattern across schools and their composition. Teachers in Fig Lane, Park Street, Dawes Point and Wattle Street appear less likely to incorporate computing facilities in their teaching, while their counterparts in Wattle Street, Hay Street and Dixon Street show lower usage of video/audio aids.

4.6.3 Assessment

The majority of teachers in all schools adopt assessment procedures such as tests, homework, oral questioning and class exercises with their first-year classes. Perhaps reflecting a more varied curriculum and the provision of more vocational programmes such as the Leaving Certificate Applied, the Leaving Cert Vocational Programme and Transition Year among older cohorts of students, teachers in Hay Street, most notably, and Wentworth Place, Wynyard Road and Fig Lane are more likely to assign project work as a means of assessment (Figure 4.21c).

With the exception of Hay Street, teachers in schools with a higher ability intake appear somewhat more likely to use tests with the first-year groups (Figure 4.21a). Again with the exception of Hay Street, homework is slightly more likely to be used as a means of assessment in schools comprising a higher ability intake (Figure 4.21b).

Figure 4.21a: Forms of assessment used with first-year students by teachers: tests

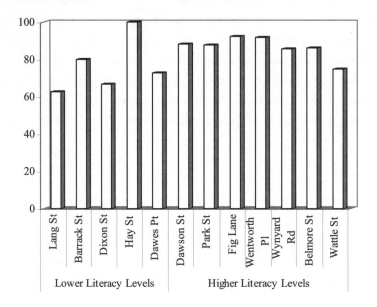

Figure 4.21b: Forms of assessment used with first-year students by teachers: homework

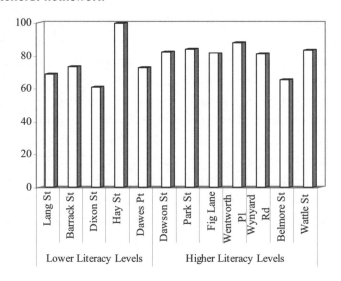

Figure 4.21c: Forms of assessment used with first-year students by teachers: project work

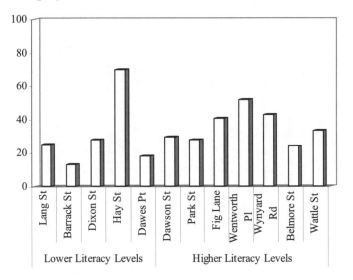

Related to issues of relevance and applicability, methods of assessment used vary across subject areas. The allocation of project work is considerably lower in Irish, Mathematics and Business Studies (Figure 4.22c). Homework is less commonly prescribed in Science (Figure 4.22b), while the use of oral questioning is less frequently employed in the practical and science subjects (Figure 4.22d).

Figure 4.22a: Forms of assessment used with first-year students by teachers: tests

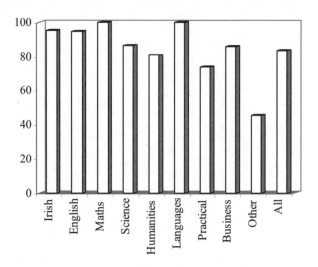

Figure 4.22b: Forms of assessment used with first-year students by teachers: homework

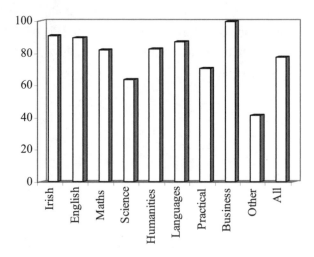

Figure 4.22c: Forms of assessment used with first-year students by teachers: project work

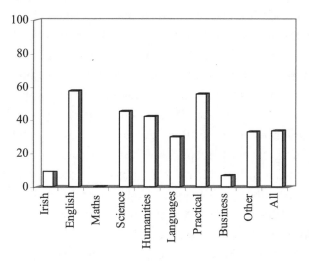

Figure 4.22d: Forms of assessment used with first-year students by teachers: oral questioning

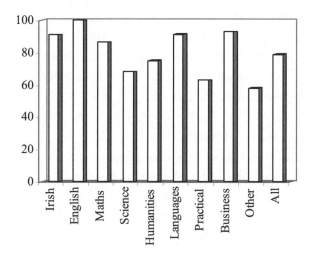

4.7 CURRICULAR PROVISION AND LEARNING STRUCTURES IN THE CASE-STUDY SCHOOLS

The twelve case-study schools included in the study showed considerable variation and important distinctions in the nature of curricular provision for first-year students, perceptions of such provision, the nature and perceived adequacy of learning supports and the nature of teaching styles. Half of the schools followed a largely mixed ability grouping approach, with Lang Street, Dixon Street, Park Street, Hay Street, Wentworth Place and Dawes Point grouping students by ability.

Regarding teacher perceptions of the curriculum, Dixon Street and Hay Street teachers considered their subject as too difficult for average ability students; these two schools also had highest levels of literacy and numeracy difficulties. Park Street teachers considered the curriculum unsuitable for lower ability students, as did Wynyard Road and Wattle Street teachers, all schools with relatively high literacy scores; with the exception of Wynyard Road, teachers in these schools also had highest levels of concern over the adequacy of learning support.

Concerns over subject overload were greatest in Hay Street, Wentworth Place and, most notably, Wynyard Road; the latter two schools offered taster programmes lasting until Christmas and for the duration of the year, respectively. Hay Street students were required to select their subjects prior to entry, although the number of such subjects appear relatively high at 13. Interestingly, schools with the fewest subjects, Barrack Street and Wattle Street, were least likely to consider that students took too many subjects.

Familiarity with the primary curriculum was perceived to be lowest among teachers in Lang Street, Wentworth Place and Belmore Street.

Finally, regarding teaching style, homework and assessment, some important distinctions are identifiable. Teachers in Hay Street were considerably more likely to hold that they adapted their teaching style when teaching first years, while their counterparts in Wattle Street were considerably less flexible in their approach. Belmore Street, Barrack Street and Belmore Street teachers were distinct in reporting higher levels of homework. The adoption of more traditional teaching styles appears somewhat higher among teachers in Lang Street, Wentworth Place and Dawes Point, while the use of group work and lower reliance on one-to-one instruction was more prevalent in Barrack Street, Fig Lane and Wynyard Road.

4.8 OVERALL SUMMARY AND CONCLUSION

In relation to the curriculum, the main concerns expressed by teachers related to the suitability of the curriculum for lower ability students and difficulties in covering the curriculum in the time available. A minority of teachers consider the primary school syllabus as a good foundation for post-primary-level education, while around half believe they are familiar with the nature of the primary curriculum. Such levels of familiarity show wide inter-school variation (partly reflecting varying levels of linkage and contact between feeder primary and post-primary schools) and also considerable variation across subjects (with low levels in History and Geography).

Satisfaction with subjects — their content and breadth — offered in the junior cycle programme varies widely. Mathematics, Science and Business Studies were more likely to be seen as difficult for lower ability students, while language teachers were most likely to consider their subject to be marked too harshly in the Junior Certificate exam. Concerns over subject overload showed no clear pattern: while overall close to half the teachers considered that students took too many subjects in first year, this was not strongly related to the actual number of subjects taken.

The timing and flexibility of subject choice varies across the schools, as does the availability and duration of taster programmes. Such taster programmes were generally perceived as beneficial, in enabling a more informed choice to be made. The opposite scenario of subject choice before entry into the school created a greater reliance on informal "outside" sources of advice, particularly parents. Students vary in their "exposure" to new subjects at primary levels: while some students had studied French in primary school, others had not, leaving them starting post-primary school with different capacities.

Given that schools vary in their intake and selection practices, the need for learning support is also variable. The vast majority of teachers viewed levels of learning support in their school to be adequate. The value of learning support for students was widely recognised. However, issues of resources and manpower needs were alluded to. There was some evidence that the role of learning support varied across schools, as did the levels of participation and extent of teamwork, with some viewing it as a discrete practice under the jurisdiction of one teacher, rather than relevant to all teachers.

Streaming is seen as useful from a teaching point of view and was perceived as benefiting more able students. However, more schools have adopted a mixed ability approach in first year taking into account the fact that young people can develop over the course of the year, errors can be made in allocating them into different streams at the beginning of the first year and it was believed that mixed ability grouping would enable the students to become more confident as learners. There was some evidence of differentiation in teacher allocation to classes according to stream location: in particular teachers employed on a part-time basis are less likely to be assigned above average groups.

There was a strong reliance on traditional, "chalk and talk" teaching styles, although teachers did believe they tailored their teaching approach to first-year groups. There was some variation in teaching style across schools. Teachers also varied in the extent to which they started at the beginning, assuming a tabula rasa, or assumed a certain level of understanding and knowledge among incoming first years.

While students entering post-primary schools encounter a largely standardised curriculum, their experiences of that curriculum have been shown to vary widely across settings and schools. Such variations in the curricular and academic environment of schools have important implications for the process of integration into the post-primary school and for the successful academic and social development of the student. Chapters Six and Seven consider the impact of the academic and curricular arrangements in schools on students' experience and adjustment to post-primary school.

APPENDIX

Table A4.1: Subject groupings

Subject Grouping	Subjects	Number of Teachers
Irish	Irish	22
English	English	19
Mathematics	Mathematics	22
Science	Science; Computer Studies	22
Humanities	History; Geography; CSPE; Art; Music; Classical Studies	52
Languages	French; German	23
Practical	Technology; Materials Technology; Technical Graphics; Metalwork; Home Economics	27
Business/Vocational	Business Studies	14
Other	Religious Education; Physical Education; Typing; SPHE; Other	24
Total		225

Chapter Five

STUDENT EXPERIENCES OF THE TRANSITION PROCESS

INTRODUCTION

Chapter Three outlined variation across the case-study schools in their approach to student integration from the viewpoint of key personnel and first-year subject teachers. This chapter draws on questionnaires completed by 916 students in the twelve case-study schools early in first year along with group interviews conducted to explore students' own experiences of making the transition from primary to post-primary school. In keeping with our hypotheses outlined in Chapter One, it is expected that students will experience fewer transition difficulties in schools with a stronger student integration programme. The first section of the chapter outlines the kind of contact students had with their post-primary school before they started first year. Section two explores their expectations of post-primary school while the third section examines the process of settling into a new school. In the fourth section, the nature of interaction between teachers and students and among students themselves is examined. The fifth section of the chapter looks at student perceptions of post-primary school and their place within it.

5.1 PRE-ENTRY CONTACT

5.1.1 School choice

This section explores school choice from the student perspective; the perspective of parents is discussed in Chapter Eight. Active school choice was evident among almost half of the students in the case-study schools, with 45 per cent reporting that there was another post-primary school closer to their home than the one they attend. This is broadly consistent with the pattern found among a national sample of Junior Certificate students in the mid-1990s (see Hannan, Smyth et al., 1996). School selection varied by social class, with students from professional backgrounds being less likely to attend their local school than those from manual backgrounds. The pattern also varied by school, with more active selection evident in Fig Lane[1] and Wattle St schools; in contrast, Lang St and Barrack St schools (both designated disadvantaged schools) drew more on students from the local catchment area. These school differences were evident even taking into account the social class background of the student intake, that is, some schools appear to be more "sought out" than others. This pattern is consistent with findings from the national survey of school principals which indicates that some schools benefit more from competition between schools than others (see Chapter Two). For the majority of students, their post-primary school represented their parents' first choice of school; four-fifths of the students reported that their parents wanted them to go to their current school, 15 per cent did not know and only six per cent reported that their parents wanted them to go to another school. This pattern varied by school with preference for another school being more prevalent in Lang St, Dixon St, Hay St, all vocational schools, and Belmore St schools, a girls' school which is mixed in intake.

Choice of school may reflect earlier decisions made about older children in the family. A third of all students had older siblings in the school; when only students with older siblings who could have attended their school[2] are taken into account, over half (55 per cent) of the students surveyed had an older sibling in the school. Having an older sibling in the school was more prevalent in certain schools (Fig Lane, Dawson St, Belmore St and Barrack St) but the pattern was not related to the social mix of the school. Female students were more likely to report having an older sibling in the school (60 per cent compared with 50 per cent); however, this pattern is due to the gender distribution over different school

---

[1] The pattern for Fig Lane is not surprising given it is a fee-paying school.

[2] For example, students in all boys' schools having an older brother.

types with no significant differences found between boys and girls within coeducational schools. Students from higher professional backgrounds are more likely than other students to have an older sibling in the school (70 per cent compared with 55 per cent for all students). The extent to which having an older sibling in the school may ease the transition process is discussed in the following sections of the chapter.

In most cases, students had at least some input into deciding on the post-primary school they would attend. Almost three-quarters (73 per cent) of the students reported that their parents discussed the choice of school with them. This pattern varied by parental social class with parents in professional occupations being somewhat more likely to discuss school choice with their children (79 per cent compared with 73 per cent for all students). This pattern also varied by school with parent-child discussion more prevalent in three of the boys' schools, Park St, Wentworth Place and Wattle St. This inter-school variation was apparent within social class groups so was not solely due to the social profile of the schools concerned. Parents were much less likely to discuss the choice of school with their children if an older sibling was already attending that school; 59 per cent of students with an older sibling in the school reported discussing the choice of school with their parents while this was the case for 80 per cent of those without an older sister or brother in the school.

The group interviews with students in the case-study schools allowed us to explore students' perspectives on school choice in a more detailed way. Parental perspectives on school choice are explored in Chapter Eight. Most of the students interviewed had discussed the choice of school with their parents. In the case of "local" schools, like Dixon St, the choice of school often seemed taken for granted, given the logistics of travelling to school and the fact that most members of the student's family had previously attended the school:

> We could have gone to another school if we wanted to but this one is nearer so it is easier for us to get there. I wouldn't be able to get a lift because I have a younger brother and he would have to go to school also. I can just walk up here myself. If I went to another school I would have to get a lift down (Dixon St School, middle group).

Interviewer: And so why did you come here?

Student 1: Because it is close.

Student 2: It is nearest to my house.

Student 3: And my uncles and all came to this school.

Interviewer: What about you? Why did you come?

Student 4: My sisters and brothers are here.

Student 5: All my friends are in it (Dixon St School, lower stream class).

A similar pattern of responses was evident among students in Dawson St and Hay St schools, where students highlighted the importance of family connections with the school:

Student 1: My sisters went here.

Student 2: My three sisters and my brother went here.

Student 3: My two sisters are here and it's closest.

Student 4: My brother is here (Dawson St School).

Student 1: My brother was in the school as well . . .

Student 2: My dad went to this school and he thought it was a good school.

Student 3: My aunts and uncles and my father went here (Hay St School, higher stream class).

In other cases, students drew on information gleaned from family and friends in order to select a "good" school (though the definition of a good school was not always clear). Reference was made to the availability of certain subjects, sports facilities and the standard of education in general:

Interviewer: Before you came here, would you have heard anything about this before?

Yeah. My brother [said] . . . that it was a good school.

Interviewer: What do you think he meant by a good school?

Alright, nothing wrong with it, the classes were okay.

I heard it was okay as well.

I just heard it was good for sports, just a good school.

I heard it was a good school (Park St School, higher stream class).

I heard it was just a good school. Loads of the people who went here said it was a good school and everything.

Yes, my cousin went here and he said it was good (Wattle St School).

Interviewer: Did any of the rest of you hear anything about the school?

My friends, people I know used to come here.

Interviewer: What did they tell you?

They said it's just a good school and you should go there.

Yeah, my friend told me that as well, that it's a good school, that I should go there.

Interviewer: When they said it's a good school, what do you think they meant?

. . . for wood and metal[work].

Education.

And it's good for basketball (Hay St School, higher stream class).

The choices of friends from primary school were also seen to influence students' preference for certain schools:

Interviewer: Why did you want to come here?

Student: Because most of my friends were coming here (Park St School, higher stream class).

It is really where your friends are going. Say if all your friends are going to [another local school] then you want to go to [that school]. That is the way it was in my school (Wentworth Place School, lower band).

Interviewer: You wanted to go to the . . . ?

Tech. Because all my friends were there . . .

Interviewer: But then you said it was your plan to come here together?

Yes, but we all decided to go to the tech and then at the end . . . I would say two weeks before the school started, we all decided to come here (Belmore St School).

However, disagreement between parents and students did arise over the choice of school:

I wasn't let go to the school where all my friends were going.
Interviewer: So you didn't have that much choice?
No, my brother came here and my mother just said you are going there as well.
Same here (Fig Lane School).

I never wanted to come to this school but my sister said I needed to come to a strict school (Barrack St School).

In some cases, it was the student's choice that prevailed over the wishes of their parents:

My mother wanted me to go to [another local school] but I don't like it. I have no friends there so then I just came here (Park St School, lower stream class).

My Mam wanted me to go to [another local school] and I said no because this was close (Lang St School, higher stream class).

It was noticeable that students in Barrack St and Dixon St schools, both designated disadvantaged schools, were more likely to report that they had wanted to go to a different school compared with students in other schools.

The students surveyed were drawn from a range of feeder primary schools. Three schools, Lang St, Barrack St and Dixon St, all designated disadvantaged schools, drew from fewer than four feeder primary schools. Furthermore, over two-thirds of the students in Barrack St and Dawes Point came from the linked primary school, that is, a primary school on the same campus. In contrast, two schools, Belmore St and Fig Lane, a girls' school and a fee-paying coeducational school respectively, drew from over 25 primary schools. These patterns are consistent with the degree of active selection of post-primary schools reported above. Figure 5.1 shows the relationship between the number of feeder primary schools and the degree of concentration of student intake, that is, the proportion of first-year students drawn from the "main" feeder primary school. As might be expected, schools drawing from a larger number of feeder primary schools have less concentration of students from any particular school. In the case of Dixon St school, for example, 95 per cent of students are drawn from a single primary school while this is the case for only 13 per cent of those in Fig Lane school. The extent to which having primary classmates in the same post-primary school impacts on the transition process is discussed in the following sections.

Figure 5.1: Number of feeder primary schools and concentration of student intake

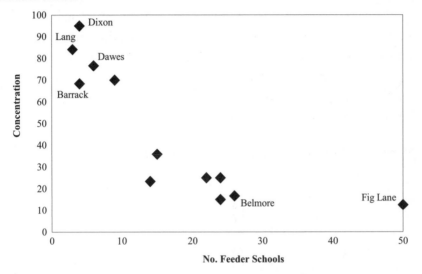

5.1.2 Pre-entry contact

A central aspect of a school's approach to student integration is the fostering of contact between the post-primary school and prospective students and their parents before entry to the school (see Chapter Three). In the survey of students, first-year students were asked about their pre-entry contact with their post-primary school. Almost all (91 per cent) had visited the school before the beginning of the school year while the majority of students reported visits from a post-primary school teacher and/or the school principal to their primary school (Figure 5.2). Only a very small number (4 per cent) of students reported a teacher (Home-School-Community Liaison Officer) had visited their parents at home. In keeping with the school approach to transition outlined in Chapter Three, schools varied in the specific approach taken to pre-entry contact. As indicated by Figure 5.2, the vast majority of students had visited their post-primary school before beginning first year. This was less common in two of the schools with a lower emphasis on student integration, Park

St and Barrack St. However, visiting their school before entry was also somewhat less common in Fig Lane school, which had a strong emphasis on integration; this appears to reflect the wide geographical spread of students and the large number of feeder schools from which students are drawn. Most students reported the school principal or another teacher visiting their primary school, with this being more prevalent in four of the "high integration" schools (Dawson St, Lang St, Belmore St and Wattle St), and very uncommon in Fig Lane school (probably because of the very large catchment of the school, see Figure 5.1). While only a very small number of students reported that their parents had been vis-ited by a teacher, this was somewhat more common in Dawes Point and Dixon St schools than in other schools.

Figure 5.2: Pre-entry contact with post-primary school

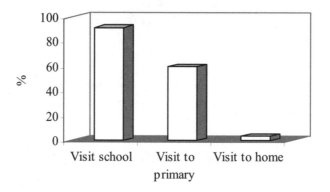

Taking the three forms of pre-entry contact together, only a very small number (6 per cent) of students had no such contact, 39 per cent had one such contact and 55 per cent had two different types of contact. The pat-tern varied by school with the highest level of contact evident in Dawson St, Lang St, Dawes Point and Belmore St schools, four of the schools that had been identified as having a strong emphasis on student integra-tion on the basis of the postal survey of school principals (see Chapter One). Lower levels of pre-entry contact were reported among students in the three schools with less developed integration policies, Barrack St, Park St and Hay St, but also in Fig Lane, most likely because of its large catchment area. It should be noted that the level of contact reflects not only the post-primary school's overall policy on integration but the nature of the linkage with specific feeder schools. In addition to the variation *between* post-primary schools, there was variation in reported pre-entry contact *within* post-primary schools depending on the primary school attended; such variation was significant in eight of the twelve case-study schools (Dawson St, Dixon St, Park St, Wentworth Place, Wynyard Road, Dawes Point, Belmore St and Wattle St). As might be expected, students in schools with a stronger emphasis on student integration tend to have had more pre-entry contact than those in schools with less of an emphasis on integration (see Figure 5.3). However, there is a good deal of variation among "high integration" schools because of the difference between schools in their focus on pre-entry contact as opposed to post-entry induction (see Chapter Three).

Figure 5.3: Pre-entry contact (2 or more contacts) by school emphasis on student integration

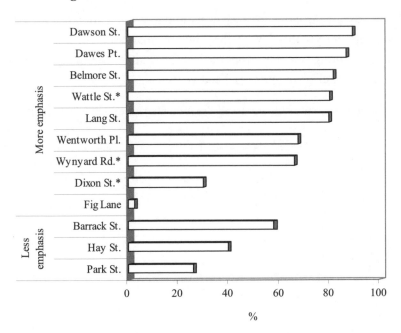

Note: * indicates a stronger emphasis on integration than was evident from the postal survey.

In the group interviews, a number of students mentioned visits made by their post-primary school teachers to their primary school. These visits were seen as giving general information about the school and the kinds of subjects available:

> Student: [The deputy principal] came into us and told all about the school and it was a bit better. They showed us a video of the school.
> Interviewer: Did that help?
> Student: Yes, it gave us an idea of what it would be like (Wentworth Place School, lower band).

> [The principal] came into talk to us and told us all about the school.
> Interviewer: What kinds of things did he say?
> He just told us all about what it would be like — what classes and what kind of students and where you would be placed and that.
> We got a little book as well of all the activities and sports (Wentworth Place School, higher band).

Open days were more frequently mentioned when students were asked about pre-entry contact with their post-primary school. These days focused on giving students a tour of the school and introducing them to key personnel, such as the principal and year heads:

> They brought us around to all the grounds and told us what subjects we would be having.
> They showed us the classrooms (Park St School, middle group).

> Interviewer: So before you came here, when you were in primary school, did you visit part of the school at all?
> Yeah, twice.
> Yeah.
> Twice, yeah.
> Interviewer: What happened when you visited it?
> They showed us around.
> We just went around, some teachers, the class teachers and some teachers said that they'd let a few people in, if you saw a door open, there was a sixth year bringing us around, if he saw a door open he went in and introduced us and then the teacher was "do you know anyone in here?" and all this.
> And you said you visited twice, what happened the second time?

> We all came in here and we sat down and met our year heads and principal . . . (Dawes Point School, higher stream class).

In some schools, students were given a demonstration of different lessons, usually focusing on practical activities:

> I thought it was good because they were showing all the Science stuff and they were doing experiments and stuff (Fig Lane School).

> They showed us all the science rooms and all the computers. We were able to go in and see the way it's taught (Wentworth Place School, higher band).

> I came to an open day.
> Interviewer: What things did you tell you there?
> Just went around the classrooms and see some of the classes going on.
> Just showing you what you would be doing in class (Wentworth Place School, higher band).

However, some students felt this gave an unrealistic picture of what the subjects would actually be like:

> I would have liked if they showed that you were doing experiments in science that you would do them but now we are just reading about animals, biology (Dixon St School, higher stream class).

In addition to the open day, many students in Fig Lane School had attended a sports camp in the school over the summer. This was seen by the students as helping them to make new friends and settle in.

5.2 EXPECTATIONS OF POST-PRIMARY SCHOOL

In spite of variation between schools in the level of contact with students before entry, students primarily relied on informal sources of information regarding the school they were going to. Siblings appeared to be the main source of information regarding issues such as discipline within the school, sports facilities and the individual teachers:

> My brother came here.
> Interviewer: What did you hear about the school from them?

The different teams.

Interviewer: Did you hear anything?

I had two brothers that came here. They told me about the soccer teams and the Gaelic ones, and what teachers were good or bad (Wentworth Place School, higher band).

My brothers and sisters just told me about all the teachers that they didn't like and that (Dawson St School).

Interviewer: What did you hear about this school first?

I have two sisters, one in sixth year and one in third year so I knew a good bit about it. I had been in here a couple of times. I used to come here every day to pick them up. And I heard about the teachers.

I just heard it was good for sports and they had good facilities.

I have a brother in fifth year and he told me about the different teachers and the sports (Fig Lane School).

However, many students also drew on information from a wider circle of family and friends:

Just everyone was telling me it would be good craic and some of the teachers are nice and some of the teachers aren't nice and some teachers you have to have all your homework in and other ones you could not do too much (Dawson St School).

Interviewer: So what would you have heard about this school before you came here?

That it was a good sporting school.

You get a good education.

I was told . . . friends would tell us, older brothers . . . it was a good school to come to for the sports and the teachers and all.

Yes and all the teachers were nice (Wentworth Place School, lower band).

While informal sources of information helped students know what to expect from post-primary school, they could also fuel anxiety as a number of students were told to expect the "first year beating"; the extent to which this "beating" was a myth or reality is discussed in a later section.

In responding to the student questionnaires, over a third of first-year students in the case-study schools reported having a good idea what to expect coming to post-primary school, just under half had some idea with 15 per cent reporting having very little idea what to expect. This pattern varied somewhat across schools with students in Hay St, Lang St and Park St schools reporting a better idea what to expect while students in Barrack St School felt relatively unprepared for post-primary school. Not surprisingly, students who had a higher level of pre-entry contact (two contacts) felt they had a better idea what to expect coming to post-primary school (39 per cent compared with 33 per cent of others), although the relationship is not as strong as may have been expected probably because of the important role of informal sources of information (see above). In keeping with the discussion in the group interviews, students with older siblings in the school had a somewhat better idea what to expect of post-primary school (41 per cent compared with 34 per cent). Girls were significantly less likely than boys to report having a good idea what to expect (31 per cent compared with 41 per cent). When this was broken down by school, girls had less idea than boys what to expect in three of the four coeducational schools (Dawson St, Dixon St and Hay St). A good deal of the gender effect was attributable to the fact that students in Barrack St, an all girls' school, reported having little idea what to expect. The pattern also varied by social class with those from semi/unskilled manual or non-employed backgrounds more likely to report having little idea what lay ahead of them. Interestingly, having attended a linked primary school did not appear to significantly influence student expectations of post-primary school.

The first day at school

Students were asked about the approach taken by their school on their first day of term. In all of the case-study schools, students had been taken into the school at least one day before the rest of the year groups returned to school. In Park St School, students were brought in for a half-day with their parents:

> There was a meeting thing in the chapel. They just told the parents what they expected from us, no messing and bullying and that stuff (Higher stream class, Park St School).

Bringing first-year students in on their own was seen as having some advantages:

> The first day we came there was barely anybody in the school, we thought it was perfect but then, when all the third and fourth years came in, it was big (Park St School, middle group).

Student accounts of the first day focus on being shown around the school, given the timetable, being divided into classes and told the rules of the school:

> The first day it was good. We didn't get any homework or anything. The teachers were just explaining to us who they were and that (Dixon St School, higher stream class).

> The first day you do a tour.
> They showed us the basic places that you really need to know, like the lockers and stuff.
> Then each group would be taken on a tour (Park St School, higher stream class).

This emphasis on imparting information about procedures has also been reported in research on the transition to secondary school in Britain (Hargreaves and Galton, 2002). The class tutor was seen as playing a key role in introducing students to post-primary school in Belmore St and Wentworth Place schools:

> Our class tutor brought us to a classroom and she let us ask any questions and explained stuff and what we needed to know for Monday and we got our timetable (Wentworth Place School, higher band).

In Wentworth Place School, older students were involved in showing the first-year students around the school.

Figure 5.4: Feelings on first day of post-primary school

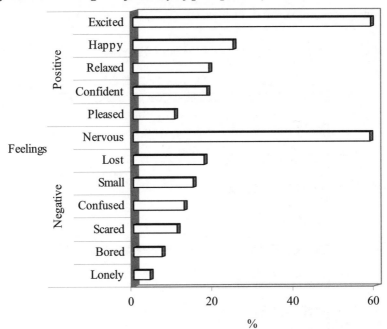

Previous research internationally and in Ireland has highlighted the "turbulent" feelings associated with making the transition to post-primary school (see, for example, Rudduck, 1996; O'Brien, 2001). In the questionnaire, students in the case-study schools were given a list of words and asked to indicate at least two words which best described their feelings on their first day in post-primary school. The responses indicate the ambiguous feelings documented in many other studies with the majority of students describing themselves as excited *and* nervous (see Figure 5.4). On the positive side, a quarter reported feeling happy with almost a fifth reporting being confident or relaxed. From a more negative point of view, almost a fifth of students reported feeling lost with over a tenth feeling confused or small.

Girls were more likely than boys to report feeling excited, nervous, happy or scared on their first day in post-primary school (see Figure 5.5). Boys were significantly more likely than girls to report feeling confident, bored, lost[3] or relaxed. There were no marked gender differences in feeling lonely, confused, small or pleased.

Figure 5.5: Feelings on first day of school by gender

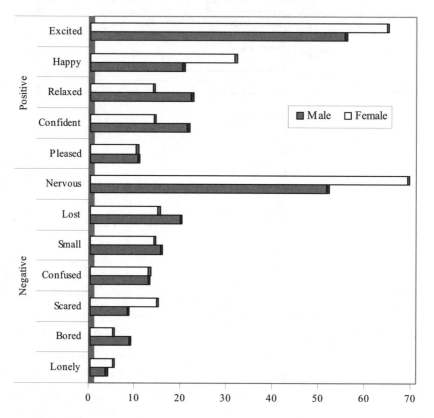

Student responses were regrouped in order to explore whether they reported negative, positive or mixed feelings on their first day in post-primary school. The largest group (56 per cent) reported a mixture of positive and negative emotions, 22 per cent reported only positive feelings (such as feeling excited, confident, happy, pleased or relaxed) while 21 per cent reported only negative feelings (such as being nervous, lonely, confused, lost, scared, small or bored) on their first day.

---

[3] The pattern for feeling lost appeared to be due to the distribution across different school types with two all-boys' schools showing a higher prevalence of these reports.

Girls were more likely than boys to report mixed feelings, mainly because of the higher proportion of girls who reported feeling nervous. Students from higher professional backgrounds were most likely to report positive feelings, in particular, feeling excited and/or confident. In contrast, those from semi/unskilled manual backgrounds were significantly more likely than those from higher professional backgrounds to report negative feelings only (34 per cent compared with 12 per cent); the pattern for students from non-employed households was similar to that for those from semi/unskilled manual backgrounds. Students from a Traveller background were somewhat more likely to report negative feelings only (28 per cent compared with 20 per cent) as were students of non-national origin[4] (31 per cent as opposed to 21 per cent). Less academically able students are more likely to report negative feelings only; that is, those with lower reading and maths scores tended to report negative feelings. The highest reading and maths test scores were found among those who reported positive feelings only. Furthermore, 37 per cent of those who felt they were at the bottom of the class in primary school report negative feelings only compared with 12 per cent of those who felt they were at the top of the class.

Students with an older sibling in the school were less likely to report negative feelings on their first day (17 per cent compared with 23 per cent). Those with no primary school friends in the *school* were more likely to report negative feelings (31 per cent compared with 19 per cent of those with three or more friends). However, the number of primary school friends in their *class* does not impact on having negative feelings, probably because most students did not know what class they would be assigned to until the first day. Those who had more contact with the school in advance (two or more types of contact) are less likely than those with no pre-entry contact to report negative feelings only (18 per cent compared with 34 per cent). Interestingly, however, increased contact with the school before entry does not increase the reports of positive

---

[4] Students from a Traveller background were defined as students who reported being "a member of the Travelling community" while students of non-national origin were defined as students with one or more parents from outside Ireland. While the numbers in these groups were relatively small (49 and 106 respectively), it is worthwhile exploring their distinctive experiences of the transition process.

feelings only. Not surprisingly, those who felt they had a "good idea" what to expect are more likely to report positive feelings, and less likely to report negative feelings, than those who had "very little idea what to expect". Students in high-integration schools were somewhat less likely to report negative feelings than those in low-integration schools, although the difference was not pronounced and there was overlap between the two groups.

In sum, feelings about coming to post-primary school are influenced by prior educational success and family background with less academically able students and those from a working-class or non-employed background reporting the most negative emotions. Mixed feelings, especially a combination of excitement and nervousness, at coming to the school are very common. Having an older sibling or primary school friends in the school helps to ease negative feelings. Having more contact with the school before entry also helps to reduce the prevalence of negative emotions. The factors shaping longer-term transition difficulties are explored in Chapter Seven.

5.3 "SETTLING IN"

5.3.1 Missing primary school

Students were asked about the extent to which they missed different aspects of primary school. It should be noted that the responses relate to the beginning of first year (approximately three to four weeks after the start of term). The extent to which students still miss primary school later in the school year is discussed in Chapter Seven. The responses focused on missing the social aspects of primary school, such as friends and school trips along with being one of the older students in the school (see Figure 5.6). However, a fifth of students mentioned aspects of school organisation, such as having one teacher or being in a small school, while a similar proportion mentioned the subjects taught or the way in which lessons were taught.

Figure 5.6: Extent to which student misses aspects of primary school

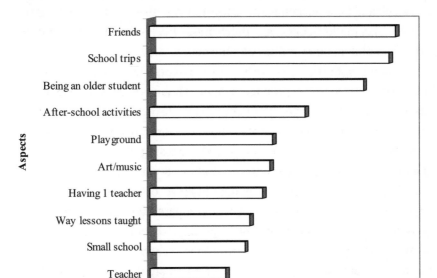

These responses were used to build a combined measure of the extent to which first-year students miss primary school.[5] This measure varied across schools with students in Barrack St and Wynyard Rd schools, both all girls' schools, more likely to miss primary school and students in Dawes Point, a boys' school, less likely to do so. Girls were significantly more likely than boys to report missing primary school, a pattern that was also evident within coeducational schools (with the exception of Hay St School which had a very small number of girls). This pattern may relate to differences between girls and boys in the extent to which they will *admit* missing primary school. However, international research has indicated the negative consequences for girls of the disruption of friendship groups involved in the transition to post-primary school (see, for example, Hargreaves and Galton, 2002). Students from a higher professional background were somewhat less likely than those from semi/unskilled manual backgrounds to miss primary school, reflecting the fact that they felt better prepared and more confident about making the transition. Students from a

---

[5] The scale is highly reliable (0.7882).

Traveller background were significantly more likely to report missing primary school. Less academically able students, that is, those with lower reading and maths scores, are much more likely to report missing primary school than other groups of students.

Students with an older sibling in the school were just as likely as other students to miss primary school. Having friends in the school makes little difference to the overall extent to which students miss primary school. However, students who have three or more friends from primary school are less likely to report missing their primary school friends "a lot" (43 per cent compared with 58 per cent of those with no friends); a similar pattern was evident in terms of having primary school friends in the same class (42 per cent compared with 49 per cent). Perhaps surprisingly, those from linked primary schools were just as likely to miss primary school as those from other schools. The length of time taken to travel to school or the mode of travel are not related to students' missing primary school.

Students in schools with a strong student integration policy were somewhat less likely to miss primary school. However, this is an average effect; one of the high integration schools (Belmore St) has the third highest prevalence of missing primary school while one of the low integration schools (Park St) has the second lowest prevalence. Furthermore, the extent of pre-entry contact with the post-primary school was not related to missing primary school. Surprisingly, students who report more positive interaction with teachers are more likely to report missing primary school (perhaps, because they are more "teacher-dependent" or "school-identified") while the opposite is the case for those who report negative interaction with teachers. Students who have experienced bullying in post-primary school are distinctly more likely to report missing primary school.

5.3.2 Differences between primary and post-primary schools

In the group interviews, students in the case-study schools were asked about the extent to which post-primary school differs from primary school. The responses focused on a number of differences including the number of teachers and variety of subjects, the size of the school, the length of the school day, being one of the smallest students in the school, the approach to discipline and the approach taken by teachers in general:

> It was a wee bit different than I thought it would be, it's a lot bigger and a lot more teachers than I thought there would be and a very long day (Dawson St School).

For many students, the main difference between primary and post-primary school was having a number of different teachers and taking a variety of (new) subjects:[6]

> You have to change around classes, because in primary school you didn't have to change (Dawson St School).

Most of the students interviewed regarded this as a positive aspect of being in post-primary school, stressing the advantages of having more than one teacher:

> You have different teachers.
> Interviewer: And you think that's better, do you?
> Yes, because you could hate a teacher for a year in primary school and you would only have a teacher here . . . once a day (Wentworth Place School, higher band).

> Do you think it's a good thing or a bad thing to have loads of teachers instead of one?
> A good thing.
> Why is that?
> Because if you don't like the one teacher you have then it doesn't matter because you've got so many other ones (Dawson St School).

> But the difference between primary and secondary, even though I get up at seven and then get home at five, it seems much shorter. The classes are shorter and we are switching around. We are only in the class and we are back out again.
> It's not as boring [as] having the one teacher, that is good (Wentworth Place School, higher band).

---

[6] Students' experiences of the curriculum in first year are discussed in greater detail in Chapter Six.

However, for a small number of students, the change was daunting:

> Do you think this school is different than your primary school?
> Yes.
> Definitely, there are too many teachers.
> Too many classes (Barrack St School).

For many students, their initial impression of post-primary school was that it was "very big":

> You get tired. Your exercise is just going up the stairs. No need to play sport here, you would be fit just doing that (Park St School, higher stream class).

Students stressed "getting lost" more in the interviews than in the questionnaires:

> You get used to where the classes are but sometimes you still get a bit lost (Dixon St School, middle group).

> You get totally lost, you don't know where to go (Dawes Point School, higher stream class).

In particular, students mentioned "getting into trouble" for being late going from class to class, which was felt to be unfair given they were having difficulties finding their way around the school:

> If you're in a class, if you come two minutes late to the class you get into an awful lot of trouble just for being that two minutes late and some of the students they get upset about that and they think they're getting in real trouble (Dawson St School).

> The teachers are always giving out to us for being late for classes but we get lost (Park St School, middle group).

> When you start school first, you get lost and you go to class late and you would be given out to by the teachers for being late (Belmore St School).

In making the transition to post-primary school, students were moving to a longer school day. This trend was reinforced by the necessity for many students to travel longer distances to reach their post-primary school.

Thirteen per cent of students across all the case-study schools took more than half an hour to get to school; this was the case for more than a fifth of the students in Dawson St and Belmore St schools.

> What is the biggest difference between your primary school and this one?
> Getting up earlier.
> What time did you get up in primary school?
> Half eight.
> And now?
> Quarter past seven (Dawson St School).

> The day is very long as well. When you get home, you are totally exhausted (Fig Lane School).

The impact of a longer school day was reinforced by many students' feeling they received more homework than in primary school:

> I get home around five and half my day is gone and then I have to do my homework (Park St School, middle group).

> And now it is twenty to four and when you go home you have to get your dinner and get dressed, do your homework.
> You would probably be out by seven o'clock (Barrack St School).

> The school is longer and you don't have time to socialise. So the only time you have is on Sunday and it might be pouring rain or you mightn't be able to get out. On Saturday your whole day is taken up by homework (Fig Lane School).

It would appear that the combination of a longer school day coupled with more homework resulted in a greater overall workload for many students. The issue of homework is discussed in greater detail in Chapter Six.

Two other contrasts between primary and post-primary school were stressed by students in the group interviews. The first is the change in status involved in moving from being one of the biggest students in primary school to being one of the smallest students in post-primary school. This was seen as making students more vulnerable to being pushed around by older students, an issue which is discussed in the section on bullying below. The second issue relates to the relationship between first-year students and their teachers; student-teacher relations are explored in greater detail in the following section.

On the whole, students appeared to be settling into post-primary school, even at this early stage (October):

> You get used to it after a couple of weeks (Dixon St School, middle group).

On the basis of the group interviews, the students who reported greatest difficulty settling in tended to be less academic students within more disadvantaged schools:

> Do you like it better here than in your primary school?
>
> It is alright but it is very strict.
>
> I don't. I would rather go to the primary school for first year and all that (Dixon St, higher stream class).
>
> Does anybody miss your primary school?
>
> Yes.
>
> I missed [the teacher].
>
> I miss it, I really do.
>
> I miss the park (Lang St, higher stream class).

In Barrack St School, students' dislike of post-primary school was seen as relating to more negative relations with teachers:

> The teachers are too cross and they give you too much homework and they pick on you for the smallest thing. And they shouldn't be picking on the students (Barrack St School).

In the questionnaires, students were asked to rate possible ways of helping first-year students to settle into post-primary school from a list of specified options. In order of frequency, responses indicated putting students in the same class as their friends,[7] stopping bullying, making lunch breaks longer, organising school trips, showing students around the school on their first day and helping students with any problems (see Table 5.1). Just under a fifth of students mentioned allowing students to

---

[7] In fact, Belmore St and Fig Lane schools endeavour to place students in the same class as (some of) their friends (see Chapter Four).

try out different subjects. However, very few students mentioned decreasing, or increasing, the number of subjects as a means of helping students settle into school (9 per cent and 3 per cent respectively).

Table 5.1: Recommendations for helping students settle into school (in order of frequency)

Recommendation	%
Put students in same class as friends	45.6
Stop bullying	42.1
Longer breaks	27.4
School trips	24.2
Show students around on first day	23.1
Help with students' problems	20.6
Teachers friendlier to students	19.9
Allow students to try different subjects	19.5
Uniform policy less strict	18.8
Lunch/after-school sports	16.2
Non-sport activities	15.5
Better equipment (e.g. PE, computers)	14.9
Listen to students before making decisions	14.0
Extra help with lessons	12.7
Improve buildings	10.4
Fewer subjects	8.6
Ensure behaviour	6.2
Explain rules	6.1
More subjects	3.4
Shorter breaks	1.5

Note: Total adds to more than 100 as students were asked to select three recommendations.

This issue was returned to in the group interviews with students in the case-study schools. Some of the comments reflected wanting less (or no) homework, a much shorter school day and no teachers!

First student: A thing that would help make the school better would be if there was no homework.

Second student: Everyone says that, you can't be saying that (Dawes Point School, lower stream class).

However, for some students, a desire for less homework appeared to be genuinely related to the time pressure they experienced:

Interviewer: And do you think there is anything that could be done to help people settle into first year better?

Student: Not so much homework. So you would have more time to study over your work (Belmore St School).

If the teacher asks you a question and you don't know it, you don't have time to study over your work at night with all the homework you get so you would be better off not to get so much (Belmore St School).

However, many of the issues raised by the students were practical ones: wanting more time to get from class to class, wanting better facilities in the school (such as PE facilities), being given a map of the school, having better or more secure lockers, preventing bullying, and improved relations with teachers:

Teachers should be kinder, more friendly (Park St School, higher stream class).

If we had nice teachers at the start of the year, we would be more interested in the work (Fig Lane School).

Many of the students had mentioned in the questionnaires the importance of having friends in the same class as helping them to settle in. However, this was seen by some students as having potential disadvantages:

Interviewer: In some schools, they try to have people from the same schools together in class to help people settle in. Is that a good idea?

No, then it's harder to mix with other people.

You would want your friends but then you mightn't make new friends (Park St School, middle group).

Some of the comments related to having a different approach to subject choice; these are discussed in Chapter Six below.

5.4 Interaction within the School

5.4.1 Student–teacher interaction

In comparing primary and post-primary school, many students stressed that teachers in post-primary school tended to be much stricter than their counterparts at primary level; the standard of behaviour expected of students was seen as different:

> Interviewer: Would you say it's a strict school?
> Yeah.
> Strict in a funny way.
> Interviewer: So more strict than primary?
> Yes. Much more.
> Not really.
> Most cases.
> Interviewer: What are they stricter on?
> Talking.
> Talking and laughing. Like if you turn around and ask for a rubber they go mad.
> If you get all giggly from someone making you laugh that is the worst (Park St School, higher stream class).

> I found in primary that I used to get away with stuff more easily than you would here. Not doing your homework — there were people in our class who never bothered and the teacher never bothered to give out to them. But now you get in big trouble for not doing your homework (Fig Lane School).

In the group interviews, students stressed the minutiae of the school's formal discipline structure, with procedures including fines, discipline entries, "stages" and a card system. In two schools, positive rewards were given as well as punishment; however, students saw the balance of emphasis as being on bad rather than good behaviour:

> But if you forget a book you get in awful trouble and you can't be expected to remember everything all the time and you hardly ever get a good tick even if you do something really good. And it is really easy to get a bad tick (Fig Lane School).

Interviewer: What does a blue card mean?

If you get three blue cards, you are expelled.

There are green cards as well [for good behaviour].

A blue card is easy to get and it's very hard to get a green card.

Interviewer: What would you get a green card for?

If you answer a very hard question in class. Or maybe just something the teacher thinks you should get a green card for.

I got one for PE for getting the highest score (Wentworth Place School, higher band).

While many students saw post-primary school as strict, other students stated that "some teachers are, some aren't" and suggested that the punishment for bad behaviour varied across individual teachers within the same school:

The only thing is that one teacher could give you fifty [lines] and the other teacher would give you about 100 and then another teacher could give you 200 (Dawes Point School, lower stream class).

Some students saw teachers as "giving out to them" for arbitrary reasons:

Some of the teachers they come in here and they might be having a bad class the class before and they take it out on us then, it's unbelievable (Dawes Point School, higher stream class).

This was especially evident among students in Barrack St and Dawes Point schools where much of the interviews centred on students' cataloguing perceived unfair treatment by teachers:

We get the blame over everything.

They just pick you out.

They say we are the worst first years (Barrack St School).

However, similar claims were made by students in some of the other case-study schools:

There are good things, most stuff is good but just some things. Some of the teachers are just awful. . . . I put my hand up to say something and he goes okay what is it, and I started to talk and then he started screaming at me: "Did I say you could talk?". You are a first year, no one has any respect for you, you are just a junior infant. It's worse than that, they are men and you are only children (Wentworth Place School, higher band).

Strict school rules were not always seen as problematic by students. In some schools, particularly Lang St and Dixon St schools, two designated disadvantaged schools which grouped students by ability, students felt they were suffering because of the behaviour of other students in their class:

> Most people in our class give cheek to the teacher and that means that the teacher has to shout and all.
> There are two boys in my class and last Thursday we got loads of homework because they kept talking and the rest of us were given more homework.
> She said "the more they keep talking, the more homework we will get".
> They know that we want to be good and not get homework, so they just do it so that we will get the homework. They don't do anything and then they get rules but they just don't do the rules. They don't care (Dixon St School, middle group).

> I would like to learn but they all mess in our class (Dixon St School, middle group).

> Interviewer: But do you think that if you have loads of messers in the class, it is really difficult to take in what the teacher is saying?
> Yes, because they are going boo, yaah, like fools in the class.
> Interviewer: Does it happen often?
> Every day.

> The teachers are always shouting and things. The class would be ruined and everything. When the teacher is reading a story or something they would be all there talking (Lang St School, middle class).

While many students focused on the strict discipline within post-primary school, for others post-primary school involved greater freedom and autonomy. In many of the schools, students were "allowed out" at lunch-time break which contrasted with the situation at primary level:

> In primary school, you couldn't go home for lunch. Here you can do whatever you want during lunch (Park St School, higher stream class).

You can buy anything in the shop.
You can go to the shops and buy comics (Wentworth Place, lower band).

Can you go into town at break time?
Yeah, you can do what you want.
Or just hang around (Park St School, middle group).

Having more control over what they ate at lunchtime was also seen as important by a number of students:

It's better. It's up to you to get to your class . . . like in primary school they tell you to eat your lunch but now it's up to you to do your own thing (Fig Lane School).

In primary school you didn't have as much freedom. You weren't allowed to eat crisps and [could] only drink water (Park St School, middle class).

In our other school we weren't allowed anything. You couldn't even bring in a carton of juice because it's not good for the environment (Park St School, higher stream class).

Others stressed the greater array of activities available to students either at lunchtime or after school:

Interviewer: Is there anything specifically good about being in first year that you really enjoy?
The extra-curricular activities, like in national school you weren't allowed to go into the computers during break and you weren't allowed to do camogie because they didn't have any camogie sticks and stuff like that there, and other stuff like that. And the cafeteria is cool because you don't have to pack your lunch and if your mammy puts in something you don't like, you don't have to dread it when you get it (Dawson St School).

However, it should be noted that in a number of schools sports activities were more or less limited to those that had been selected for particular teams:

Everybody loves football and they can't all get picked for the team.
But you have to try out for a team and you mightn't make it.
I thought there would be team A, B, C, but no, it's just one team.

> If you don't get picked then there is nothing (Wentworth Place, higher band).

Information from the student questionnaire allows us to place these responses in the context of experiences among all first-year students in the twelve case-study schools. In the questionnaires, students were asked about the extent to which they had experienced different types of interaction with teachers in the two weeks prior to the survey. These responses were used to form measures of positive and negative teacher-student interaction.

Positive student–teacher interaction

Positive teacher–student interaction was based on the extent to which students had been told their work was good by a teacher, had asked questions in class, had been praised for asking a question, and had been praised for doing their written work well. Over half of students had asked questions in class often or very often while around half had been told their work was good by a teacher often or very often (see Figure 5.7). Fewer than forty per cent of students had been praised frequently by a teacher. Furthermore, a significant minority (over a fifth) of students had never received such praise.

Figure 5.7: Reports of positive student–teacher interaction

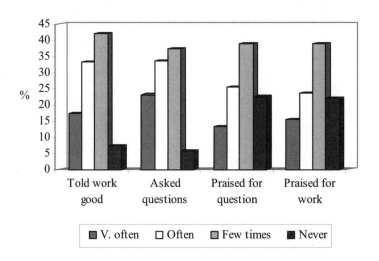

These different aspects of student–teacher interaction were used to form a composite measure of positive student–teacher interaction.[8] The extent of positive interaction varied by school but the pattern did not relate to the school's approach to student integration; more positive interaction was reported in Lang St and Hay St schools and somewhat less positive interaction was reported in Fig Lane and Wynyard Rd schools. This is consistent with previous research which shows variation in school climate over and above differences in formal organisational structure (Smyth, 1999). Boys were more likely than girls to report positive interaction; on closer investigation, this was due to the gender distribution across different schools with no significant differences apparent between boys and girls attending the same school. The pattern of positive interaction did not vary by social class background. Students who had reported being top of the class in primary school were more likely to experience frequent positive interaction with teachers than those who had been at the middle or bottom of their class. Perhaps puzzlingly, students with lower reading scores reported more positive interaction with teachers; this may reflect teacher strategy to encourage less academically able students.

Negative student-teacher interaction

This measure was based on reports of interaction with teachers in the two weeks prior to the survey. Most students had not experienced negative interaction with their teachers; only a minority of students had been given out frequently for their work or for misbehaving while over a quarter had been given out to by teachers "a few times" (see Figure 5.8).

---

[8] The resulting scale had a reliability of 0.719.

Figure 5.8: Negative teacher–student interaction

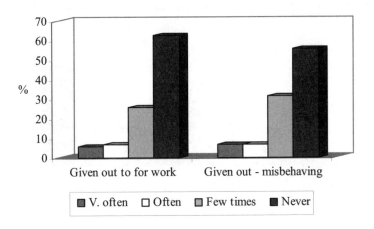

The pattern of negative interaction[9] varies across schools with more negative interaction reported in Lang St, a boys' school, and less negative interaction in Belmore St, a girls' school. Girls report less negative interaction with teachers than boys on average, a pattern that is evident within coeducational schools (with the exception of Hay St School). The pattern varies by social class background with students from higher professional and farming backgrounds less likely to report being given out to by teachers and higher levels of negative interaction among those from non-employed backgrounds. Students with lower reading and maths test scores tend to report more negative relations with teachers. Similarly, students who reported being bottom of their sixth class were more likely to experience negative interaction with teachers. In keeping with previous research (see Hannan et al., 1996), there is no significant relationship between the frequency of positive and negative interactions, that is, students who have positive interactions with their teachers are not markedly less likely to be given out to. Classroom climate is found to vary by class allocation with the highest level of negative student-teacher interaction reported among male students assigned to lower stream classes in streamed schools (see Figure 5.9), a pattern that is consistent with that found by Lynch and Lodge (2002).

---

[9] The composite measure of negative student–teacher interaction has a reliability of 0.6761.

Figure 5.9: Negative student-teacher interaction for male students by class allocation (per cent been given out to one or more times)

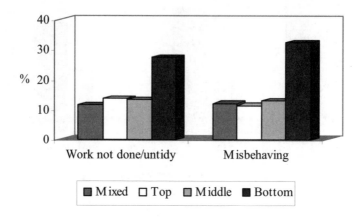

5.4.2 Interaction with other students: Being bullied

Students in the case-study schools were asked about their experience of being bullied in the two weeks prior to the survey. There were gender differences in the prevalence of different types of bullying with girls suffering more from verbal rather than physical aggression. The most common form of bullying reported by boys was being jeered by other students while among girls being upset by things said behind their back, being jeered or being ignored were equally common forms of bullying. Boys were significantly more likely than girls to report being jeered or physically pushed around while girls were significantly more likely to report being ignored or being upset by things said about them (see Figure 5.10). A significant minority (a fifth) of boys reported being physically pushed around by other students with under a tenth experiencing being pushed around on the way to or from school.

Figure 5.10: Experience of being bullied (per cent one or more times)

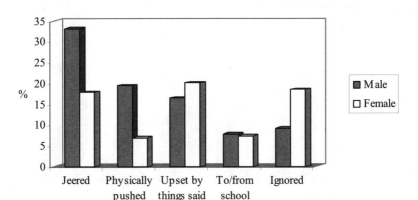

The case-study schools differed in the extent of bullying but the form of bullying which was most prevalent varied from school to school. Being physically pushed around was more commonly reported in Hay St (a co-educational school with a predominantly male intake) and Park St (a boys' school), both schools with less emphasis on student integration. Being physically pushed around was less frequently mentioned in two of the girls' schools, Wynyard Rd and Belmore St, but also in one of the boys' schools, Lang St; school-level differences in the prevalence of physical bullying was evident for both boys and girls.

A composite measure of being bullied was constructed. Girls tend to report less bullying than boys on average. While the incidence of being bullied does not vary consistently by social class background, students from professional backgrounds are slightly less likely to report being bullied and those from non-employed households are more likely to do so. Students from non-national backgrounds are significantly more likely to report being bullied as are students from a Traveller background (see Figure 5.11), indicating that bullies may single out students who are somehow "different" as targets.

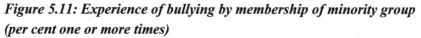

Figure 5.11: Experience of bullying by membership of minority group (per cent one or more times)

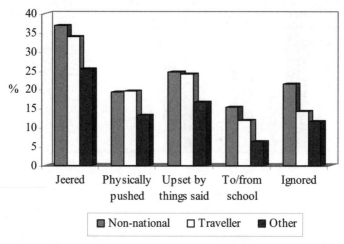

Students with no primary school friends in the school are slightly more likely to experience bullying but having an older sibling in the school appears to make no difference to the risk of being bullied. Students in lower classes in streamed schools were significantly more likely to report bullying than students in other classes; this pattern is evident among both girls and boys. Students with higher reading or maths scores were less likely to report being bullied; this is partly because these students are not allocated to lower stream classes. There was some variation across schools in the overall prevalence of bullying with the highest levels reported in Hay St, a "low integration" school with a high proportion of boys, and the lowest levels in Belmore St, a girls' school with a strong emphasis on student integration.

A major theme emerging from the student interviews was the change in status associated with being the smallest students in the school:

> You see in sixth class you were the biggest boys, now in secondary you're just tiny lads (Park St School, lower stream class).

In the boys' schools, in particular, students had heard about "the first year beating" before they came to school and many had experienced some degree of being physically pushed around, usually referred to as being "thrown in the bins" or "thrown in the bushes":

If you give cheek to the fifth years they won't get you but if you give cheek to the third or second years they will get you. You just have to act real big.

Some people just walk up to you and grab you and punch you and walk off again.

It's like first year beating, it's funny to them (Park St School, higher stream class).

When you are in the shop line, it's huge and then everyone goes in front of you and they all just push you out the way (Park St School, middle group).

You'd be going upstairs . . . and you'd be here and you go down and they'd be pushing you and kicking your bag in front of you (Dawes Point School, lower stream class).

While this was somewhat less evident in the coeducational schools than in boys-only schools, boys in coeducational schools did report a similar rite of passage:

At the start of the year when we came first in we got our beatings (Dixon St School, lower stream class).

This was not seen as happening to girls in the same way:

Interviewer: And what about the girls, do the girls push you around a bit as well?

No it's just mainly the boys.

Interviewer: So the older girls, do they react to the first year girls at all?

If there was something wrong with you they'd come over and ask you are you alright or whatever (Dawson St School).

However, a number of girls did report being pushed or shoved:

We were back, the first years and the sixth years.

And me and you were walking down the hall. . .

Yes, we were walking down the hallway and this girl goes "yes, thanks a lot for bringing us back to school" and we didn't know what to say and then she came up to me one day and started pushing me back because I was at the vending machine. She pushed me back. So there is a lot of bullying.

> Yes, that is what they do. If there is a really big queue and you come to the top they just push you (Belmore St School).

Students differed in how they perceived the "beating". Some argued that it only happened to students who knew older students, for example, the friends of older brothers:

> If you didn't know anybody coming to this school then you wouldn't get hit at all it's when you know them, and they know your brothers (Park St School, higher stream class).

For some students, being pushed around happened in the first week and was then "over":

> We used to get digs going down the corridor but now that has stopped.
> The first years would be going down the corridor and all the fifth years would be coming down and we would get squashed into the wall.
> Interviewer: Would they do that on purpose?
> Yeah. They only done it for the first week (Park St School, middle group).

Others maintained that this was just "messing" and did not involve being hurt in any serious way. These students seemed to see it as an integral part of being in first year:

> First student: Most of them are only after you for the laugh because you're a first year, you see that's all part and parcel of it coming into secondary school, you're going to get your first year beating like, so there's no point in going mad telling the teachers because you know they're only doing what's going on.
> Second student: It is a kind of a tradition in one sense (Park St School, lower stream class).

> I got about ten slaps over the head . . .
> Interviewer: Who gave you the ten slaps over the head?
> Older students.
> Everyone, I'd be walking through the corridor.
> Anyone that you might know they come along and they give you an old shove.

> Interviewer: Other first years or older?
>
> Second years.
>
> Third years.
>
> His brother is in second.
>
> I'm not going to say their names because I don't mind, it didn't hurt or anything and it's only a laugh.
>
> . . . [W]hen you're in primary it's like a rumour going around that when you come over here you're going to get such a beating and you come over and it's like a mess, they're messing (Dawes Point School, higher stream class).

However, it is difficult to determine whether these comments represent bravado on the part of students; a number of other students did seem to be hurt by older students:

> Interviewer: And is it really bad?
>
> No, they just mess.
>
> It is only messing.
>
> I got worse than him.
>
> I got worse. I got bruises all over me and the side of my head, and bounced my head off walls and all.
>
> Interviewer: Was it very painful?
>
> No.
>
> Yes.
>
> You would be crying on the ground (Dixon St School, lower stream class).

> Interviewer: But what does it actually mean, the first year beatings?
>
> Banging your head and . . .
>
> Kicking you and stuff.
>
> I got thrown into thorn bushes.
>
> Interviewer: It seems very severe to me. It must be very hurtful?
>
> I got the thorns in me.
>
> Yes, I got the thorns in my leg and it bled when they took them out.
>
> I couldn't sit down for ages (Lang St School, middle group).

Some first-year students felt that they could then take their "turn" the following year:

> But when we are in second year we will be killing the first years that
> come in.
> Interviewer: So do you think that you will do the same now when
> you are into second year; you will give the first years their beatings?
> Yes.
> We got it and they have to get it (Dixon St School, lower stream class).

While others felt their own experiences meant they would be less likely
to pick on other students:

> I'm not going near them [first years] because people did go near me
> and I know how it feels (Park St School, lower stream class).

The incidents reported here tended to happen on the corridors while students were moving from class to class or in the school grounds during
break time. In some schools (Dawson St and Fig Lane schools), first-
year students were allowed on break before other students in order to
avoid students being pushed around.

5.4.3 Talking to someone about problems

Chapters Two and Three have outlined the kind of support structures
available to first-year students across different school contexts. However,
such structures are only likely to be effective to the extent that students
are aware of them and prepared to approach the relevant personnel for
help. In the survey, first-year students were asked to whom they would
talk if they had a problem; almost two-thirds said they would talk to
someone at home, 19 per cent said they would talk to someone at school
while 16 per cent of students reported that they would not talk to anybody about their problem. There were no significant gender differences
in potential sources of help, although girls were somewhat less likely
than boys to report having no-one to talk to (14 per cent compared with
18 per cent). Sources of help did not vary by social class background.
However, students were more likely to say they would talk to someone at
school (or no-one) if they had lower levels of parental involvement, that
is, if their parents do not frequently talk to them about school and their
life in general. A matter for concern is the fact that students who report
being bullied are more likely to say there is no-one (at home or school)

they would talk to if they had a problem. In addition, students who do not like their school or teachers and have a negative view of their own abilities are more likely to say they have no-one to talk to.

Students were also asked to whom they would talk if they *had* to talk to some-one at school about a problem. Class tutors and year heads were most often seen as potential sources of help for students (see Figure 5.12). However, a significant proportion of students (over a fifth) mentioned their student mentor, "buddy" or prefect while a similar proportion indicated their informal network of friends at school as a source of support. Students were less likely to mention a subject teacher, guidance counsellor or the chaplain/matron as potential sources of help. Eight per cent of students directly stated that they would not have anyone to talk to at school, which is potentially a matter of concern. Potential sources of help varied across the case-study schools; class tutors were most frequently mentioned by students in Wentworth Place, Dixon St and Dawson St while student mentors were most frequently mentioned in Belmore St and Fig Lane.

Figure 5.12: Potential sources of help at school

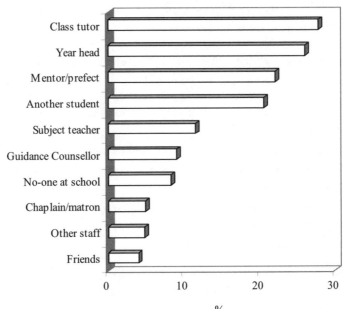

Note: Total adds to more than 100 as students could mention more than one source of help.

In the group interviews, some students reported feeling they could go to their teachers, usually their class tutors about any problems. However, students generally appeared to be reluctant to report bullying to teachers either because they felt it would make the situation worse or because teachers would be unable to help:

> Interviewer: But is there anybody that you can actually go to when it gets really out of hand?
>
> No, that's called ratting.
>
> If you tell on them they will get you worse.
>
> They will go at you for the rest of your life (Lang St School, middle group).

> The teachers, you feel a bit uneasy talking to them about it.
>
> Because then the teachers could say . . . "your name was told . . . they said that you hit them" but then they would give you more grief for telling the teacher on them (Wattle St School).

> And if someone was bullying you, do you think you'd go and tell a teacher?
>
> I'd tell the teacher but then the teachers don't really do much about it (Park St School, lower stream class).

Students were somewhat more likely to feel that their student mentor was more approachable than the teachers:

> Interviewer: You mentioned prefects — so what are the prefects there for?
>
> They are the older students and they would look after you.
>
> If something was robbed on you, you tell them and they would tell it to your form teacher.
>
> Interviewer: Would you go to your prefect if you had a problem or you wanted to know something?
>
> Yes, you would (Barrack St School).

> Yeah, we've mentors and prefects just to take care, if anything happens and we don't want to go to talk to a teacher about it we can go and talk to them and they can say such and such or whatever.
>
> Interviewer: And do you find them quite friendly and approachable?

> Yeah, I'd rather talk to them than the teachers, I feel more comfortable because they're still around our age (Dawson St School).

In sum, first-year students are more likely to go to their family about a problem. However, within the school context support structures such as the year head and class tutor system along with student mentors are seen as potential sources of help. Nevertheless, a certain number of students, especially those who are experiencing bullying or are disaffected with school, are more likely to report having no-one to talk to if they had a problem.

5.5 PERCEPTIONS OF SCHOOL

This section explores student perceptions of school life in general. Students were given a set of statements about school and asked whether they agreed or disagreed with these statements. On the basis of their responses, a number of different dimensions of school-related attitudes could be distinguished:[10]

1. The extent to which students reported liking school life;

2. The extent to which students reported liking their teachers;

3. Academic self-image, that is, the extent to which students felt they could cope with school-work;

4. Isolation, that is, the extent to which students felt isolated in their new school and consequently anxious about their situation;

5. Self-image.

5.5.1 Liking school

The extent to which students were considered to like school was derived on the basis of the statements:[11]

- I find school-work in this school really interesting.

---

[10] Factor analysis was used to analyse the interrelationships among the different statements.

[11] The scale derived is highly reliable (0.7771).

- I am excited about being at this school.

- I like being at this school.

- I usually feel relaxed about school.

- I look forward to coming to school most days.

- I like school better than most other students in this school.

In general, students tend to have very positive attitudes towards school at the beginning of first year (see Figure 5.13). However, a significant minority of students do not find school-work interesting, do not feel relaxed about school and do not look forward to coming to school.

The extent to which students reported liking school varied across the case-study schools, although this pattern was not related to the school's approach to integration or subject choice; more positive views were reported in Park St and Hay St schools and less positive views were reported in Barrack St and Dawes Point schools. On average, there were no significant gender differences in liking school. However, within coeducational schools, girls tend to have somewhat more positive attitudes than their male counterparts. Interestingly, the pattern did not vary markedly by social class background, although those from higher professional backgrounds did have more positive views. Having primary school friends in the school and being from a linked primary school did not make a difference to whether students said they like school. Students who have already experienced success in the educational system, that is, those who described themselves as at the top of their sixth class and who have higher reading and maths scores, have a significantly more positive orientation to school. Interaction with their post-primary school teachers has a significant influence on their attitudes to school; students who have experienced positive interaction with teachers are more likely to report liking school while the opposite is the case for those who have experienced negative interaction. Interaction with peers is also an influence on whether students like school; students who have been jeered or physically pushed around by other students have more negative attitudes to school.

Figure 5.13: Extent to which students like school

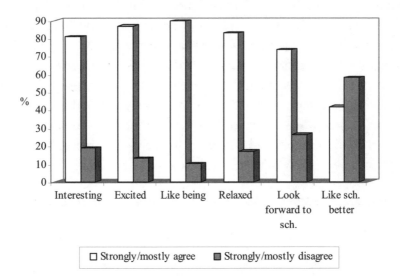

5.5.2 Liking teachers

This measure was based on the following statements:[12]

- I think most of my teachers are friendly.

- My teachers would help me if I had a problem with my school work.

- I could talk to at least one of my teachers if I had a problem.

- Most of the time there is a good working atmosphere in the class.

- I like most of my teachers.

Figure 5.14 indicates that first-year students generally have positive views of their teachers. In contrast to liking school, the extent to which students reported liking teachers did not vary markedly by school, although somewhat higher values were reported in Hay St and Belmore St schools and somewhat lower values in Barrack St School. No noticeable gender or social class differences were apparent in the extent to which students like their teachers. As might be expected, students who report

---

[12] The scale has a reliability of 0.7284.

liking school are also likely to report liking teachers. While liking school is positively correlated with reading and, to a lesser extent, maths score, there is no relationship between prior performance and liking teachers. On the other hand, students who report being at the top of their class in primary school are more likely to report a positive view of their post-primary teachers. As might be expected, students who have experienced positive interaction with teachers are more likely to report liking teachers in their school while the opposite is the case for levels of negative inter-action. Perhaps surprisingly, however, students who report having been bullied are less likely to have a positive view of teachers.

Figure 5.14: Extent to which students like teachers in their school

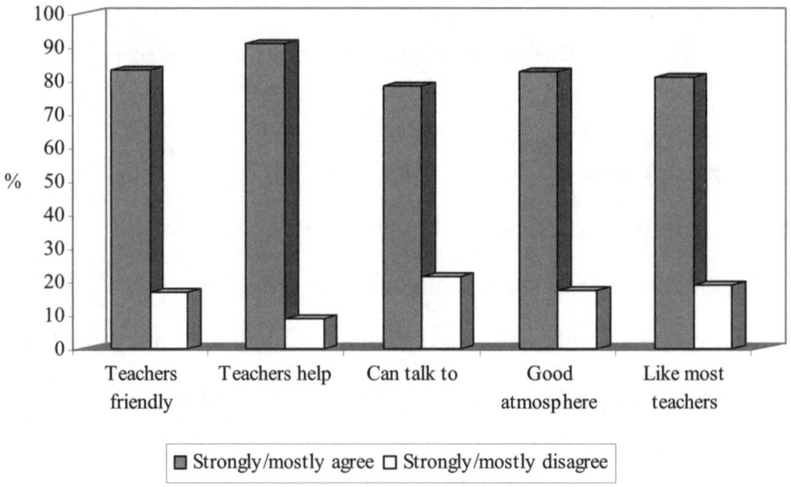

5.5.3 Academic self-image

The measure of academic self-image was based on the following state-ments:[13]

- I think I am doing well at this school.

- I think the work is quite easy at this school.

- I think I am working hard at this school.

---

[13] The scale is highly reliable (0.7539).

- I am able to do my school work as well as most other students.

- I do better at school work than most other students in my class.

- I'm quite pleased with how my school work is going.

- I have trouble keeping up with my school work (disagree).

The majority of first-year students report doing well, being pleased with their school work and not having trouble keeping up (Figure 5.15). Furthermore, the vast majority feel that they are working hard at school. However, a significant proportion (43 per cent) of first-year students do not find the work easy.

Figure 5.15: Academic self-image

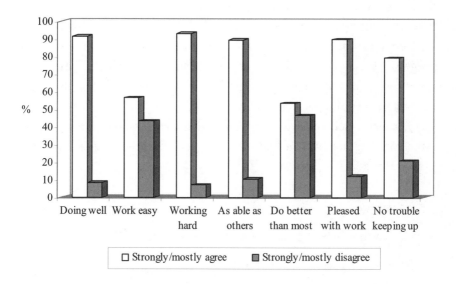

Boys have a somewhat higher academic self-rating than girls, a pattern that is consistent with previous research on Junior and Leaving Certificate students (Hannan et al., 1996). Academic self-image varies by social class background with more positive self-images found among those from higher professional or farming backgrounds and less positive ratings reported by students from semi/unskilled manual or non-employed households. Students who report liking school, liking teachers and having a positive academic self-image are more likely to report that their parents spend more time interacting with them.

As might be expected, academic self-image is influenced by prior educational success. Students with higher reading and maths scores are more likely to have a positive academic self-image. Those who felt they were top of the class in primary school are more likely to have a positive academic self-image than those who reported being in the middle or bottom of the class. Students who were spending longer on homework at the time of the survey (September) were less likely to report being able to cope with their school-work; these students appear to feel "swamped" by the academic demands of first year. Students who have experienced positive interaction with teachers are, as might be expected, more likely to have a positive view of their academic progress; the opposite is the case for those who have reported negative interaction with teachers. In addition, students who reported only negative feelings on their first day at school tend to have a more negative view of their subsequent academic progress. The different dimensions of attitudes to school life are interrelated; students with more positive academic self-images are also more likely to report liking school and liking teachers.

Academic self-image varied somewhat across schools with higher ratings among students in Park St and Wattle St schools and lower ratings in Barrack St school.

5.5.4 Isolation

This measure was based on the following statements:[14]

- Being at this school scares me.

- Nobody at this school seems to take any notice of me.

- At times I feel down about my life.

- I often feel lost and alone at school.

- I don't have many friends at this school.

- I'm afraid that I'll make a fool of myself in class.

---

[14] The measure has a reliability of 0.7603.

- I am afraid to tell teachers when I don't understand something in class.

A minority of students report feeling very isolated in terms of feeling alone, without friends, being scared by school or being ignored (see Figure 5.16). However, a significant group of students are inhibited by the potential judgments of others with almost a third of students being afraid to make a fool of themselves in class and being afraid to ask teachers if they don't understand something. In addition, almost a third of the students surveyed reported feeling down about their life at times.

Figure 5.16: Extent to which students feel isolated at school

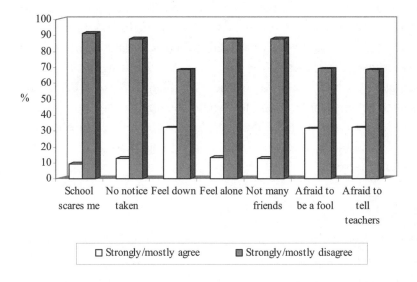

There was some variation across schools in reported isolation among students, although this pattern is not clearly related to the prevalence of support structures for first-year students; somewhat higher levels were reported in Wynyard Rd, Barrack St and Dawes Point schools and somewhat lower levels were reported in Lang St and Belmore St schools. Girls were somewhat more likely to report feelings of isolation than boys; this pattern holds within all coeducational schools, with the exception of Fig Lane School. There was significant variation by social class background with those from professional backgrounds much less likely to report feeling isolated in school than those from non-employed backgrounds. There was some variation by household structure with students living with neither parent most likely to report isolation and those living with both parents least likely to do so. Furthermore, students with higher levels of parental involvement were less likely to report feeling isolated at school. Students from a Traveller background or with non-national parents were significantly more likely to report feeling isolated within school.

Students with higher reading and maths scores were less likely to feel isolated while those who had a negative perception of their performance in sixth class and those who had experienced bullying were more likely to report such feelings. No marked difference was apparent between those in high and low integration schools. Pre-entry contact or having an older sibling in the school had no significant relationship with reported isolation. As might be expected, those with three or more friends from primary school in their *school* were less likely to report isolation. However, the relationship with number of friends in their *class* was insignificant.

Students who report isolation are less likely to like school and/or teachers. Liking school, liking teachers or feeling isolated does not vary markedly by type of class, although those in lower stream classes are slightly more likely to report feeling isolated than those in higher stream or middle classes.

5.5.5 Self-image

Students were asked about three aspects of their self-image in terms of the following statements:

- I like the way I look.

- I am good at sports.

- I am liked by most of the other students in my class.

While factor analysis identified the different aspects of self-image as clustering together, the resulting scale did not have a high reliability (0.55) so the dimensions are analysed separately here.

In general, the first-year students surveyed had a positive self-image in terms of their appearance, their sporting prowess and their popularity (see Figure 5.17). Body-image (a student liking the way they look) varied significantly by school with more positive reports in Lang St School, a boys' school, and less positive views in Barrack St School, a girls' school. This is partly related to gender with schools varying significantly for girls but not for boys (however, boys in Lang St school have a more positive body-image than boys in other schools). In keeping with previous research, girls are found to have more negative body-images than boys, reflecting wider social pressures rather than the school context per se (Figure 5.18) (see Hannan et al., 1996). There is no significant variation in body-image by social class background. Students who had been bullied have a more negative body-image, a pattern that is consistent with that found in Hannan et al. (1996). This may relate to the fact that bullying behaviour may target some aspects of students' appearance. Students who have a more positive body-image also have a more positive experience of school in general; they are more likely to like their school and teachers, rate their academic performance more positively and are less likely to feel isolated.

Figure 5.17: Student self-image

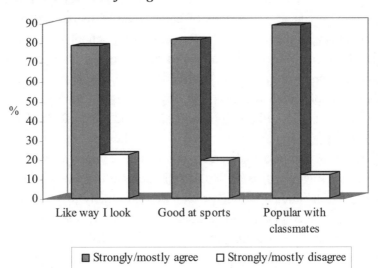

Strongly/mostly agree ☐ Strongly/mostly disagree

Figure 5.18: Body image by gender ("I like the way I look")

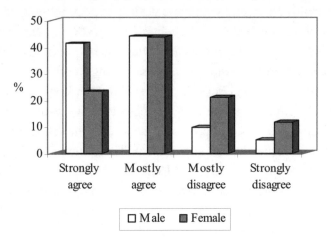

Schools varied markedly in the extent to which students reported being good at sports. Since girls are significantly less likely than boys to report being good at sports (see Figure 5.19), views were more positive in all boys' schools (such as Lang St and Park St) than in all girls' schools (such as Belmore St School). There is no discernible variation by social class background in perceptions of being good at sports. Students who reported being at the top of their class in primary school are significantly more likely than those in the middle or bottom of the class to report being good at sport (56 per cent compared with 32 per cent); this pattern is apparent among both the girls and boys surveyed. Students who have been bullied are less likely to report being good at sports. Students who report being good at sport are more likely to be involved in sports both within school and in outside clubs; this pattern is more marked for boys than girls. However, it is difficult to disentangle the relationship on the basis of available data; young people are more likely to get involved in sports if they feel they are good at them but being involved is also likely to boost their view of their sporting abilities. Students who report being good at sports are generally more positive about their lives; they are somewhat more likely to like their school and teachers, rate their academic performance more positively and are less likely to feel isolated.

Figure 5.19: Being good at sport by gender

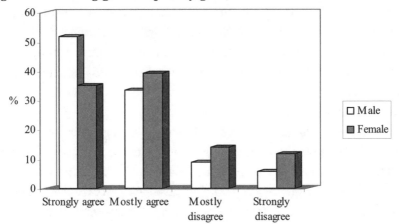

There was no significant variation across schools in self-reported student popularity, that is, whether students felt they were liked by their class-mates. This pattern did not vary significantly by gender or social class background. Students who have been bullied, as might be expected, are less likely to report being popular with their classmates. Students who see themselves as popular are more likely to like school and their teach-ers, rate their academic abilities highly and are, as might be expected, less likely to feel isolated at school.

5.6 CONCLUSIONS

This chapter has outlined experiences of the transition from primary to post-primary school among first-year students in twelve case-study schools. While the schools have not been selected to be representative of the total population of post-primary schools in Ireland, they capture im-portant dimensions of how schools handle the transition process and therefore provide a useful insight into the nature of the adjustment proc-ess for students in different school contexts.

It was hypothesised in Chapter One that students would experience a somewhat easier transition in schools with more developed integration programmes. This hypothesis was at least partially borne out by the find-ings in that the degree of contact with their post-primary school before entry helps to some extent to reduce student anxiety about making the transition. However, students' expectations of their post-primary school appear to be based mainly on informal sources of information, such as siblings and the wider family circle. These informal sources of information and support (for example, having siblings and/or friends in the same school) also appear to be important in reducing negative feelings about moving to post-primary school. Students themselves feel that putting them in the same class as their friends and reducing bullying would do most to help them settle into the new school.

In keeping with previous research, the prevailing pattern is of mixed emotions around the transition process, with most students feeling a combination of nervousness and excitement on their first day at school. Nevertheless, a significant minority of students have very negative feelings about school from the outset and this group is disproportionately made up of students who have not experienced educational success at primary level.

For first-year students, the main differences between post-primary and primary school centre on having more teachers and subjects, being one of the youngest students, having different relations with teachers, being in a "big" school and having a longer day. A major downside for many students was the change in status associated with being one of the youngest and smallest students in the school; a recurring theme in the student interviews highlighted "the first year beating" as a rite of passage for boys in first year. However, many students stress the advantages of post-primary school over primary school in terms of wider experiences and greater autonomy. Over and above the influence of the school's approach to handling the transition process, school climate, that is the nature of interaction among teachers and students in the school, appears to play a significant role in influencing not only student attitudes to school but students' own view of themselves. In particular, students who have experienced bullying have a more negative view of themselves, feel more isolated and have a more negative attitude to school and their teachers. It appears, therefore, that a school's formal structures to assist student integration may be insufficient to ease the transition process unless they are underpinned by a positive school climate.

This chapter has focused on the early stages of students' transition into the post-primary school; the extent to which long-term transition difficulties are evident among first-year students in the case-study schools is discussed in Chapter Seven.

Chapter Six

STUDENT PERCEPTIONS OF THE LEARNING PROCESS

INTRODUCTION

Chapter Five examined students' perspectives of the transition into post-primary school. Previous research has highlighted the significant differences between the primary and post-primary sectors in the subjects taught and the approach to teaching (see Chapter One). This chapter explores student perceptions of the learning process within first year. Students were surveyed in September and May of first year (see the ESRI and NCCA websites for the questionnaires used); analyses in this chapter are based on the 750 students included in both waves of the survey along with 38 group interviews conducted with students in October to explore their perceptions of the learning process within first year. Because Wynyard Rd. school discontinued their involvement in the research, analyses are based on students in a total of eleven schools. The first section examines the approach to ability grouping in the case-study schools and students' views on class allocation. The second section analyses student perceptions of subject choice and the number of subjects they take. Continuity in curriculum between primary and post-primary school is explored in section three while student perceptions of particular subjects are examined in section four. Student views on the pace of instruction are analysed in section five and the amount of time spent on homework is discussed in section six. Section seven examines the different forms of learning assistance available to students.

6.1 ABILITY GROUPING

Chapter Two has indicated a decline over time nationally in the proportion of first year base classes which are grouped on the basis of ability. The case-study schools varied in their approach to ability grouping. Mixed ability base classes were employed in first year in five of the schools: Dawson St, Barrack St, Fig Lane, Belmore St and Wattle St. In Fig Lane and Belmore St, students were allowed to specify friends with the schools attempting to group some friends in the same class in order to facilitate the settling-in process. In Wentworth Place, classes were banded, that is, divided into two bands on the basis of assessed ability. In five of the schools (Lang St, Dixon St, Park St, Hay St and Dawes Point), classes were streamed from higher to lower by assessed ability.

Students were asked whether they agreed or disagreed with a number of statements regarding class allocation (see Figure 6.1). Over three-quarters of the students in the case-study schools agree with the statement that "students should be put in the same class as their friends". Support for this view was highest in Belmore St, Wattle St and Fig Lane, all mixed ability schools, but it was also relatively high in Lang St, which was streamed. Interestingly, there was quite a high level of support for ability-based differentiation among the students surveyed, with 63 per cent agreeing with the statement that "test results are a good way of deciding which class students should be in". Support for this view was highest in schools which used streaming/banding, particularly Hay St and Wentworth Place. However, the majority of students in mixed ability schools also supported ability-based grouping; the exceptions to this pattern occurred in Fig Lane and Belmore St. Within streamed schools, students in lower stream classes were more likely to oppose ability-based differentiation; 31 per cent disagreed with the statement compared with 16 per cent of those in the higher stream classes.

Figure 6.1: Attitude to class allocation approaches

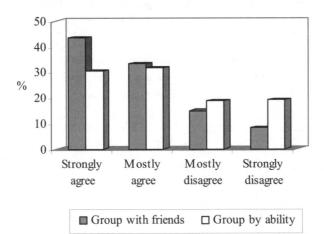

Attitudes to ability grouping were further explored within group interviews with students. As in the questionnaire responses, students were divided in their opinions of ability grouping but overall responses tended to be positive. The main justification given for ability grouping was that it would mean a more appropriate pace of instruction within class, with teaching tailored to the group taught:

> You should be with people of the same ability.
> You don't want to be in a class that have people going at a slow pace and you want to go quicker (Park St, higher stream class).

> You might end up in a class that is too fast (Park St, middle class).

> Because if you aren't really that smart, it is easier if you learn it slower than quicker.
> But the smart lads go way ahead of you. And it wouldn't be fair to the smart people (Wentworth Place, higher band).

> Some people couldn't keep up with the others and some people are too smart for the others (Lang St, middle class).

However, such grouping was sometimes seen as resulting in extra pressure for those in the higher stream classes:

> You know the way when you get into [the higher stream class] and if you didn't get placed into different classes, you would be really behind because imagine all the slow things they would be teaching people.
>
> [But] They are much more strict [with the higher stream class]. They think we are brain boxes and we are only kids. We don't know all the scientific stuff (Dixon St, higher stream class).

One of the main disadvantages of class allocation based on ability from the students' point of view was that they would not be in the same class as their friends:

> It was weird waiting to see what class you were in, you were nervous, you wanted to be put in with your friends (Wentworth Place, higher band).

Almost two-thirds (63 per cent) of students in the case-study schools agreed with the statement that "teachers treat the different classes in first year differently". Students in streamed schools were more likely to agree with this statement, although over half of those in mixed ability schools also did so. Students in Belmore St, a mixed ability girls' school, were most likely to see the classes as being treated equitably. Those in the lower class within streamed schools were most likely to perceive treatment as inequitable, perhaps because they report more negative interaction with teachers (see Chapter Five). Interestingly, a number of students in higher classes reported unfair treatment, focusing on the fact that students in the lower classes were under less pressure in terms of academic work and discipline and had greater access to subjects with a practical orientation:

> And young people get a reward for being dumb.
>
> They get to go swimming and bowling every week.
>
> They get a reward for being dumb. What do we get? Hard work.
>
> They [the teachers] are not too strict with them [the lower stream class].
>
> If they say curses to the teachers all they do is write a note and that's it. If I did that, I would be expelled on the spot (Dixon St, higher stream class).
>
> But the dumb people always get games and everything.

We have metalwork once a week and they have metalwork twice a week (Lang St, higher stream class).

All of us are in [the higher stream class] now and the amount of homework we get.
Because we're the smartest (Dawes Point, higher stream class).

In contrast, students in the lower stream class mentioned issues such as restricted choice of subjects:

We are not allowed to pick.
Because we are slow.
Yes, we are in a slow class.
[Somewhat later.]
When you are in C and D you can't pick. When you are in A or B you are allowed pick.
Interviewer: Do you think that it is fair that only…?
It is not. Because then people are saying to you that you are slow and all (Dixon St).

The language used in these quotes, contrasting "dumb" and "smart" students, was evident in many of the interviews held in streamed schools. Even at this early stage in the school year (October), class allocation appeared to be strongly linked to the labelling of students on the basis of ability and these labels seem to have been internalised by students:

Interviewer: Can I ask how are you divided into classes? Do you know?
Student: Who's smart goes into [this class] and who is dumb goes into [that class] or [that class] or something (Dixon St, higher stream class).

They are clever and we are dumb (Dixon St, lower stream class).

A2 and A1 are smart classes and B1 and B2 are normal classes, then C1 and C2 are stupid classes (Park St, lower stream class).

The brainy people are in the brainy classes.
And then if you are in the stupid class, they call you a dope and all that (Wentworth Place, lower band).

> They [the lower stream class] think that they are mad.
>
> They are just all scumbags really (Lang St, middle class).

An interesting issue which emerged from the interviews was the fact that some students in higher classes within streamed schools felt their position was precarious. Students in the higher stream classes in two boys' schools, Park St and Wentworth Place, reported that mid-term tests were being held which could result in students being reassigned to different classes. This possibility led to some concern and anxiety among students in these schools who preferred not to be transferred out of an already established group:

> I dread tests.
>
> We have them at mid-term as well.
>
> They are all added up on an average. Then every subject's average is added up and then you have an overall average and you have to get over 85 per cent to stay in [the higher stream class].
>
> Interviewer: Are you worried about that?
>
> Yeah.
>
> We don't want to drop down (Park St, higher stream class).

> We did a test yesterday to see if everyone should still be in this class.
>
> But we have made friends now but we might be sent to different classes because of the test. That is not fair (Wentworth Place, higher band).

However, for some students in the lower stream classes the possibility of moving classes was seen as a "second chance":

> It's good in that way because you've a second chance. Then really if you just try and you've a good chance then of getting into a higher class (Park St, lower stream class).

In actuality, among the sampled students, there was no "downward" movement from the higher stream class in Park St with a small amount of "upward" mobility from the middle and lower stream classes. In Wentworth Place, 6 per cent of those in the higher band moved "downwards" while 12 per cent of those in the lower band moved "upward".

6.2 SUBJECT CHOICE

The case-study schools differ in their approach to subject choice for students (see Chapter Four). In four of the case-study schools (Barrack St, Dawson St, Wattle St and Dawes Point), students pick their subjects before entry to the school. In two other schools, Park St and Hay St, students select their subjects before entry to the school but the choice of subjects was somewhat more restricted. In Wentworth Place and Dixon St, students try out the different subjects through a "taster" programme for part of the year. In Lang St, Belmore St and Fig Lane, students take subjects for all of the first year before selecting their Junior Certificate subjects.

First-year students were asked about the sources of advice they draw on in making decisions about subject choice. Parents emerge as the most important source of advice for first-year students, followed by teachers and friends (see Figure 6.2); the Guidance Counsellor is a very important source of advice for only a minority of first-year students in the case-study schools. As might be expected, the source of advice differs according to the stage at which students have to choose their subjects. Friends are a less important source of advice, and teachers a more important source, when subject choices are made at a later stage (that is, after sampling subjects). There is some variation across schools over and above that related to the school's approach to subject choice. Parents are a very important source of advice for the vast majority (85 per cent) of students in Barrack St and teachers and friends are more highly rated as a source of advice in this school than any other. It would appear that students in this school are highly "other-directed" in their selection of subjects.

Figure 6.2: Sources of advice for subject choice

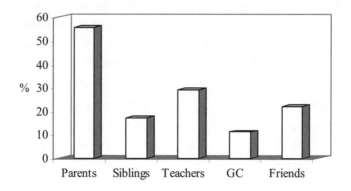

As well as being asked about potential sources of advice on subject selection, students were asked about the factors influencing their choice of
subjects. Needing the subject for a course or job at a later stage and finding the subject interesting emerged as the most important reasons put
forward by students in the case-study schools (see Figure 6.3). Almost a
third of students said they were influenced by their parents' views on
which subjects they should take. A quarter of students selected subjects
they thought would be easy while a fifth of students were influenced by
what their friends were picking or what their teachers recommended.
There was some variation across the schools surveyed. The intrinsic interest of the subject was a more important influence in Fig Lane and
Wentworth Place than in the other schools. The choices of friends were
seen as more important in Barrack St, Hay St and Dawes Point than in
other schools; these three schools were all designated disadvantaged
schools in which subjects were chosen at an early stage. Parents were
seen as more important influences in Wattle St, Hay St and Park St,
again all schools with early subject selection. Not surprisingly, therefore,
friends and parents represent a more important influence in schools
where students pick subjects before entry. This pattern may have implications for the kinds of subjects chosen; if parents and primary school
friends are not very familiar with the post-primary curriculum, they may
encourage the selection of more "traditional" subjects. Unfortunately, the
effect of different sources of advice cannot be disentangled from the im-

pact of school-level subject provision within the relatively small number of schools included in this study.

Figure 6.3: Influences on subject choice

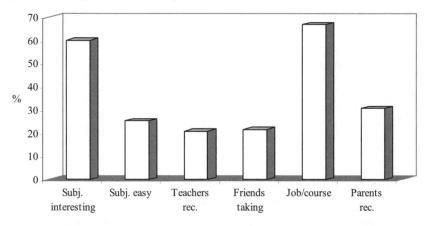

The influences on subject choice are also related to the class placement of students. Intrinsic interest is a more important influence for those in mixed ability or higher stream classes than for those in middle or lower stream classes (see Figure 6.4). The perceived ease of the subject is more influential for those in middle or lower stream classes as are the recommendations of teachers, friends or parents. The pattern of variation by class placement is partly, but not wholly, due to the over-representation of students with lower reading test scores in lower stream classes.

Figure 6.4: Influence on subject choice by class placement

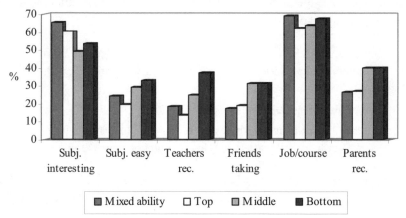

The issue of influences on subject choice was explored in greater detail with students in the group interviews. As was apparent from the questionnaire responses, students who chose their subjects before entry to post-primary school tended to be more reliant on informal sources of information:

> Interviewer: And when you had to pick the subjects, how did you make up your minds what you wanted to do?
>
> Student: Asking everybody like.
>
> [Another student interrupts.]
>
> Interviewer: Sorry, you said you asked people; who did you ask?
>
> Student: Like the people that were in this school that had those subjects.
>
> Interviewer: And what did you ask, what was the best?
>
> Student: Yes. What was the hardest and what was the easiest.
>
> People were saying "go and do business studies and all and you will get a good job out of it" but then you have to do so much work.
>
> I just picked whatever my friend was picking (Barrack St).

The rumoured workload was also a factor for some students in the lower stream class in Park St school:

> Interviewer: When you had to pick between French, German and Home Economics, how did you decide which one to pick?
>
> Student: Because Home Ec. is dossing and in French and German you have homework (Park St, lower stream class).

Lack of knowledge about subjects meant that sometimes students regretted their choice subsequently:

> Interviewer: And have any of you picked subjects that you think you would rather not have done if you knew something about them?
>
> Student: Yeah.
>
> Interviewer: Like what subjects?
>
> Student: Like business studies or something, I picked it because I didn't know what it was about (Hay St, higher stream class).

Although students in Dawes Point chose their subjects before entry, they had a discussion about subject choice with the school principal and were given a talk on the different options by the subject teachers. While students reported finding this helpful ("because it helped us really to pick our subjects"), they did not always feel that subjects turned out to be what they expected.

Students who had a chance to try out different subjects before making their choice mentioned a number of factors as influencing their choice, including the particular teacher involved, the perceived workload as well as the content of the subject itself:

> I like the subject . . . but I won't pick it because of the teacher (Wentworth Place, higher band).

> I will keep Art because you get no homework (Lang St, middle class).

Some students felt that subjects should be chosen in terms of what they would "need" in the future, perhaps combined with some subjects taken for interest's sake:

> You should do some [subjects] you know you will need and then other ones that maybe you like or something. Like in fifth year . . . you sort out your subjects for what you want to do when you are older but like you should sort them out from first year, and you can drop some like have a few which you don't know exactly what you are doing but have the ones that you kind of know what you are doing (Belmore St).

The school's approach to subject choice naturally has implications for the number of subjects taken by first-year students; students take more subjects if their school has a taster programme in operation. However, even among schools with a similar approach to subject choice, there is variation in the number of subjects taken. Schools with "early" subject selection tend to take 12 subjects compared with 16 for those in schools with some sort of taster programme. However, among the "early choice" schools, students in Hay St tend to take more subjects than those in the other schools. Among schools with a taster programme, students in Fig Lane and Lang St, schools with quite contrasting student intakes in terms of social background and prior ability levels, tend to take more subjects (17) than those in other schools. The number of subjects taken also varies within schools. In three of the streamed schools (Dixon St, Park St and Dawes Point), students in the lower stream classes tend to do slightly fewer subjects than those in the higher stream classes. In some cases, students receiving learning support take fewer subjects than other students. In addition, a number of students appear to have an exemption from taking Irish; for instance, students with non-national parents are less likely to be studying Irish than other students. In general, students with higher reading and mathematics scores tend to take more subjects.

Over half of the students surveyed reported that there was a subject that they would like to have taken but couldn't. This pattern varied markedly by school with restricted choice more prevalent in Dawson St and Fig Lane schools and less prevalent in Lang St and Hay St schools. The subjects students would like to have taken tended to be more practical in orientation and included Materials Technology (Woodwork) (33 per cent), Metalwork (21 per cent), Home Economics (17 per cent) and Spanish (17 per cent). Restricted choice did not vary by gender or mathematics/reading test score. However, in a number of schools (Dixon St, Park St and Lang St), students in lower stream classes were more likely to report not being able to take a subject they wanted to do (see above).

Over half (57 per cent) of first-year students reported that they got to take all of the subjects they chose, just over a fifth did not while a similar proportion did not yet know if they been granted all their choices.[1] Among students who knew the outcome of their selection, not getting their choices was more common in Hay St, Dawes Point, Dawson St and Dixon St. Constrained choice was more prevalent in middle or lower stream classes than in higher stream or mixed ability classes (37-40 per cent compared with 21-24 per cent). This pattern was especially evident in Dixon St, Park St and Dawes Point.

At the beginning of the school year, twenty-nine per cent of students agreed with the statement that "I am taking too many subjects at the moment"; thirty-one per cent of students did not know while forty per cent of students disagreed with the statement. The pattern did not vary markedly across the school year, even though some students (those in

---

[1] This arose in schools where students were in the process of subject selection for second year.

Dixon St and Wentworth Place) were taking fewer subjects in May than in the first term; twenty-nine per cent of students felt they were doing too many subjects in May. This pattern did not vary by gender, social class or class type. However, the pattern varied significantly by school with those in Lang St, Barrack St and Fig Lane schools more likely to feel they were taking too many subjects. As might be expected, students who agreed with the statement were taking more subjects than those who disagreed with the statement (15 compared with 14.3 subjects in September; 14.4 compared with 13.9 subjects in May). However, considerable variation was apparent among students taking the same number of subjects; among those taking 13 subjects, for example, 23 per cent of students felt they were taking too many subjects while 42 per cent disagreed with the statement. This appears to be related to the differential capacity of students to cope with a variety of subjects since students with lower reading scores were more likely to feel they were taking too many subjects in both September and May.

Figure 6.5: Preferences regarding subject choice

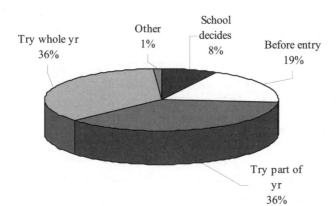

Students were asked about their preferred approach to subject choice. The majority of students surveyed opted for a "taster" approach, where they would get to try subjects before having to choose; students were equally divided between being able to try subjects for part of the year and taking the subjects for the whole of the year. Almost a fifth of students would prefer to pick their subjects before entry to post-primary school while 8 per cent would like the school to decide on their subjects. Students with lower reading and mathematics scores, those in middle or lower stream classes in streamed schools, and those from manual, non-employed or Traveller backgrounds were more likely to report preferring school allocation of subjects, most likely reflecting less confidence in their ability to choose among the subjects provided.

Not surprisingly, students' preferred approach to subject choice appears to be influenced by the actual approach taken in their school. Support for sampling subjects for the whole year is most strongly advocated in Belmore St and Fig Lane, where such an approach is employed. Sampling subjects for part of the year is most strongly favoured in Wentworth Place, where this is the approach taken. However, over half of the students in schools where subject choice is made early would like the opportunity to sample subjects. Perhaps surprisingly, over a fifth of students in three schools, Barrack St, Dixon St and Hay St, would like the school to decide on their subjects for them.

In keeping with the questionnaire responses, students in the group interviews tended to favour having at least some opportunity to try subjects out before they selected them. This approach was seen as having some advantages, mainly in terms of the opportunity to make a more informed choice regarding subjects:

> If you had less subjects, you might be missing something that you didn't realise you really liked (Student, Fig Lane).

> I wanted to do one [subject] and then like I had a class and I hated it (Belmore St).

> You get four weeks of each subject before you get to choose.
> Interviewer: And do you think that's a good idea?
> Student: Yes.
> [Otherwise] you could pick a dreadful subject that you hate and you could be stuck with it for three years (Wentworth Place, higher band).

Some students reported picking (or going to pick) subjects that they might not otherwise have thought of selecting:

> When I came here I was thinking I would do French but I don't
> really like French now. I think I prefer German so it's good to see
> which one you prefer and then decide after that (Fig Lane).

However, an increased amount of homework and the perceived difficulty
of the "new" subjects were seen as disadvantages of having more (new)
subjects:

> If you don't do homework one night, say you are too tired and you
> just do the bare amount that you have for tomorrow, then it all builds
> up for the next day.
> I always do that. I used to leave the homework I needed for the next
> day and you would have about 15 subjects to do (Fig Lane).
>
> It's nice getting a chance [to take] other subjects, learning new sub-
> jects but some of them are really hard or difficult (Dawson St).
>
> Science is quite hard because you've all different things ... you
> never really did science in primary and it's just like a big step from
> doing nothing into all these different . . ., everything has a different
> symbol and everything. It's hard in Science.
> It's a big difference because woodwork and metal work, you never
> did them in primary, you have to learn the grip of the saw and all
> that, it's way harder (Dawson St).

Another disadvantage was the difficulty in maintaining continuity in a
very varied set of subjects:

> If you have business, you only get two classes a week and you forget
> the stuff.
> You can't take any of it in. It is just really hard to take it all in (Fig
> Lane).

In Dawson St, where students selected subjects before entry, this approach was seen to have some disadvantages:

> Here we were coming in, we just had to go by what people were tell-
> ing us, what Business was like. You don't get a chance to actually
> see what they're like. You could have chosen different ones if you
> had of seen what they [the teachers] were doing (Dawson St).

Some students in Park St, Barrack St and Hay St also said they should have been allowed to choose their subjects:

> It's a good idea [to try out subjects] because at least then you're not missing out on any subjects. You do the subjects you're strongest at (Park St, lower stream class).

However, a number of students said they would prefer to pick the subjects before starting post-primary school:

> I would rather just pick them, because you lose out on a lot of work on other subjects when you are doing about twenty. Then you would have to work really hard so I would prefer to pick them at the start (Park St, middle class).

In sum, students in the case-study schools tend to favour the opportunity to try out subjects before selecting them, mainly because it allows them to make a more informed choice. Students who had to choose subjects before entering post-primary school were more likely to rely on informal sources of information, such as the views of parents and friends. However, a potential downside to the taster approach was seen to be the increased workload involved and students in "taster" schools were more likely to feel they were taking too many subjects. The relationship between the number of subjects taken in first year and student integration and progress within the school is assessed in Chapter Seven.

6.3 CURRICULUM CONTINUITY

6.3.1 Perceived standards in Irish, English and Mathematics

Chapter Five has described how the transition from primary to post-primary school involves an encounter with new subjects and different teaching methods. At the beginning of the school year, students were asked to compare their experiences of Irish, English and Mathematics in post-primary school with the standard of these subjects in primary school. Students tended to see these subjects as "the same" or "harder" than at primary school level (see Figure 6.6) with a small proportion finding the subjects easier.

Figure 6.6: Perceived standard of Irish, English and Mathematics at post-primary level compared with at primary level

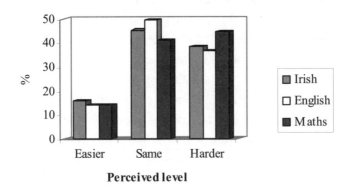

Perceived level

Only a small minority (16 per cent) found Irish easier with 45 per cent reporting it was "about the same" and a significant group of students (39 per cent) finding it harder than in primary school (see Figure 6.6). Boys were much more likely than girls to report Irish as harder *or* easier. However, this pattern was due to the distribution of boys and girls across school types with no significant gender difference found among students in the same school. The perception of differences between primary and post-primary subject standards did not vary markedly by social class background. Interestingly, finding Irish easier was much more common in lower stream classes within streamed/banded schools while those in higher or middle stream classes were more likely to find the subject harder. This would appear to reflect the way in which subject content is tailored to the different ability groups with greater academic demands made on students in higher stream classes (see Chapter Four). Students with lower reading scores were somewhat more likely to see Irish as harder in post-primary school. As well as varying across the case-study schools, there was variation within schools in terms of where students had gone to primary school; significant variation was evident within half of the case-study schools: Dawson St, Lang St, Barrack St, Hay St, Fig Lane and Belmore St schools.

Fourteen per cent of students found English easier than in primary school, almost half found it "about the same" while 37 per cent found it harder (Figure 6.6). Boys were significantly more likely than girls to find it harder; this pattern was evident within coeducational schools, although the difference between girls and boys is not statistically significant within these schools. As with Irish, those in lower classes in streamed schools were likely to find English easier than at primary level, indicating differential standards across the class groups. In contrast to the pattern for Irish, students with *higher* Mathematics and reading scores were significantly more likely to see English as harder; this is apparent across class types. It may be related to more challenging material being targeted at more academically able students. The pattern varied significantly by school with some variation within schools by primary school attended (to a significant extent in Dawson St, Lang St, Hay St, Fig Lane and Dawes Point schools).

Students were significantly more likely to see Mathematics rather than Irish or English as harder in post-primary than in primary school (see Figure 6.6). As with Irish and English, boys were more likely to see Mathematics as harder than it had been. This pattern is due to the gender distribution across school types with marked gender differences evident only in Fig Lane school. Students with lower Mathematics and reading scores were significantly more likely to see Mathematics as harder in post-primary school. Furthermore, students in the lower class in streamed schools were likely to see Mathematics as easier than it had been. The pattern for Mathematics varied by case-study school and variation by the primary school attended was apparent within schools with significant differences evident in Dawson St, Lang St, Hay St, Fig Lane and Dawes Point schools.

Measures of the perceived level of Irish, English and Mathematics in post-primary school were moderately intercorrelated ($r=0.1-0.2$), that is, students who found one subject harder were somewhat more likely to report finding the other subjects harder. However, this relationship was not very strong, indicating that some students felt "better prepared" in some subjects than in others. Over a tenth of students find all three subjects harder than in primary school. Students in higher or middle stream classes are more likely to find all three subjects harder, indicating increased academic demands for these students compared with primary level. A significant minority (36 per cent) of students in Lang St, a streamed school which is designated disadvantaged, find all three

subjects harder. There was significant variation in finding all three subjects harder within two schools (Wentworth Place and Belmore St) in
terms of the primary school attended, a pattern which makes it difficult
for teachers to tailor curricular standards according to the needs of in-
coming students.

In sum, a significant minority of students find Irish, English and/or
Mathematics harder in post-primary school than it was in primary school.
There are marked differences by class allocation; students in higher stream
classes tend to find the subjects harder while those in lower stream classes
often find the subjects easier. This reflects the different pace and standards
applied in different ability groups within streamed schools. Another interesting pattern was the differences among students in terms of the primary
school they had attended; it appears that there are variable standards across
the feeder schools with greater curriculum discontinuity for some students
than for others.

The issue of variable experiences of primary subjects was also raised
by students in the group interviews:

> I was in an Irish school and they spoke Irish and we were way ahead.
>
> In the Maths . . . they went straight into sets and we skipped it last
> year.
>
> My old teacher, he only did about twenty minutes of Irish every day
> (Wentworth Place, higher band).
>
> Our school in primary, we did nothing in Irish, five minutes a week
> on Irish.
>
> We were really bad at Irish in our school (Park St, higher stream
> class).

6.3.2. Views on the post-primary curriculum

At the end of the school year, students were asked to reflect on their perceptions of the post-primary curriculum as compared with their experiences in primary school. The majority of first-year students in the case-
study schools reported that they enjoyed the subjects in first year more
than they had subjects in sixth class within primary school (see Figure
6.7). The majority also felt that primary school had prepared them well
for post-primary school and that most of the subjects had followed on

well from the primary curriculum. However, almost a third of students felt that many subjects in first year just repeated what they had already learnt in primary school:

> The geography down there is just the exact same in primary, and the history. And the English. We are getting the exact same work and some of the work that we get in history and geography we already did in 6th class (Dixon St, lower stream class).

Figure 6.7: Views on the post-primary curriculum (% agree)

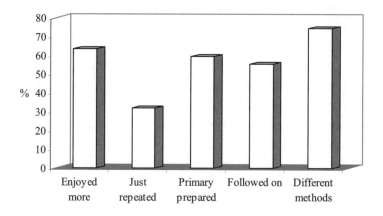

Furthermore, three-quarters of students felt that subjects were taught in a different way in post-primary than in primary school:

> You see in primary the teachers used to stay 'til everyone knows it and then you have a test on it and then she'd start a new thing and then wait then 'til everyone else knows it and then she'd do a test on that and then she'd do a big one on everything that we done and see did you remember it. Because I think it's fair the way it is at primary because they wait 'til everyone knows it.
>
> Interviewer: And now what happens?
>
> They just keep on, the teachers just go on and wait, or say our teacher, she does maths pages by maths pages and then she gives us a test and then she thinks that we're not learning it but then you feel embarrassed then saying to them I don't know how to do it, I find it hard (Park St, lower stream class).
>
> They [Mathematics] are not explained as well as they were in primary school (Fig Lane).

Students who *felt* they were taking too many subjects were less likely to report enjoying first year more, were less likely to feel primary school had prepared them for post-primary or that subjects followed on from primary school; the pattern did not vary by the *actual* number of subjects taken by students, however. Students with a higher reading score were more likely to report enjoying first-year subjects and that the subjects had followed on from primary school.

Student views on curriculum continuity in general and in relation to English, Irish and Mathematics in particular were interrelated. Those who felt that primary school was a good preparation and/or there was continuity in many subjects were also likely to report finding Irish, English and Mathematics easier or about the same in post-primary as in primary school. In contrast, students who found teaching methods quite different at post-primary level were more likely to report finding the core academic subjects more difficult than at primary level.

Curriculum continuity is likely to depend on a number of factors, including the structural (mis)match between the primary and post-primary curricula, post-primary teachers' familiarity with the primary school syllabus and their awareness of the specific material covered by their students in sixth class. In keeping with the reports by subject teachers in Chapter Four, teachers were seen as differing in their approach to teaching first-year students. Many students reported in the group interviews that their teachers had not asked them about what they had covered in primary school:

> Interviewer: In Irish, would they have tried to find out what you did in primary school?
>
> They just started.
>
> They just assume that we did all the stuff in the primary...
>
> Interviewer: And would you have done it?
>
> No (Wentworth Place, higher band).

> Interviewer: When you came into first year and with your Irish teacher, did they ask you what kind of Irish you'd done in primary school?
>
> No.
>
> No.

They said that doesn't matter anymore; he said that doesn't matter anymore because we're here now and we get all the words, because none of us knew any Irish (Dawes Point, lower stream class).

Interviewer: At the beginning, did [the Irish teacher] not ask you how much Irish you had?
No.
She just expected that we all knew buckets of Irish.
She thinks we know everything in the Irish language, we know nothing (Park St, higher stream class).

However, there were exceptions in which teachers asked about the approach taken in primary school and revised some of the material, taking account of the varying backgrounds of the students:

Interviewer: What about Maths? Did the teachers try to find out what you had done in primary school?
Student: Yes, well she asked us . . . which way did you do this in primary school? And we would say one way. She is really good, [she said] well this is the way we do it now up to sixth year (Belmore St).

Interviewer: And say . . . Maths when you came into first year, did the teacher try to find out what kind of things you did in primary school?
Student: Yes, in most stuff at the beginning of the book some of us had already done in primary school.
Interviewer: So they checked that?
Student: Yes.
Interviewer: And did they go over that for some of the people who hadn't done it?
Student: Yes.
Interviewer: And say in English then, would they have done the same thing or what kind of things have they been doing?
Student: Like if you punctuate — punctuation marks and stuff like that.
And if some didn't do it, she, the teacher we had, would tell them what the meaning [was] and where you would put them (Belmore St).

> Some people from other schools had done it [the Mathematics] before and some people were more ahead and some people weren't. So that was hard on some.
>
> Interviewer: So was it difficult in class that some people knew it and some people didn't?
>
> Student: Yes and the English . . . the answers all are more detailed.
>
> Irish was basically the same but Maths was a bit harder because some people didn't know [it] . . . Our teacher, she just went over it even though some people knew what they were doing, and she just went over it so that the people who didn't know would catch up (Fig Lane).

In sum, students were generally positive about the post-primary curriculum, especially in relation to the range of subjects. However, a significant minority of students, especially those with lower literacy levels, felt that the curriculum at primary level had not provided them with a good foundation for their post-primary studies.

6.4 PERCEPTIONS OF SUBJECTS

6.4.1 Subject preferences

In both waves (September and May) of the survey, students were asked which two subjects they liked most. It should be noted that at the time of the first survey, students would have had very little exposure to the "new" post-primary school subjects. Because of variation in take-up of the different subjects, responses relate only to those students taking the subjects. Materials Technology (Woodwork) was most frequently mentioned as students' favourite subject in both September and May (see Figure 6.8). Other popular subjects included PE, Art and Home Economics. Subject popularity does not vary markedly over the course of first year; subjects with a practical orientation maintain, if not increase, their popularity. Gender differences were apparent with girls much more likely than boys to nominate Art, English or languages. Boys were much more likely than girls to name Materials Technology, other practical subjects or PE.

Figure 6.8: Most popular subjects (among students taking the subjects)

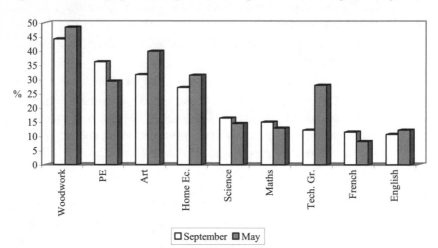

Students were also asked to name the two subjects they liked least. Irish was the most commonly mentioned subject at both the beginning and end of first year, although its unpopularity declined somewhat over the course of the year (Figure 6.9). Negative attitudes to Irish were also evident in the group interviews with students:

> It is our language — it is our nationality or whatever. But it is really hard. You have to get to know everything — all the grammar and everything. If you could just speak it and it didn't matter — if you write, say spell it wrong or leave out a fada — people that would read it would kind of know what is what you are trying to say. Yes but like say — you don't even need Irish. No one speaks Irish. All the grammar and everything. They make it hard in Junior Cert. and Leaving Cert. when you don't even need it (Belmore St).

> You need French for going on holidays, which you do.
> But you have a choice of doing French in the Leaving Cert. You don't have a choice in Irish. We are the only ones [only country] that use it so there is no point (Park St, higher stream class).

> There is no point in learning it [Irish], it's not like you are ever going to use it (Park St, higher stream band).

Figure 6.9: Least popular subjects (among students taking the subjects)

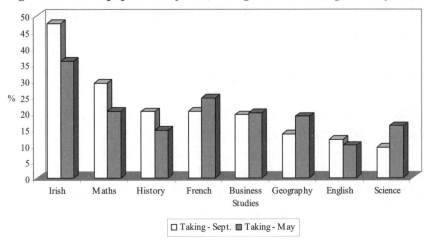

Much of these negative attitudes appeared to be related to the fact that students did not see Irish as useful for their future lives:

> Interviewer: Well, do you think you should have to do English?
> Yes.
> Yes. Irish next year is going to be poetry and stuff like that. Yes, but you don't need poetry anyway. English is different. You are doing Irish for 14 years and then if you decide to go to college in England or America, you are not going to need it. And you will have just wasted fourteen years doing Irish. Or so if you weren't even going to go to college like, that is a total waste. And you are going to work somewhere or own a business, like. Yes, fourteen years like gone down the drain (Belmore St).

Other relatively unpopular subjects included: Mathematics, French, History, Business Studies, Geography, English and Science. Mathematics and History became somewhat less unpopular in the course of the year while the reverse was the case for Geography and Science. Boys were somewhat more likely than girls to name Irish, Mathematics or English as their least favourite subjects.

At the beginning of first year, almost two-thirds (63 per cent) of students in the case-study schools agreed with the statement that "I prefer more practical subjects where I can work with my hands". This proportion did not change over the course of first year. Girls and boys were equally likely to agree with this statement. At the beginning of the year, this pattern did not vary markedly by social class, class type or reading/ mathematics scores. However, by the end of first year, students from higher professional backgrounds and students with higher reading and mathematics test scores were somewhat less likely to prefer practical subjects than other students. Students with higher test scores are less likely to prefer subjects with a practical orientation, even when actual take-up patterns for these subjects are taken into account.

At the beginning of first year, a quarter of students agreed with the statement "I prefer more academic subjects where I have to work out problems"; almost half of all students disagreed with this statement. The pattern of responses was similar at the end of first year. The pattern of responses did not vary by gender or social class. However, students in higher stream classes were twice as likely as those in lower stream classes to prefer more academic subjects. Furthermore, those who considered themselves top of the class in primary school were three times more likely to prefer academic subjects than those at the bottom of the class. Students with higher reading/mathematics scores were more likely to report preferring academic subjects at both time points.

6.4.2 Subject difficulty

At the end of first year, students were asked about the extent to which they found a specified set of subjects difficult. These subjects included: Mathematics, Science, English, History, Geography, Home Economics, Business Studies, Foreign Language, Materials Technology (Wood), Art, Computers, Irish and Physical Education (PE). Responses relate only to students taking the subjects in question.

In general, academic subjects were seen as more difficult than those with a more practical orientation. Irish was seen as the most difficult subject followed by Science, foreign languages and Mathematics (see Figure 6.10). Almost half (49 per cent) of the students reported finding Irish difficult while only a small minority (12 per cent) of first-year students in the case-study schools find English difficult. There is no overall gender variation in the perceived difficulty of Mathematics; however, girls in coeducational schools (with the exception of Hay St) are somewhat more likely than boys to find Mathematics difficult. Girls are much less likely than boys to find English or Irish difficult, patterns that are also evident within coeducational schools.

Figure 6.10: Perceived difficulty of different subject areas

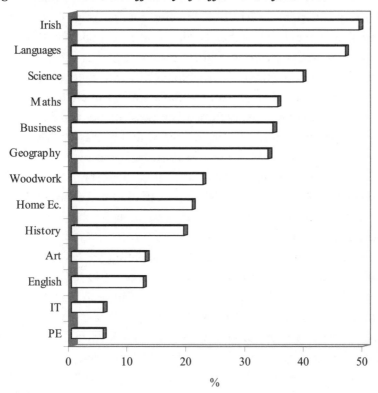

Students with lower mathematics and reading scores and those who considered themselves to be bottom of the class in primary school were more likely to report finding Mathematics and Irish difficult. In contrast, the perceived difficulty of English does not appear to be related to prior educational success. In fact, students who find English difficult tend to have higher Mathematics scores than those who do not. The perceived difficulty of Mathematics, English and Irish does not vary across class types but it does vary across schools. In particular, students in Dawes Point, a designated disadvantaged school, were quite likely to find Irish and Mathematics difficult. Students in Park St, Lang St and Wattle St, all boys' schools, were more likely to find English difficult.

Looking at the perceived difficulty of other "academic" subjects, forty-seven per cent of students find foreign languages difficult (more than for any other subject except Irish), forty per cent find Science difficult, a third find Geography difficult while under a fifth of first-year students find History difficult. Girls are somewhat more likely than boys to find History difficult and less likely to find foreign languages difficult, patterns that are evident within coeducational schools. Students with lower reading scores were more likely to report finding these academic subjects (with the exception of Geography) difficult. Students in middle or lower stream classes in streamed schools are less likely to find Geography difficult, and more likely to find Business Studies and Science difficult, than those in higher stream or mixed ability classes. Those who said they were bottom of the class in primary school were much more likely than those at the top of the class to find Business Studies and foreign languages difficult. There was some variation by school in the perceived difficulty of these academic subjects, although the pattern varied depending on the particular subject.

In general, subjects with a practical orientation are less likely to be seen as difficult by first-year students. Just over a fifth of students find Materials Technology (Woodwork) difficult, a fifth find Home Economics difficult, thirteen per cent find Art difficult while only five per cent of students in the case-study schools find Computer Studies or PE difficult (see Figure 6.10). The perceived difficulty of Woodwork, Computers and PE does not vary by gender. However, girls are somewhat more likely than boys to find Home Economics difficult; it should be noted, however, that the number of boys taking the subject is very small. Girls are less likely to find Art difficult than boys.

There is no marked variation in the perceived difficulty of the practical subjects by initial reading or mathematics test scores. However, those in lower stream classes are somewhat more likely to find Art and Computer Studies difficult. This pattern is also apparent for PE, although the difference across class groups is not very marked. Those who reported being at the bottom of the class in primary school are somewhat more likely to find Home Economics, Computers and PE difficult; the reverse is true for Art. There is no such variation for Woodwork.

It was possible to compare attitudes in September with those in May for a selected group of these subjects. In most cases, students who found particular subjects difficult in September tended to find these subjects difficult in May; the perceived difficulty of Mathematics, Science, English, History, Home Economics, Woodwork and Irish in September is predictive of the perceived difficulty of that subject in May. The exception to this is Computer Studies; the vast majority of students found this subject "not difficult" by May, including 90 per cent of those who had found it difficult in September. This remarkable shift may be related to differences among students in their initial exposure to, and familiarity with, computers; as the year progresses, students become much more positive about the difficulty of Computer Studies. In spite of a relationship between student attitudes at two points in time, there were some shifts in the perceived difficulty of certain subjects. Science and, to a lesser extent, Home Economics were seen as more difficult in May than in September whereas students saw English and Computer Studies as becoming less difficult over the course of the year. No appreciable changes in the perceived difficulty of Mathematics, History, Woodwork and Irish were evident.

6.4.3 Interest in subjects

Student interest appears to be highest in subjects with a practical component, with the highest levels of interest evident in relation to Woodwork, PE, Art, Computer Studies, Science and Home Economics. The lowest level of interest was reported in relation to Irish (see Figure 6.11).

Figure 6.11: Student interest in specified subjects

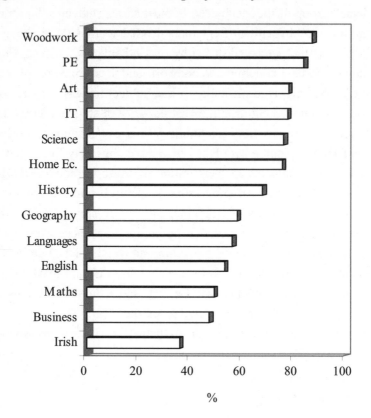

Among the "core" academic subjects, over half of first-year students find English interesting, forty-nine per cent find Mathematics interesting while only a minority (39 per cent) of students find Irish interesting (Figure 6.11). There are no marked differences overall in the level of interest reported by girls and boys. Students with higher Mathematics test scores and those who were top of their class in primary school are more likely to find Mathematics interesting. Those in lower stream classes in streamed schools are slightly more likely to find English and/or Irish interesting than those in other class groups, perhaps indicating the tailoring of subject content to the ability level of students. There is some variation across the case-study schools in the interest reported in these core subjects.

Among the other academic subjects, the highest interest levels are evident for Art and Science with over three-quarters of first-year students reporting finding these subjects interesting. This high level of interest may relate, at least in part, to the practical aspects of the subjects. There are no gender differences in interest in Science or Geography. Boys are significantly more likely than girls to find History interesting and less likely to find languages interesting, a pattern which is evident within co-educational schools. Interest in these academic subjects does not vary markedly by initial reading or mathematics score. However, those with higher reading scores are somewhat more likely to report being interested in languages and less likely to report being interested in Art. Students in lower stream classes in streamed schools are most likely to report being interested in Geography and, to a lesser extent, Business and Art. There is variation across the case-study school in reported interest, although the pattern varies by subject.

The majority of first-year students find the practical subjects interesting. Girls are much more likely than boys to find Home Economics interesting while boys are more likely to find PE interesting than girls. There is no marked variation by reading or mathematics test score, although those with lower reading scores are somewhat more interested in Woodwork and Computer Studies. Within streamed schools, those in lower stream classes are more likely to find Home Economics interesting, although the numbers are quite small and should be interpreted with some caution.

It was possible to compare interest in specified subjects in September and May. While attitudes to the subject at the beginning and end of the year were closely related, some shifts over time were evident. Interest levels in Mathematics were lower at the end of the year while those for Science and Home Economics were higher.

6.4.4 Perceived utility of subjects

Figure 6.12 indicates the proportion of first-year students who consider the specified subjects to be useful. It is worth noting that for all of the subjects, including academic subjects, the majority of first-year students in the case-study schools find them useful.

Almost all (91 per cent) of students consider Mathematics useful, eighty-two per cent of students find English useful while just over half of students see Irish as useful, the lowest rating among the specified subjects. Those who saw themselves at the top of the class in primary school and those with higher initial Mathematics test scores are more likely to see Mathematics as useful.

Figure 6.12: Perceived utility of subjects

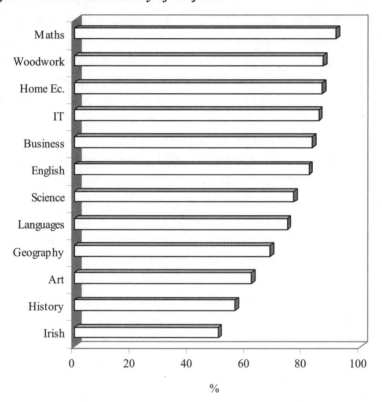

In relation to the other academic subjects, four-fifths of students find Business Studies useful, three-quarters find Science useful, almost three-quarters find foreign languages useful, over two-thirds find Geography useful while fifty-six per cent find History useful. Girls are more likely to see languages as useful than boys, a pattern that is evident within coeducational schools (with the exception of Dixon St). Boys are somewhat more likely to see History as useful, a pattern that is also evident within coeducational schools. Students in lower stream classes are less likely to see Science as useful and more likely to see History, Geography and Art as useful than those in higher stream or mixed ability classes. Students with higher Mathematics and reading scores are more likely to see Science as useful and students with higher reading scores are more likely to see languages as useful. In contrast, students with higher Mathematics scores are less likely to see History as useful. Students with lower reading and Mathematics scores are more likely to see Art as useful.

The vast majority of first-year students see Woodwork, Home Economics and Computer Studies as useful. Girls are more likely than boys to find Home Economics useful while finding Woodwork useful is more common among boys than girls. Those in lower stream classes are more likely to find Home Economics useful than those in higher stream classes.

Students were less likely to see Science, English, History and, to a lesser extent, Irish as useful in May than they had been in September.

The group interviews with students in October allowed us to explore attitudes to post-primary school subjects in greater detail. In general, students were not terribly forthcoming about why they liked particular subjects. However, they were generally positive about taking on the "new" school subjects, especially the subjects with a more practical orientation. One advantage was seen to be the "clean slate" these subjects provided:

> The new ones [subjects] are quite easy because you have to start at
> the very start. You are not expected to know so much (Fig Lane).

First-year students in the case-study schools were somewhat more forthcoming about why they disliked particular subjects. Students' perceptions of particular subjects were often influenced by who was teaching the subject:

> The subjects I hate are because of the teachers (Fig Lane).

> If you get a new subject and you don't know what it's like and you
> get a bad teacher, then you just think it's a horrible subject (Fig
> Lane).

> If you have a teacher that gives you a hard time in a subject, then you
> won't like it (Barrack St).

A major complaint appeared to be that he or she "doesn't explain things" along with unfair treatment by particular teachers (see Chapter Five):

> You are kind of out on your own and you are trying to figure it out.
> It is like swimming. It is like starting off swimming or something (Fig Lane).

> But English, [X] doesn't really teach much. For the past week we just read through the book, and [s/he] just says do it, but doesn't explain anything. Then [s/he] gives you a test on it and doesn't even explain anything (Park St, higher stream class).

This was contrasted against individual teachers who did take the time to explain lessons:

> [Y] explains it so everybody knows it. And she comes around and everything.
> And she gets you to write down what you did so you will remember it.
> Then you can go back and look at it (Fig Lane).

Another complaint was that the teacher was "boring", by which students often meant that the teachers "just read from the book":

> One of the teachers reads all the time and doesn't let any of us read. It's all her. She just reads the book and doesn't explain anything. She talks really fast as well, there is no stopping and asking do we understand (Fig Lane school).

Students also tended to dislike subjects that they found too difficult (see above).

In sum, first-year students were generally positive about the subjects they took, especially subjects with a more practical orientation. However, a significant minority of students found some of the academic subjects difficult and perceived difficulty along with teaching style contributed to their overall perceptions of junior cycle subjects.

6.4.5 Time allocation to subjects

First-year students were asked whether they felt too much time, about the right amount of time or too little time was allocated to the specified subjects. In general, the majority of students considered the right amount of time was allocated to the academic subjects (see Figure 6.13). More students reported that too much time was spent on academic subjects, particularly Irish and foreign languages, than reported that too little time was spent on these subjects. The pattern for subjects with a more practical component was quite different. A considerable proportion of students felt that too little time was devoted to Materials Technology, Art, Computer Studies and PE in their school timetable.

Figure 6.13: Time allocation to specified subjects

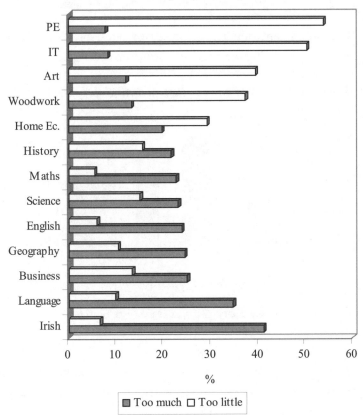

6.4.6 Pace of instruction

At the beginning of the year, students were asked about the pace of instruction across subjects in general. Student perceptions of the pace of instruction are associated with their class placement. Different standards appear to apply across different class groups since half of those in lower stream classes agree that "teachers go too slowly with my class" compared with less than a fifth of those in higher stream or mixed ability base classes (see Figure 6.14). Students in higher stream (or middle) classes are more likely to agree with the statement that "teachers go too quickly with my class":

> In every class they always do a chapter of a book and then go onto a different chapter even if you don't understand it.
>
> Interviewer: OK, so it is too quick?
>
> Student: Yes. You just get mixed up (Dixon St, higher stream class).

However, a significant minority (a third) of those in lower classes in streamed schools also find the pace of instruction too fast.

Figure 6.14: Perceptions of pace of instruction (September)

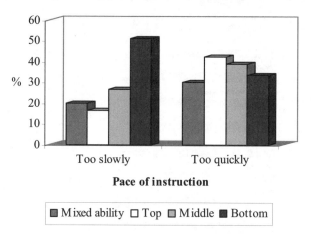

First-year students in the case-study schools were asked in May whether their teacher went too quickly, about the right speed or too slowly in a number of specified subjects. The majority of students felt that their teachers went at about the right pace (see Figure 6.15). However, almost a third of students considered that the pace of their Irish and languages classes was too quick. This was the case for around a quarter of students in the case of Science and Mathematics. In contrast, twelve per cent of students felt their English teacher went too quickly. Only a minority of students felt that their teachers went too slowly; this was somewhat more prevalent in English than in the other subjects.

Figure 6.15: Perceptions of pace of instruction (May)

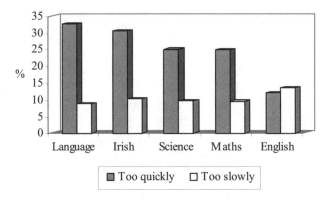

Views about the pace of instruction varied by class allocation in May as in September. A third of students in mixed ability or higher stream base classes reported their Irish teacher went too quickly compared with 19 per cent of those in lower stream classes (Figure 6.15); on the other hand, those in lower stream classes were more likely than those in the higher stream classes to report their teacher moved too slowly. In the case of English, students in lower stream classes were more likely than those in higher stream classes to think that the teacher moved too quickly or too slowly. There was very little variation in Mathematics. In Science and foreign languages, those in lower stream classes were slightly more likely to report teachers went too quickly. In general, students with lower reading scores were more likely to feel the teacher was going too quickly. However, this pattern was not evident in relation to foreign languages.

6.5 HOMEWORK

Students were asked about the average amount of time they spend on homework on a weekday night in both waves of the survey. Over three-quarters of students in the case-study schools spend more than one hour on homework per night while around a quarter spend more than two hours. There is a slight reduction in the average time spent on homework between September and May of first year from 87 minutes to 83 minutes.

This may reflect the somewhat greater necessity for students to get to grips with new subjects or "catch up" in other subjects at the beginning of first year. Alternatively, students may have a more realistic view of teacher demands in relation to homework by the end of first year.

Figure 6.16: Amount of time spent on homework per evening in September and May

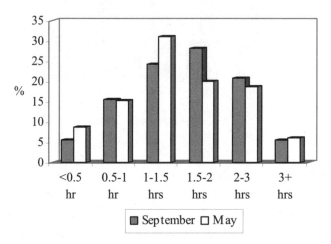

Girls report significantly longer homework times than boys (97 compared with 82 minutes in September; 90 minutes compared with 78 minutes in May). This gender difference is evident within coeducational schools. There is no marked variation by social class background among students in the case-study schools. Students in lower stream classes report the least amount of homework in both September and May; those in mixed ability classes report the most time in September while those in higher stream classes report the most time in May. This pattern was evident within all streamed schools, with the exception of Hay St where those in the lower stream class appear to spend more time on homework than those in the higher stream class. At both time points, the relationship between time spent on homework and reading score is complex with homework time being somewhat greater for the middle ability group. The lowest reading scores are found among those who spend less than half an hour on homework/study. Homework time is longest in Belmore St and Park St and lowest in Hay St. Students who spend more time on homework in September are also likely to spend more time on homework in May.

At both time-points, those who spend longest (that is, three or more hours) on homework are less likely to like school or teachers and report more isolation. There is no significant relationship between the frequency with which parents check homework and the amount of time spent at either time-point; however, in May those whose parents never or only rarely check their homework tend to do less homework.

Over half of students agreed with the statement that "I get too much homework at this school". As might be expected, students spending longer on homework were more likely to agree with the statement that they get too much homework in their current school. Students who feel they get too much homework like school and their teachers less than other students, have lower ratings of their own abilities and tend to report feeling more isolated.

When interviewed in September of first year, the majority (70 per cent) of students in the case-study schools reported getting more homework than in primary school, even at this relatively early stage in the school year. Seventeen per cent reported getting "about the same" amount of homework while twelve per cent of students reported getting less homework. Those in mixed ability or higher stream classes were more likely to report increased homework while around a fifth of those in middle or lower stream classes reported receiving less homework. Students with higher mathematics and reading test scores were more likely to report increased homework but this pattern is primarily due to their over-representation within higher stream classes. The amount of homework varied significantly by school with students in Dawson St and Lang St reporting increased homework. Reduced homework was most common in Barrack St, Dixon St and Hay St schools. As might be expected, those who reported receiving more homework than in primary school spent the most time on homework (93 minutes).

In the group interviews, responses also varied concerning the amount of homework received. Some students reported that they got very little homework or had the opportunity to do some of it in class. In contrast, other students emphasised the increased workload compared with primary school:

That is the biggest thing, the homework. In primary it takes about five minutes and it's all done. Now here it's hours. And you have to study as well (Student, Park St, higher stream class).

One teacher in post-primary school wouldn't know what the other teachers are giving you so they just give you homework. In primary school, they would know how much you are getting (Student, Park St, middle class).

We don't finish here some days 'til five and then it's seven before you can even start your homework and finish [it] then about nine or ten, then you go to bed (Student, Fig Lane).

In Wentworth Place and Dawes Point, both streamed schools, some students reported differences between the classes in the amount of homework given:

We are in the highest class and we get homework from every class. . . .
My friend is in one of the lowest classes and he said he didn't get homework once yet.
It's not fair (Wentworth Place, higher band).

We don't get as much homework as we did in sixth class.
That's because we're in the stupid class.
Because we're in the stupid class, of course we don't get homework.
Interviewer: So you think you get less homework because of the class you're in?
Well, when we're going home, there's about two books in our bag.
When [the higher stream class] is going home, there's about seventeen books in their bag (Dawes Point, lower stream class).

6.6 LEARNING SUPPORT

A number of different sources of help and support for student learning were investigated: school reports of the students receiving learning support; student reports of receiving learning support within school; family help with homework/study; and take-up of grinds or other private tuition. Figure 6.17 indicates the proportion receiving different sources of assistance.

Figure 6.17: Prevalence of different forms of learning support

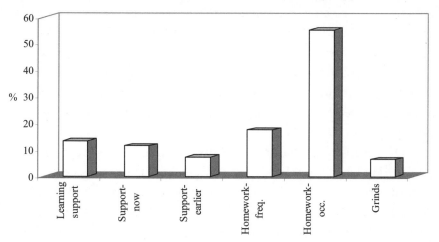

According to reports from the case-study schools, thirteen per cent of the students in the sample had received some form of learning support in first year. The proportion of students involved varied markedly across schools; 44 per cent of students in Dixon St received learning support[2] while this was the case for around 5 per cent of those in Park St, Fig Lane and Wattle St.

Almost a fifth of the students surveyed reported that they had received help at some point in the school year; this includes seven per cent of students who received support earlier in the school year but where help had been discontinued by the time of the survey in May. The discrepancy between school and student reports may relate to students' interpretation of "extra help within school" which students may take to include informal help from teachers as well as the provision of formal learning support. The pattern of student reports also varies across schools with, in keeping with school reports, students in Park St, Fig Lane and Wattle St least likely to receive such help. Those in Dawes Point and Hay St were most likely to report receiving help at the time of the survey. As might be expected, those allocated to the lower stream class in streamed schools were more likely to receive learning support than those

---

[2] The high proportion receiving help was possible because of the use of additional teachers within specific classes.

in higher stream, middle or mixed ability classes. Extra help was most frequently received in Mathematics (55 per cent) or English/reading (41 per cent), although 29 per cent of students reported receiving extra help in Irish. The form of assistance was most frequently in small groups (64 per cent) or on a one-to-one basis (34 per cent). Almost two-thirds (63 per cent) of students found this support helped them "a lot", a quarter found it helped "a little" while 12 per cent reported the help was "not really" useful.

Of those who had not received extra help in school, over one-third reported that they would have liked such help. The most frequently mentioned subjects with which students would have liked help were: Irish (48 per cent), Mathematics (34 per cent) and French (17 per cent). Those who would have liked extra help have lower reading and mathematics scores than those who would not. However, the difference is not nearly as pronounced as between those who received extra help and those who did not. Students in lower stream classes were somewhat more likely to report wanting extra help than other students (43 per cent compared with 31 per cent of those in higher stream classes).

Almost a fifth (18 per cent) of students in the case-study schools reported receiving help often with homework/study from their parents or siblings while over half (55 per cent) received help "sometimes". Students in middle or lower stream classes were more reliant on family help than those in higher stream or mixed ability classes (28 per cent compared with 11 per cent in higher stream and 14 per cent in mixed classes). As might be expected, students with low initial reading and mathematics scores were more reliant on frequent help from family with homework. However, those who received occasional help did not differ from those who received no help whatsoever. Students most frequently receive help from their family with Mathematics (44 per cent), Irish (36 per cent) and French (10 per cent).

Seven per cent of students in the case-study schools had received grinds or some other form of private tuition in the course of first year, usually in Mathematics, Irish or English. This pattern did not vary markedly across schools. Students who took grinds tended to have lower initial reading and mathematics scores than other students.

6.7 CONCLUSIONS

The case-study schools vary in their approach to class grouping and sub-ject choice (see Chapter Four). In general, the students surveyed tend to support ability-based grouping because they see it as yielding a more appropriate pace of instruction. In practice, however, many students in streamed classes report that their teachers move too quickly or slowly in covering subject material. The majority of first-year students support the idea of having some exposure to subjects before selecting them, princi-pally because this would facilitate a more informed choice. Where stu-dents did select their subjects before such exposure, they were more likely to rely on informal sources of advice, such as family and friends.

For most students, the opportunity to take new and diverse school subjects is a welcome one with students tending to enjoy post-primary subjects overall more than primary ones. However, the different teaching methods at post-primary level appear to require some adjustment on the part of students and a significant minority of students find Irish, English and/or Mathematics harder than in primary school. Curriculum disconti-nuity appears greater for some students than for others, depending on the primary school they attended.

In general, first-year students in the case-study schools are more positive about subjects with a more practical orientation, including Mate-rials Technology (Woodwork), PE, Art and Home Economics with more negative attitudes evident in relation to Irish, Mathematics and foreign languages. Many students would prefer more time to be allocated to the practical subjects with less time spent on Irish and foreign languages.

Around one-tenth of first-year students in the case-study schools re-ceived learning support in the course of first year. These students gener-ally found such assistance helpful. However, one-third of students who had not received formal learning support would have liked additional help in one or more subjects.

Chapter Seven

EXPERIENCE OF FIRST YEAR: STUDENT INTEGRATION AND ACADEMIC PROGRESS

INTRODUCTION

Chapters Five and Six have explored students' experiences of the transition from primary to post-primary school and their perceptions of the first-year curriculum. This chapter looks at their experiences over first year as a whole by drawing on questionnaires completed by 750 students in eleven schools along with 38 group interviews with students. In Chapter One, it was hypothesised that students would settle into school more quickly and experience fewer difficulties in schools which had stronger student integration programme. In addition, it was hypothesised that a more developed approach to student integration would have positive effects on students' academic progress over the course of first year. This chapter examines the extent to which these hypotheses are supported by data from the case-study schools. The first section examines the extent to which students feel "settled in" to post-primary school and the factors which facilitate their integration into the new school. The second section looks at changes in their attitudes to school over first year. Section three uses reading and mathematics test scores in September and May to analyse the extent to which student performance changes over the year.

7.1 SETTLING INTO POST-PRIMARY SCHOOL

In May of first-year, students were asked how long it had taken them to get settled into post-primary school (Figure 7.1). Almost one-fifth reported that they had settled in immediately, 43 per cent got used to post-primary school within one week, almost a quarter took a month to get settled in while 14 per cent of the students in the case-study schools took longer than a month to feel used to post-primary school. Figure 7.2 indicates the variation across the case-study schools. In keeping with the hypothesis, students tend to settle in quicker in schools with a stronger emphasis on integration. However, there is considerable variation within the two groups of schools. Students in two schools, Barrack St and Fig Lane, are more likely than those in other schools to report that the settling in process took longer than a month. The two schools are quite different in their student intake and approach to the transition process: Barrack St draws on students from more disadvantaged backgrounds and has somewhat less of an emphasis on integration while Fig Lane is predominantly middle-class in intake and places a strong emphasis on student integration. In the case of Barrack St, the higher prevalence of transition difficulties appears to reflect lower levels of pre-entry contact with the post-primary school and more disaffection with school among the students. In the case of Fig Lane, students also had relatively low levels of pre-entry contact with the school and the fact that students came from a large number of feeder schools appeared to disrupt friendship patterns established at primary level.

Figure 7.1: Settling into post-primary school (student reports)

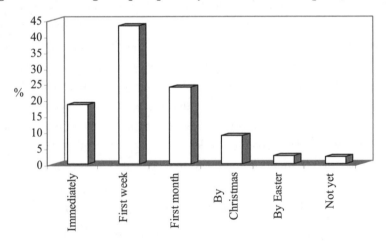

Figure 7.2: Proportion taking longer than a month to settle by school approach to integration

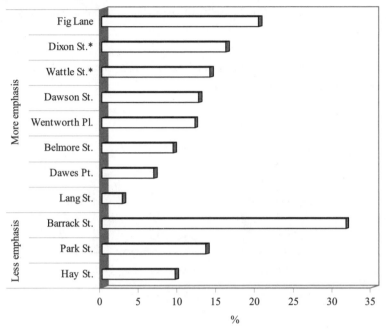

Note: * Schools initially classified as "low integration" which were found to have more developed integration policies.

There are differences among groups of students in their reported ease of transition. On average, boys tend to report settling in quicker than girls, a pattern that applies within coeducational schools (with the exception of Dixon Street). There is no marked variation by social class background. However, members of two minority groups, students from Traveller and non-national backgrounds, appear to take longer to settle into post-primary school. On closer investigation, the pattern for Traveller children is differentiated by age with the most marked differences evident among students aged 13 years or older (see Figure 7.3). Transition problems are more evident among older students from a Traveller background which may reflect their difficulty in integrating into a group of much younger students. Although students vary in their age at transition with over two-thirds of students in the case-study schools aged under thirteen, for students in general age is not associated with transition difficulties. As might be expected, students who are less self-confident, that is, those who have more negative views of their own academic or sporting abilities and body-image, tend to experience greater transition difficulties.

Figure 7.3: Proportion of students taking longer than a month to settle in by minority group membership

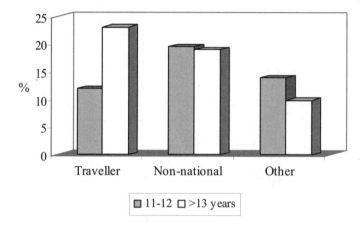

The way in which the transition process is managed by the school and the student's own social networks appear to play a role in easing the transition for students. The amount of pre-entry contact a student has with their post-primary school makes some difference to the ease of transition; over half (53 per cent) of those with no contact report settling in immediately compared with almost two-thirds (64 per cent) of those with two or more contacts with the school. Having three or more friends from primary school in the new school also makes a difference; two-thirds of those with three or more primary friends in the school settle in immediately compared with 58 per cent of those with no friends. Having a sibling in the school was found to ease students' anxiety about making the transition (see Chapter Five). However, having a sibling in the school does not appear to shorten the settling-in process. It may be that having a sibling in the school is not enough to prevent transition difficulties where there are other risk factors for the students involved. Students who have little idea what to expect from post-primary school take longer to settle in; less than half of those who had very little idea what to expect settled in immediately compared with almost three-quarters who felt they had a good idea what to expect (see Figure 7.4). The extent to which students feel they had a good idea what to expect in post-primary school is partly related to the amount of contact they have with the school beforehand but students also appear to draw on more informal sources of knowledge (such as parents and wider family) in forming their expectations of post-primary school life (see Chapter Five).

Figure 7.4: Student expectations of post-primary school and length of settling-in period

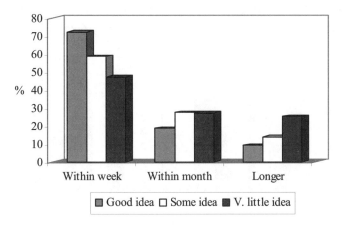

The informal climate of the school, that is, relations between students and their peers and with their teachers at the beginning of first year, is predictive of how students will settle in over the year as a whole. Chapter Five has indicated that a significant proportion of students experience some form of bullying within the first month of starting post-primary school. Those students who experience bullying at the start of first year take longer to settle in as do those who report feeling isolated in September. Students who have been jeered or mocked by other students, physically pushed around, upset by things said behind their back, upset by being ignored or bullied on the way to/from school are much more likely to take longer than a month to settle in compared with those who have not experienced such bullying (see Figure 7.5). The informal climate of the school is influential with students who report negative interaction with teachers in September experiencing greater transition difficulties.

Furthermore, those who are disaffected with school or their teachers early in the year take longer to settle in. It is difficult to establish the causality involved; some students may come to post-primary school with negative attitudes to school life while for others, their disaffection may be a reaction to the school climate in their new school. For over a third of students, the move to post-primary school involved a change from a single-sex to a coeducational setting (or vice versa); there is no evidence that a change in the gender mix of the school was associated with greater transition difficulties among girls or boys.

Figure 7.5: Proportion of students taking longer than a month to settle in by experience of bullying in September of first year

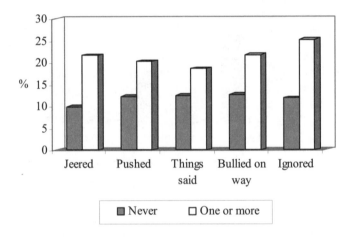

The degree of continuity between the primary and post-primary curriculum is found to impact on the ease of transition into first year. Students are more likely to experience transition problems if they feel their primary subjects did not prepare them for post-primary school, if they feel the subjects do not follow on from their primary subjects and if they are not enjoying first year subjects (see Figure 7.6). Perceived lack of curriculum continuity reflects the feeder school attended only to some extent since students who have attended the same feeder school also differ in their preparedness. In contrast, feeling that subjects were taught very differently in post-primary school was not associated with transition difficulties; this may be related to the fact that the vast majority of students felt teaching methods were very different at post-primary level. Further-more, students who found Irish or English harder at post-primary level took slightly longer to settle in. Chapter Six indicated that students as-signed to higher stream classes within streamed schools face increased academic demands and this pattern is associated with taking longer to settle into post-primary school than students assigned to lower stream classes. Initial reading and mathematics scores per se were not strongly related to settling in; the crucial factor appears to be the extent of (dis)continuity between the primary and post-primary curriculum. Being changed from their class group represented a source of anxiety for some students in the case-study schools. In fact, a small number of the students surveyed changed classes between September and May; over one-third (37 per cent) of these students took more than a month to settle in com-pared with over one-tenth (13 per cent) of other students.

Figure 7.6: Transition difficulties and curriculum continuity (per cent taking longer than a month to settle in)

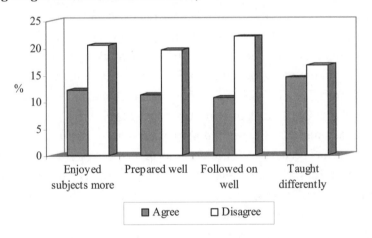

Taking a taster programme as such does not seem to impact on the settling-in process. However, students who *feel* they are taking too many subjects in September tend to report more difficulties (see Figure 7.7).

Figure 7.7: Length of settling-in period and perceptions of number of subjects

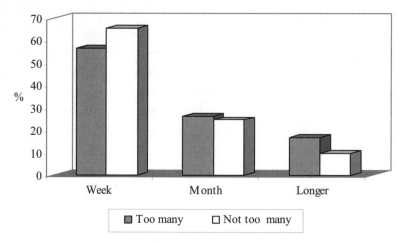

These analyses relate to how long students feel it has taken them to settle into post-primary school. Students were also asked about the extent to which they missed various aspects of primary school. The pattern of responses captures another aspect of integration into post-primary school and, as might be expected, students who report taking longer to settle in are more likely to report still missing primary school in May of first year. Figure 7.8 indicates the extent to which students miss various aspects of primary school in September and May of first year. There is some reduction over time in the proportion who report missing primary school "a lot", especially in relation to their teacher, friends and after-school activities. However, there is remarkably little change in relation to more "structural" issues, such as having one teacher, the teaching methods used and the subjects taught.

There was some variation by school with students in Barrack St and, to a lesser extent, in Belmore St, both girls' schools, more likely to report missing primary school. Girls are more likely to report missing primary school than boys, especially their teacher, friends and the way subjects were taught. This is consistent with international research which indicates that the transition to primary school causes greater disruption to girls' friendship groups (Hargreaves and Galton, 2002). Those from a semi-skilled or unskilled manual background are more likely to report missing primary school while students from a higher professional or farming background are least likely to do so. Furthermore, students from Traveller families are more likely to report missing primary school than other students. As with ease of transition, students who report having very little idea what to expect coming to post-primary school are more likely to report missing primary school. Those who felt they were at the bottom of the class in primary school, those with lower reading scores and students who reported in September that they were taking too many subjects were more likely to miss primary school. In general, students who appear to be at greater risk of academic underperformance are more likely to report missing primary school, although a significant proportion of all students surveyed miss at least one aspect of the primary experience.

Figure 7.8: Student reports of missing primary school

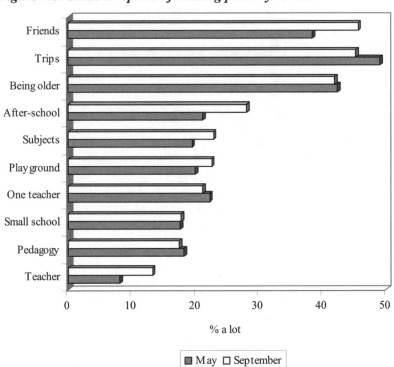

% a lot

■ May □ September

In the May survey, students were asked which factors from a selected list helped them to get used to post-primary school. The responses are out-lined in Figure 7.9. Almost all students reported that social networks helped to integrate them into post-primary school; over four-fifths mentioned having friends from primary school, over two-thirds mentioned involvement in extracurricular activities while thirty per cent cited having an older sibling in the school. The next most prevalent responses related to induction-type programmes within the post-primary school with two-thirds of students mentioning such programmes; half of the students in the case-study schools reported that the open day helped them settle in, with forty per cent mentioning an induction programme and a third mentioning visits by teachers to their primary school. A significant group (61 per cent) of students saw school personnel as playing a key role in their transition; almost half mentioned their class tutor or student mentor while over a third mentioned subject teachers (see Figure 7.9).

Figure 7.9: What students saw as helping them to settle in

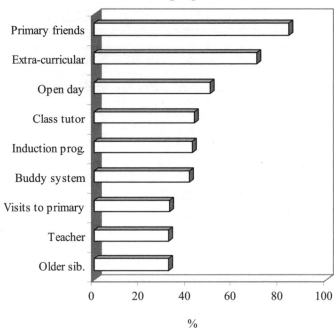

Note: Students could mention more than one factor.

Students from a Traveller background were more reliant on school personnel in the integration process while students from a professional background were somewhat less likely to mention school personnel. Furthermore, those with lower reading and mathematics scores were more reliant on school personnel while those who considered themselves to be top of the class in primary school were less reliant on school personnel. This indicates the potential to target "at risk" groups of students through identifying key personnel responsible for easing their transition to post-primary school.

7.2 CHANGES IN ATTITUDES TO SCHOOL OVER FIRST YEAR

The factors associated with student attitudes to school were discussed in Chapter Six. Students' attitudes to school and to their position within school in September are predictive of their attitudes by the end of first year. Students who have positive attitudes to school in September of first year tend to have positive attitudes by the end of the school year. Thirty-six per cent of the variation in liking school in May is accounted for by liking school in September, with a similar pattern for students' view of their own abilities (academic self-image). Twenty-five per cent of the variation in liking teachers in May is accounted for by attitudes to teachers in September with similar patterns for reported isolation and body-image. Students who regard themselves as good at sports in September are highly likely to do so in May, with initial attitudes accounting for half of the variation at the later stage. The relationship between the responses in September and May is weaker for reported popularity with classmates, indicating some fluctuation in relations with peers over the course of the year.

While attitudes at the beginning and end of first year are strongly interrelated at the student level, it is worth exploring whether any general changes occur in attitudes to school over first year. Table 7.1 indicates the average level of reported attitudes in September and May of first year. At the beginning of first-year, students are generally positive about school and their teachers (see Chapter Five). By the end of first year, attitudes to school and teachers have become somewhat less positive on average and students are less positive about their own academic abilities. This may reflect the end of a "honeymoon" period and the fact that students are becoming more realistic about their ability to cope with schoolwork at post-primary level. The pattern is consistent with research in Britain and elsewhere which indicates that attitudes to school become less positive over the course of the schooling career (Keyes and Fernandes, 1993; Hargreaves and Galton, 2002). There is a slight decline in body image for both girls and boys over the course of first year which is most likely related to general adolescent development rather than the school environment per se. There is no overall change in the extent to which students report feeling isolated, (un)popular or good at sports.

Table 7.1: Changes in attitudes over first year — all students

	September	May	Change
Academic self-rating	3.07	2.97	Decline (p<.05)
Liking school	2.97	2.68	Decline (p<.05)
Liking teachers	3.16	2.94	Decline (p<.05)
Isolation	1.73	1.70	No change
Sports self-image	3.21	3.20	No change
Body image	3.08	3.02	Decline (p<.10)
Popularity	3.24	3.21	No change

Note: Figures relate only to those with valid information at the two time-points.

Tables 7.1a and 7.1b indicate that attitudes to school and teachers become less positive for both boys and girls in the case-study schools. Girls report slightly more negative views of their efficacy at sports in May than at the beginning of the year; no such pattern is evident for boys in the case-study schools.

Table 7.1a: Changes in attitudes over first year — male students

	September	May	Change
Academic self-rating	3.10	3.00	Decline (p<.05)
Liking school	2.96	2.64	Decline (p<.05)
Liking teachers	3.15	2.90	Decline (p<.05)
Isolation	1.71	1.68	No change
Sports self-image	3.31	3.34	No change
Body image	3.22	3.17	No change
Popularity	3.25	3.22	No change

Table 7.1b: Changes in attitudes over first year — female students

	September	May	Change
Academic self-rating	3.02	2.91	Decline (p<.05)
Liking school	3.00	2.76	Decline (p<.05)
Liking teachers	3.17	3.03	Decline (p<.05)
Isolation	1.75	1.74	No change
Sports self-image	3.01	2.92	Decline (p<.10)
Body image	2.82	2.73	No change
Popularity	3.21	3.19	No change

For "liking school", there was a decline across all the items within the scale, with a decrease in the proportion of first-year students finding schoolwork interesting, being excited about being at school, liking being at school, feeling relaxed about school, looking forward to coming to school and liking school better than other students. Thus, by the end of first-year, students are somewhat less likely to find schoolwork interesting or like being at school, although it should be noted that student attitudes are generally positive overall. For "liking teachers", there was a decline across all the items in the scale, with a decrease in the proportion of first-year students finding most teachers friendly, feeling teachers would help with a schoolwork-related problem, feeling the student could talk to a teacher, reporting a good working atmosphere in class and liking most of their teachers. This pattern is somewhat surprising as it might be expected that students would be more likely to go to a teacher with a problem when they knew the teacher better. For academic self-rating, there was a decline in the proportion of students who reported doing well in school, working hard at school, being able to do schoolwork as well as other students, doing schoolwork better than other students and being pleased with schoolwork. There was no significant change in the numbers finding the work quite easy or having trouble keeping up with schoolwork.

Figure 7.10: Decline in "liking school" by school approach to integration

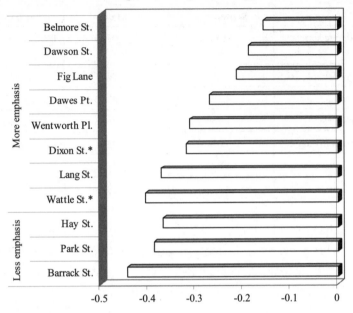

Note: * Schools initially classified as "low integration" which were found to have more developed integration policies.

The change in attitudes to school over the course of the year was more evident among some groups of students than others. The decline in "liking school" was greater in five of the case-study schools: Wattle St, Park St, Barrack St, Hay St and Lang St. In general, the greatest decline in "liking school" was evident in schools without a strong emphasis on student integration, although there was some variation among "high integration" schools (Figure 7.10). In contrast, Belmore St and Dawson St schools appeared to be more successful in preventing student disaffection with school. Students who reported preferring academic subjects were somewhat more likely to report a decline in school attitudes than those who preferred subjects with a practical orientation. Furthermore, those who reported finding English harder in post-primary than in primary school reported more negative attitudes to school by the end of the year. The decline in attitudes was somewhat more evident in streamed/banded schools than in those with mixed ability base classes. As might be expected, students who have taken longer to settle in have less positive attitudes to school by the end of first year.

Figure 7.11: Decline in "liking teachers" by school approach to integration

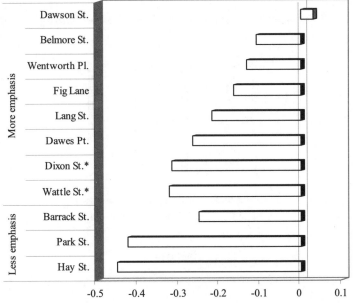

Note: * Schools initially classified as "low integration" which were found to have more developed integration policies.

On average, students were somewhat less likely to report "liking teachers" in May of first year than in September. The decline was greatest in Hay St and Park St schools and least evident in Dawson St and, to a lesser extent, Belmore St (Figure 7.11). The decline was somewhat greater among boys than girls, a pattern that was also evident within co-educational schools (with the exception of Fig Lane). Those who reported finding English harder in post-primary than in primary school reported more negative attitudes to teachers by the end of the year. Schools with a strong emphasis on student integration were generally more successful at maintaining positive attitudes to teachers among first-year students (Figure 7.11). Furthermore, attitudes to teachers tended to become somewhat more negative in schools where students made their choice of subjects at an earlier stage, perhaps indicating dissatisfaction with their choice of subjects by "blaming the teacher". Among boys, students in higher and middle classes in streamed schools had a greater decline in the proportion "liking teachers" than those in mixed ability base classes (Figure 7.12).

Figure 7.12: Decline in "liking teachers" by class allocation — male students

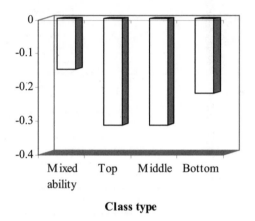

Class type

Students had more negative perceptions of their abilities at the end of first year than at the beginning. The pattern varied across the case-study schools, although changes in perceptions were not clearly related to the integration practices of the school; the decline was greatest in Barrack St school and least evident in Dawes Point, Fig Lane and Belmore St (see Figure 7.13). Those who reported being at the top of their class in primary school experienced a greater decline, indicating potentially different standards between the primary and post-primary levels. Students who prefer subjects with a practical orientation report less of a decline in academic self-image. The decline is slightly greater among students in higher and middle classes in streamed schools. Students who received learning support within school tended to have an improvement in their academic self-image. In contrast, those who changed class had more negative views of their own abilities. Students who have taken longer to settle in report a greater decline in their academic self-image.

Figure 7.13: Decline in perceived ability to cope with school-work (academic self-image) by school approach to integration

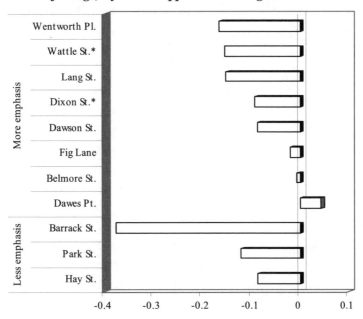

Note: * Schools initially classified as "low integration" which were found to have more developed integration policies.

7.3 READING AND MATHEMATICS PERFORMANCE

Drumcondra Level 6 tests in reading and computation were administered to first-year students in September and again in May.[1] Thus students were given the same test at the two time-points in order to see if their raw score improved over the course of first year.

Table 7.2 indicates the factors associated with higher test scores in reading and computation in September of first year. On average, there were no significant differences by gender in reading or computation scores among students in the case-study schools. In keeping with previous research, reading and mathematics scores were found to be strongly differentiated by social class background with the highest scores found

---

[1] Of the 750 students included in both waves of the survey, 726 took the reading test in September and May while 741 students took the computation test in September and 746 students took it in May.

among students from higher professional backgrounds and the lowest scores found among those from manual and non-employed backgrounds. Students from Traveller backgrounds were found to achieve significantly lower scores in both reading and computation than those from working-class backgrounds.[2]

Table 7.2: Factors influencing reading and numeracy scores at entry

	Reading	Computation
Constant	28.877	14.739
Female	-0.039	0.049
Social class:		
Higher professional	14.030***	5.613***
Lower professional	9.514***	3.967***
Other non-manual	8.148***	2.438*
Skilled manual	3.479	0.301
Farmer	7.055***	4.661***
Not employed	-0.352	-2.165
No information	-2.036	-0.230
(Contrast: Semi/unskilled manual)		
Non-national parent	-0.311	-0.480
Traveller background	-9.919***	-3.943***
Adjusted R^2	0.143	0.135

Note: ***p<.001, *p<.05.

Figure 7.14 indicates variation across the case-study schools in the entry reading test scores of first-year students. The pattern is depicted in the form of box-plots; the black line within each box refers to the average (median) score within the school. The length of the box is influenced by the difference between the 75th percentile (75 per cent of students in the school are below this score) and the 25th percentile within each school; the "whiskers" show the largest and smallest observed scores. Average entry scores are highest in Wattle St and Fig Lane and lowest in Dixon St, Lang St, and Hay St. In addition to varying in the average reading

---

[2] It is worth noting that the representation of students from Traveller backgrounds varied by school with a somewhat higher representation in Barrack St and Dixon St schools, both designated disadvantaged schools.

ability of their students, the case-study schools also vary in the range of reading scores found among in-coming first years. Dawson St, Fig Lane and Wattle St deal with the most varied range of reading abilities. In contrast, reading scores in Dixon St are relatively low and distributed across a fairly narrow range.

Figure 7.14: Reading test scores (raw scores) in September by school

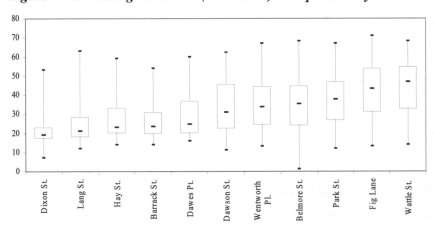

Computation test scores also vary by school with the highest average scores found in Wattle St, Fig Lane and Park St and the lowest scores found in Dixon St, Lang St, Hay St and Dawes Point (Figure 7.15). Scores are more varied in Wattle St and less varied in Lang St school. The average computation scores among students in the case-study schools are lower than those among a national sample of sixth class students.[3] This may indicate a fall-off in computation performance over the transition between primary and post-primary school. However, without sixth class test scores on the individual students included in the sample, it is impossible to determine the reason for this pattern.

---

[3] Twenty-nine per cent of students in the case-study schools were at or below the tenth percentile in computation. This ranged from 16 per cent to 65 per cent across the schools included in the study.

Figure 7.15: Computation test scores (raw scores) in September by school

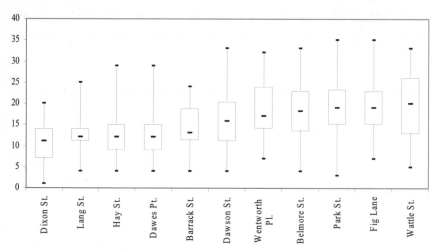

Reading and computation test score analyses from a national sample in- dicate the confidence intervals for the scores, that is, the scale of per- formance difference which would be needed to say the change in scores would be unlikely to result from chance (Shiel, 1994, 1998). Figure 7.16 indicates the proportion of students who experienced a significant im- provement in their reading or computation test scores between Septem- ber and May of first year, that is, students who achieved a higher score in May than in September and where the scale of the difference was such that it could not be attributed to chance. For the majority of students, test scores in reading and computation are broadly similar in September and May of first year. In other words, the majority of students *do not* appear to make progress in reading or computation. There are more changes in reading scores than in computation with almost a fifth of students im- proving their reading compared with one tenth for computation. How- ever, given that it would not be unreasonable to expect students to make some progress in reading and mathematics over the course of the year, the improvement depicted in Figure 7.16 may actually overestimate the extent of progress. The pattern in the case-study schools is similar to that found in a British study which found first year in post-primary school represented a hiatus in academic progress (Hargreaves and Galton,

2002). This may be due to the focus on a greater range of subjects in first year along with the need for students to adjust to different styles of teaching. However, it could be argued that exposure to new subjects and textbooks might be expected to improve students' vocabulary and hence their reading scores.

Figure 7.16: Change in reading and computation scores over first year

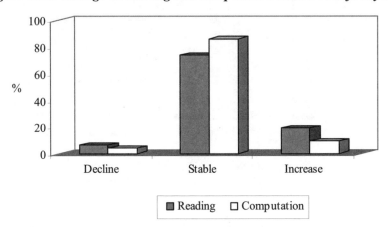

7.3.1 Trends in reading scores

Trends in reading scores varied across the case-study schools with a higher decline in Park St and Lang St, both boys' schools, while an improvement was more common in Dawson St, Fig Lane and Belmore St schools. Overall, girls in the case-study schools are more likely to have an improvement in their reading performance than boys, although this pattern is due to the fact that the greatest improvements were found in two all-girls' schools and there is no significant difference in progress between boys and girls in the same school. Students from farming or higher professional backgrounds make more progress but the difference by social class background is very slight. Furthermore, students from a Traveller background are less likely to make progress. In general, students with higher reading scores at the start of first year are less likely to make progress than others, indicating some "catching-up" by students with initially lower reading scores. Students who report recurring misbehaviour over the school year are more likely than others to experience a

decline in their reading score and less likely to experience an improvement (see Figure 7.17).

**Figure 7.17: Progress in reading score by misbehaviour during first
year**

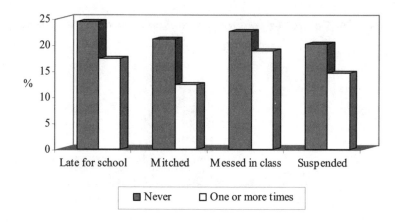

Among students, there is no marked relationship between the amount of
time students reported taking to settle into post-primary school and their
progress in reading. The relationship is slightly stronger for girls than for
boys; 17 per cent of girls who take longer than a month to settle in make
progress in reading compared with 23 per cent of other female students.
However, progress in reading is more common in schools with a strong
emphasis on student integration, a pattern that is evident for both boys
and girls (Figure 7.18). This pattern is not due to the initial reading
scores of in-coming students. In fact, while students with higher initial
reading scores tend to make less progress, students in schools with
higher average reading scores tend to make slightly more progress over
the course of the year.

Figure 7.18: Improvement in reading scores by school approach to student integration

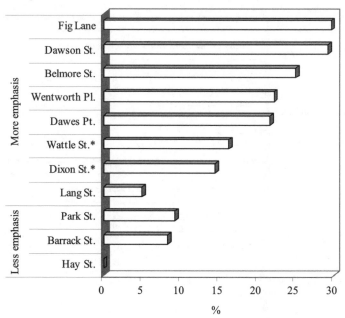

Note: * Schools initially classified as "low integration" which were found to have more developed integration policies.

At the individual level, the number of subjects taken by students is not related to their progress in reading. At the school level, there is little difference in improvement in reading scores between schools with a taster programme and those where students choose their subjects before or on entry to post-primary school (see Figure 7.19).

Figure 7.19: Improvement in reading score by approach to subject choice

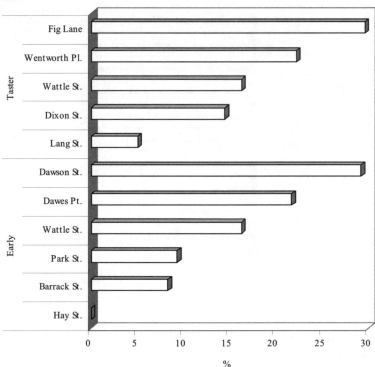

Progress in reading is less common overall in streamed schools due to the lower progress among students in middle or lower stream classes. Figure 7.20 indicates the pattern for boys due to the small number of girls in streamed schools.

Figure 7.20: Progress among male students in reading and computation by class allocation

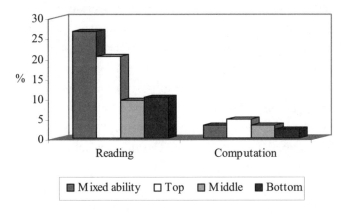

7.3.2 Trends in Mathematics scores

While test scores in computation were more stable than those in reading, some factors are associated with an improvement in computation scores. A decline in mathematics scores was somewhat greater in Dawson St, Lang St, Fig Lane and Wattle St schools with significant progress more common in Belmore St and Barrack St, both girls' schools. As with reading, girls were more likely to improve their computation scores than boys but the pattern is largely due to their distribution across school types rather than differences between boys and girls in the same school. In general, students with lower initial computation scores make the most progress. Students who report greater parental involvement make more progress in mathematics than other students.

As with reading, there is no marked relationship between the length of time it takes to settle into post-primary school and trends in mathematics scores; twelve per cent of students who settle in within a month make progress compared with eight per cent of those who take longer. Progress in mathematics is slightly more common in later choice schools but the difference is very slight. Progress in mathematics is not strongly differentiated by approach to ability grouping, although students in the lower stream classes in streamed schools tend to make less progress (see Figure 7.20).

7.4 CONCLUSIONS

Findings from this study indicate that a minority of first-year students in the case-study schools experience sustained transition difficulties. However, some groups of students are found to experience greater difficulties than others. Female students, those from minority groups and students who are less self-confident are more likely to encounter difficulties in making the transition from primary to post-primary level. Students who feel well prepared in terms of having a good idea what to expect and seeing a connection between the primary and post-primary curriculum are less likely to experience difficulties. The informal climate of the school plays a role with positive relations with teachers and peers fostering student integration. In keeping with our initial hypothesis, the existence of developed integration programmes within the school helps students to settle into school with greater ease. However, a school's *formal* policy on student integration appears to be successful only to the extent that it is underpinned by a positive informal climate and provides students with a realistic view of what to expect from post-primary school. Contrary to our initial hypothesis, there is no evidence that being exposed to a taster programme in first year leads to greater transition difficulties.

While the majority of students successfully settle into post-primary education, student attitudes to school and to their teachers are somewhat less positive at the end of first year than at the beginning. There is tentative evidence that schools with a strong emphasis on student integration and with mixed ability base classes are more successful in fostering positive attitudes to school among their students.

Among the majority of students, test scores in reading and computation do not improve over the course of first year; only one-fifth of students experience a significant improvement in reading and one-tenth experience a significant improvement in computation. This lack of progress in core competencies may be related to the fact that the first year curriculum focuses on the development of a broader set of competencies across a greater range of knowledge areas than reading and computation and that first year represents a period of adjustment for students. Contrary to our initial hypothesis on the effect of the school's approach to subject choice, there is no evidence that exposure to more subjects in first year has negative effects on reading or mathematics performance. However, progress in reading was found to be somewhat more apparent in schools with a strong emphasis on student integration, in keeping with the hypothesis in Chapter One. Furthermore, progress in reading tends to be greater in mixed ability schools than in those using streaming or banding. While test scores in reading and computation give some insight into student progress over the course of first year, further information on longer term performance in junior cycle subjects would be needed to fully explore the relationship between the school's approach to the transition process and student achievement.

Chapter Eight

PARENTS' EXPERIENCE OF THE TRANSITION FROM PRIMARY TO POST-PRIMARY EDUCATION

8.1 INTRODUCTION

Academic research shows that there is a strong relationship between pupil adjustment and achievement levels in schools and parental support and involvement (see Desforges and Abouchaar, 2003). Such support takes many forms including providing children with a stable and secure environment, supporting their aspirations and getting involved in school-related issues and activities. Parental support may be especially relevant when children are moving from one school setting to another. Transition from primary to post-primary education is a significant event for parents as well as their children. Research on transfer-related issues in other countries has emphasised the importance of parental support and involvement in reducing the incidence of learning and behavioural difficulties during the transfer period (Grolnick et al., 2000). In Ireland, little is known about parents' perceptions of the transition process from primary to post-primary school. One of the few studies to date, carried out by O'Brien (2001), indicates that Irish parents are concerned that their children will make new friends and not encounter bullying in the new school. They also express concern that their children will adjust to the level and variety of schoolwork at post-primary level.

In order to build on the previous Irish study and further explore parental perspectives on the transition process, interviews were carried out with eighty-one parents (mostly mothers) across eleven case-study schools. The interviews were semi-structured and were conducted over the phone in order to facilitate participation. In some cases the research-ers contacted parents directly with the school's permission, in others the school mediated the contact (see Chapter One). On average, the inter-views lasted twenty minutes and the topics covered included school choice, pre-entry contact with the school, the settling-in process for their child, school-work in general, and parents' hopes for the future of their child. The interviews were recorded with parents' permission.

While these interviews cannot be taken as representative of all par-ents in the case-study schools, they provide a valuable insight into par-ents' experiences of the transition process and practices at a family level. A number of international studies focus on transition experiences at a school level failing to provide the perspective of the parents who, it can be argued, also experience a period of "turbulence" together with their children (Lucey and Reay, 2002). This study addresses the gap by draw-ing on interviews with parents to explore their perceptions of the transfer process. The chapter starts by looking at reasons for selecting the school in question and examines parental contact with the school before entry. This is followed by a section which looks at parental concerns about the transition, both from a social and an academic perspective. The fourth section explores perceptions of the support structures for first-year stu-dents in the case-study schools.

8.2 PRE-ENTRY CONTACT WITH THE SCHOOL

8.2.1 School choice

The factors influencing choice of school have been the focus of much research in Britain and elsewhere (see, for example, Gorard, Taylor, Fitz, 2002; Lucey and Reay, 2002). O'Brien (2001) and Lyons et al. (2003) refer to the lack of systematic research in Ireland on how and why stu-dents and their families choose second-level schools and the implications of these choices for school climate and students' future life chances. While interviews with parents in this study are not concerned with issues relating to school choice in particular, they provide a valuable insight into the factors shaping such choices and provide a useful complement to the views of students presented in Chapter Five.

Chapter Five indicated that the majority of students had discussed the choice of school with their parents. On the basis of the interviews with parents, two broad groups of parents could be identified: "laissez-faire" parents who allowed their child to have a strong input into the choice of post-primary school and in relation to their future educational career; and "directive" parents who took a more active role in school selection and had more clear-cut aspirations for their child's future.

As already discussed in Chapter Five, drawing on students' experience, various factors inform the choice of post-primary school. The variety of reasons for choosing a particular school was also evident from interviews with parents in the current study. In most cases, choice was informed by a combination of factors. Many parents mentioned closeness to home and access as relevant factors in choosing the post-primary school. For them it was important that the school was on a bus route or that the school was close enough to allow the child to come home for lunch:

> Because it was the nearest school to me and lots of his friends went from the primary school to that school as well. I am living in the centre of town and if I was to send him anywhere else, he would need to get a bus and at this point he can come home at lunch time (Wentworth Place).

Having an older child already in the current school or the parents having attended the school themselves were also influences on the choice of school.

In the case of "laissez-faire" parents who allowed their child a strong input into the choice of school, the school selected by their child's friends became a significant factor followed by convenient locality and reputation of the school:

> Well it is in the locality, and some of his friends were going, and also you know I would have been happy with the school. I suppose the biggest factor was the friends but I was quite happy with the school, we were quite happy with that (Park St).

The reputation of the school and the facilities, especially sports facilities, for students were considered important factors in choosing schools by many parents, both "laissez-faire" and "directive". Parents who wanted their child to go on to third-level education emphasised the academic reputation of the school: "the subjects are more academic than other schools that were on offer for him" (Wattle St). In some cases, having attended an open day or evening for parents helped to inform parental choice of school:

> When we went to the open day, I just liked the look of it and it had a good reputation and everything. . . . She does every subject in the first year (Belmore St).

> Having our interview with the principal, I think that was very much a deciding factor, first of all the rapport between [my child] and the principal on the day would have to be heard to be believed. There just was an instantaneous rapport between them, they just linked into each other very quickly (Fig Lane).

The gender composition of the school was also a factor for some parents and students:

> One of the reasons was it was an all-girls' school (Belmore St).

> He actually went to an all-boys' primary school and he wanted to go to an all-boys' school (Wattle St).

In sum, parents relied on a combination of factors in choosing a school for their child. Proximity to home, family tradition, the reputation of the school along with school facilities played a role in their decision. In addition, a group of parents relied strongly on their child's preferences in selecting the school attended.

8.2.2 Pre-entry contact with the school

Chapters Two and Three have described differences between schools in the amount of contact with parents and students before entry. The importance of pre-entry contact in informing school choice was also touched upon in the previous section. Most of the parents interviewed for the study had visited the school at least once in the pre-entry period, usually at an open day or evening for parents.

All case-study schools offered an open day or an open night for parents in order to familiarise them with the rules and regulations of the school. In some schools, more than one meeting was provided:

> We had a good few meetings before we actually went and signed up for it [the school]. We had about three meetings and they went through the curriculum, we were introduced to the teachers and then we were given information on different subjects. We actually got a fair bit of information from them. We met them [the teachers] all individually which was great (Dawes Point).

There were strong similarities in the topics discussed at such meetings with parents which included school discipline (including rules on school uniforms, jewellery, and possession of mobile phones), sports facilities and other activities in the school, along with information on the subjects taken by students. A small number of parents did not attend a meeting, mainly because they had an older child in the school:

> I didn't need any information because when you have three gone to the school already (Park St).

Information given at open days/evenings was supplemented by the provision of booklets or information leaflets for parents in many of the schools:

> It contains a booklet with maybe ten or twelve pages describing the school and what is involved and an enrolment slip and there is other stuff, . . . where you get uniforms and insurance and all that kind of stuff on it, . . . what is involved in the sports and the achievement of the students and how they got on (Belmore St).

A number of parents mentioned the way in which the schools had initiated contact with their child before the transfer to post-primary school. One parent of a child in Barrack St school mentioned visits by the primary children to the post-primary school:

> The children were brought up, when they were in sixth class they were brought up for I think it was nearly say one day every week for a month. The sixth years brought the sixth class up and they brought them around the school and that and then I think I went to a meeting on my own. And then I think it was before she went in, the two of us

went up together and we seen the teachers so that was quite nice
(Barrack St).

The visits took place in non-disadvantaged as well as disadvantaged
schools. Such pre-entry contact seems popular across all school types
and "takes an edge off" the transition to post-primary school as discussed
in Chapter Three. A positive relationship and co-operation between the
two school settings was seen by parents to ease the anxiety related to
transition experiences.

In addition to open days and information nights, schools often organised additional activities for the new students. One parent described a
summer camp that had been provided for students to get to know other
students before starting school:

> We were invited, yes, for the day of the interview. Then they ar-
> ranged what I thought was very good, a summer camp for all intend-
> ing first years, on their own for four days. So [my child] during that
> time would have got to know a lot of the boys and girls; they were
> by themselves just the first years so that made the transition then
> much easier. They were also taken in, first years I think when the
> school year opened and then gradually the other years were intro-
> duced so it wasn't like 800 children all of a sudden that they had to
> contend with, there was probably 200 or 300 initially (Fig Lane).

Contact with the school before the official start of the school year was
seen by parents as reducing anxiety on the part of their children:

> I thought a lot of the steps they took made that transition much easier
> for the child (Fig Lane).

> She wasn't really anxious because [her teacher] out of the national
> school had already brought them up to the secondary school (Barrack
> St).

8.3 PARENTAL CONCERNS ABOUT THE TRANSITION

All of the parents interviewed reported some degree of nervous anticipa-
tion on the part of their children regarding transferring to post-primary
school. However, they felt that there was less anxiety involved when
older siblings were already attending the school. Concerns about the

transition centred broadly on social adjustment and on the (lack of) continuity between the academic approach taken at primary and post-primary levels.

8.3.1 Social adjustment

As discussed in Chapter Five, there are various factors that have an impact on students' adjustment to a new school setting. According to the parents interviewed, their children expressed concerns about meeting new friends, being bullied by other students,[1] getting lost moving between different classrooms, different teachers and the change of status involved in the move to post-primary school:

> I think the kids themselves would worry a bit about it, yeah. I think they go from . . . like being the top students, the age group in their primary school and then go into secondary without knowing an awful lot about it (Barrack St).

> She did worry about . . . would there be bullying or would she fit in or would she know her way from place to place, various worries like that (Dawson St).

> They all knew where they were going anyway so it was just the first day walking in that gate. Then they hear about these bashings and all that (Dixon St).

> I suppose he would have been anxious, yes, because it is a culture shock really going from primary school to secondary school you know because you have to go to a different class for each different subject and even finding your way around the big school like that you know is traumatic (Hay St).

These issues were seen as worrying first-year students irrespective of their socio-economic background or the level of integration at the post-primary school even when they were generally excited about moving to a "Big School". The information from parents' interviews is consistent with the information on students' and school personnel's perspectives

---

[1] "First year beatings" as a form of bullying was high on the list of students' worries about transition, according to their parents.

presented in Chapters Three and Five according to which over half of the pupils feel excited and nervous before moving to a new school for a variety of reasons. Information drawn from the interviews demonstrates that parents generally have a good idea about the emotional turmoil of their children at transfer.

An additional factor contributing to nervousness, according to the parents, was not knowing what to expect in the new school and not knowing anybody in the school:

> Just not knowing any of the kids and meeting all the different teachers and all different people and the overall situation. She has one teacher as you know in primary school. And then she has nine or ten teachers now and the overall situation, [it is] a big transition really from primary to secondary (Barrack St).

On the other hand, knowing somebody in the school beforehand or having an older sibling already there was seen to have a positive impact on children's adjustment:

> A good core group of that class that were his class in primary school; that was a huge thing (Park St).

> I think it helped having other children his own age that he knew. There were two more going with him. That helped him (Hay St).

In most cases, uncertainties and fears were short-lived and the children were generally happy to move into the new school as it was generally perceived as a sign of becoming more "grown up":

> I felt very, very strongly this time with this child in particular that he was ready for secondary school that he needed this challenge and the step up and he was very happy about it himself and he took to it straight away and just loved it (Park St).

In general, the majority of the parents interviewed reported that their child had adjusted to post-primary school relatively quickly:

> They get over it quick enough. I don't see any problems, they all seem quite happy. I'd see them as groups coming out when I'm collecting her. They seem a happy bunch to me, that's the impression I get (Barrack St).

According to the parents, how well students settle in depends very much on the child's personality and their maturity. The age of pupils transferring from primary school was cited by some parents as a factor in adjustment. While most parents were of the opinion that students are old enough and prepared to move on, there were some who considered the age of eleven as too young for the transfer into post-primary education.

As the transfer coincides with the onset of puberty, some parents referred to children's "difficult age" during the transition from primary to post-primary school. One parent remarked "[our child] has changed since he went into post-primary school in the sense that he is cheekier, that comes with the age as well, he has come out of himself". This is supported by Hirsch and Rapkin (1987) who argue that the onset of adolescence is closely linked with psychological, cognitive, social and environmental changes. In the present study any difficulties in making the transition were generally seen as related to a lack of confidence on the part of the child:

> The anxiety didn't disappear for a long time. He is a very nervous child, it is very easy to worry him. He hasn't as much confidence in himself as what the others [siblings] would have had (Park St).

It could be argued that parental support and involvement is particularly important for shy and less outgoing children. One mother stressed the role of parental support in minimising the disruption caused by the transition process:

> If they are helped and supported to get along with it, they will get on fine, and if you make a big fuss about it and tell them this is going to be a big adjustment and, you know, make them think it should be a big adjustment and you make them start worrying. I think if you are just there for them and if you can support them as much as you can, you are aware of it yourself without frightening the life out of the child. I think we fuss far too much, I really do (Park St).

8.3.2 Academic adjustment

The previous chapters have referred to the different nature of the primary and post-primary sectors in the Irish educational system. The issue of discontinuity was also commented on by the parents. Most of the parents interviewed perceived marked differences between the primary and post-primary systems. They were aware of the challenges their children had to face in terms of increased number of subjects, being grouped into classes by ability in some schools and the increased amount of homework.

Curriculum continuity and subject choice are discussed in Chapters Four and Six. They show that the case-study schools differ in their approach to subject choice. Some schools enable the students to "sample" a large number of subjects in their first year, which is often accompanied by an increased amount of homework. It could be argued that in some schools the academic strain is greater, as could be seen in Fig Lane school which provides a great variety of subjects for their first-year students:

> It's a huge difference because the curriculum now there's a lot more lessons, a lot more subjects than there would be at primary school and I think it's a bit confusing. When you've only got five subjects to learn, it's fine, you can keep on top of it but suddenly then when you've ten subjects to learn and you don't know which ones to pick. I'd say she's finding it a bit difficult with the amount of subjects. . . . What you learn in secondary school is a lot more complicated than what you learn in primary school (Fig Lane).

However, while being concerned about the academic challenges in post-primary school and stating that "more is expected of pupils", the majority of the parents, both "laissez-faire" and "directive", perceive the differences between primary and post-primary levels as "natural" and "part of the secondary system". As with the pupils interviewed, most parents reported that children liked the variety of subjects available within post-primary school:

> The impression he seemed to give was one of being pleased that there was such a breadth of subjects. It was interesting. He found it challenging but interesting, not negative (Wattle St).

> He loves the variety of the different subjects (Hay St).

Parents tended to report that their child received more homework than in primary school:

> In sixth class in primary school they get very little homework and suddenly they're landed with homework in ten subjects (Fig Lane).

> He gets more homework than he used to. So he has to sit down a bit more and do it (Dixon St).

However, some parents found their children were resistant to spending the required amount of time on homework:

> But he [the principal] said an hour and a half. Now normally she would spend about forty minutes. But they want a bit more. I can't get that out of her, she is not willing (Dixon St).

> If he sat down and got through it, I suppose you are talking about around an hour, but we lose a pencil, we go to get something and then I find him in front of the telly. . . . I found the first term was better, you know, and it is a battle. And you know the first term the rule was that half four he was out here in the kitchen with me, no telly, no radio, I make the dinner he does the homework, now that has drifted a little (Park St).

Furthermore, a number of parents reported that their child was spending less time on homework than at primary level:

> I think she done more homework in primary school than she's doing in secondary school (Barrack St).

> That is one of my worries now they don't have a lot of homework; my nine-year-old has more homework than he has (Wentworth Place).

This could be explained by some schools easing their students into post-primary level and a possibility that some students are permitted to do their homework at school. A number of parents reported that their child could do homework during "free" classes and so had little work to do in the evening:

> He doesn't do homework at all. He has a lot of free classes, a lot of free classes and teachers out sick so he does it in school. He would say to me such a body wasn't in today so I did that homework in that class. Or for his break if the weather was bad and couldn't go outside he would do some homework in the study hall. So as regards home-

work he can't believe that in primary school he would have sat for an hour every evening, now he seems to be getting it done in school (Wattle St).

The study skills programme in Belmore St school was seen as assisting students in planning their homework and study time:

She does out a bit of a timetable for herself and spends so long on each one. And then if she is not finished on one, she goes on and she goes back to what she hasn't finished (Belmore St).

A number of schools provided homework clubs for students to engage in supervised study after regular school hours. This was seen as a valuable resource by parents, especially where they themselves had difficulties in helping their children with their schoolwork:

I think it's brilliant. Because they do what they have to do. ... I can't help him, I could help him with Irish, and English or maybe Geography but I could not help him with Maths. I can't do that. They have changed so much. And the teacher is there and if they are stuck they can ask him (Hay St).

The homework club is very good with him. If they need any help at all the teacher comes down and sits with him and I think some of the sixth years do be there as well to give him a hand (Dawes Point).

Research carried out in other countries suggests that students often experience a drop in grades moving from primary to post-primary school (Gutman and Midgley, 2000). However, some parents interviewed for the present study reported an improvement in their child's grades compared with primary school:

Well, they said all her grades were up very good but as I said it was an early test and they would have got maybe higher grades than they would if it was further on in the year. I think they sort of give them that little bit extra because it's their first test and they're only starting (Barrack St).

Yes, he is delighted with it. . . . Results are doubled. . . . They were actually getting on to us now they want to try and move him up a grade in school because he never did as well as he is doing now (Dawes Point).

> She's about the same now. In fact she may have come on a little bit better in secondary. Well I don't know whether it is a variation in teachers or what. I don't know why but . . . she might have more of an interest this year than she had in the last year in national [school] (Belmore St).

Others, consistent with Gutman and Midgley (2000), found that their child was receiving lower grades than they had been used to:

> I think in the primary school he probably got slightly better grades than he has now but it's hard for me to say, that might be just part of the settling down period and different subjects (Hay St).

> I was disappointed in his grades and some were good and some were I won't say bad but you are looking at D plus type thing. I don't even compare now [with primary], it is a different ball game altogether I think with secondary (Wentworth Place).

> They [the grades] were lower. You know a lot of them science, wood-work they hadn't done those before in the primary school (Dawes Point).

Previous chapters demonstrated that in some schools there is generally a strong link between primary and post-primary schools that facilitates movement from one school level to another. However, some parents commented on lack of academic preparation at primary level, which was seen as accounting for some difficulties in adjusting to new academic demands:

> I think he would feel it's more difficult. The subject he didn't do in national school, which would be language. And more is expected of them. They are supposed to show what they know more and perhaps if you weren't so good in national school it's not there, you haven't got it (Wattle St).

> I feel that they didn't have enough of the basics really going into secondary in the Irish from the national [school]. . . . I thought she should have been more up with the Irish going into secondary than she really is. And she did remark to me there at one stage that girls that came from different national schools are much better at the Irish than the girls from her national school (Belmore St).

The children were seen as having different capacities to cope with post-primary schoolwork because of their different experiences at primary level:

> He had already done French in national school. It was a good help to him because languages would not be his strong point. And he had a grounding in French before he went in (Hay St).

> She had done a little course in German, not last year but the year before when she would have been in fifth class, it was just an introduction to German. And I think because she knew a few little phrases going into the class, she feels more at home with the German than she does with the French (Fig Lane).

As with the students and teachers, a number of parents stressed the different standards in subjects at post-primary level compared with those at primary level:

> I had to do English homework with him and some of the questions were just unbelievable, very hard. I mean I couldn't understand them myself — or some of them. You were kind of reading through the story to see if you could make sense of the questions but it is very difficult going from what they were doing in primary school, like a straightforward question, and then going into this and they were kind of asking a question but it was very complicated. There is a big jump (Lang St).

Discontinuity was seen as even more of an issue for students who had moved to Ireland from other countries with very different school curricula:

> There are certain subjects she finds difficult, such as history. [There] the history syllabus is different and focuses more on [that country's] history and that of neighbouring countries. But here it is Bronze Age etc (Barrack St).

> He doesn't have to learn Irish. But he does stay in the class. The teacher says it is better if he stays in the class and just listens. And French he finds very difficult. Because, obviously they don't learn French in [his country] (Hay St).

As seen in earlier chapters, teachers' approaches differ when teaching first-year students. Some build upon what the students already know from primary school, others start from the beginning. This obviously puts the students who have done the subjects already at an advantage. It was also pointed out by several parents that different teaching methods in primary and post-primary schools can cause initial problems for the new students:

> Always from day one, even like years ago we learned our tables by singing them. I think in a boys' school maybe it's just that bit differ-ent. They don't and he couldn't figure this out at all, from the day he started with tables (Dawes Point).

Another potential source of tension in the first year is organising students into different class groups. Chapter Four has indicated that a number of the case-study schools group students by ability in their first year classes. Being divided into classes was seen as a source of anxiety for some chil-dren who were anxious not to be separated from their primary school friends (see also Lucey and Reay, 1998). On the whole, parents felt that grouping by ability would result in a more appropriate pace of instruc-tion with less pressure on students:

> Although people are in the same class in primary, some kids are bet-ter at some subjects than others. . . . If they're put into a higher class or all into one class and there's other kids better than them and they're expected to keep up which is hard for the kids . . . so I think it's a good idea, yeah (Barrack St).

> I don't know how else they would do it really because they could put weak and strong together and then the weak would get intimidated and the strong would get frustrated so there has to be some system and it seems the only way (Park St).

> He is under no pressure because he is in the middle class. He is not in the top class, he is in the middle. He is not under any pressure and he is finding it OK. He did very well in his Christmas exams. There is no pressure thanks be to God, because I wouldn't want him under pressure (Lang St).

However, one parent reported mixed feelings about ability grouping depending on the needs of their child:

> I suppose as a parent if I had a good child I would like them to be with a goodish group. If I had a weak child I [would have] liked them in the mixed ability so that they would be brought on (Park St).

This corresponds to students' views in Chapter Six whereby students in lower streams showed uneasiness about labelling by other students.

Parents across all schools, both designated disadvantaged and non-disadvantaged schools, wanted their children to stay on to complete the Leaving Certificate. More "laissez-faire" parents said that they are going to leave the ultimate decision to the children, while the remainder stated that their children were "not allowed to leave" without the Leaving Certificate. Parents differed in the extent to which they aspired to third-level education for their children. However, across all schools, qualifications were seen as an asset:

> Just try to better yourself. Make something of yourself in the world. There is good jobs out there if you have a good qualification, great jobs. Brilliant jobs. But you have to have the brains. The only way you are going to get the brains is to go to college. Going into a 9 to 5 job and what have you got for it at the end of the day but a week's wages (Dixon St).

> I want to try to get him to go to college before they start out looking for work or anything (Dixon St).

8.4 SUPPORT STRUCTURES FOR FIRST-YEAR STUDENTS

Chapter Three has indicated differences between the case-study schools in the support structures available for first-year students. A combination of induction programmes for first years along with a class tutor system was seen as a useful approach by some parents:

> To give them an introduction to the school and from a student's point of view to be shown around and taken care of is a very good option as well, I think the combination of both is good (Fig Lane).

> They have their day, they go up there and have a look around and see everything. Then they have their tutors and they also have year heads that if they are having problems, they can go to them. I feel there is enough for them really (Dixon St).

However, another parent found that one person may not be enough for first-year pupils:

> I don't think they realise the big step [transition is] . . . I think they always have a year head but I think there should be more than one assigned, I think they should have a few others, you know, even if it is only parents like I mean from the parents' association, that can go in there . . . and more talks (Belmore St).

The statement also demonstrates that not all parents are always familiar with the support structures offered by schools (or the schools may not make them transparent enough). In fact, Belmore St school provides other supports in addition to the year head.

Many parents mentioned student mentors as important in helping first-year students settle into school. Their role is to be there for any problems first-year students may encounter as well as helping teachers: "call the roll if the teacher wants them to and they give them the notebook and the pen and they look out for bullying and stuff like that" (Barrack St). Parents felt that students might approach another student rather than an adult within the school: "because I think sometimes they feel if they involve the teachers, it might make the thing worse, you know what I mean" (Dawson St).

However, not all parents were happy with the support provided by the school with a feeling that students were left to "sink or swim":

> I found myself in the first couple of weeks that the first years were very much left to their own devices. I didn't think they got enough support. Yes. I would find it would be nice for the first years to have somebody because it's all new to them and because it's all so difficult, yeah, there should be someone they can turn to. They were thrown in at the deep end with no help (Wattle St).

In one case, a parent intervened because they were dissatisfied with the situation:

I had to take [my child] out the second day because he couldn't even find his way around. They were just left to follow the crowd. It's like a maze [. . .]. He was exhausted when he came home the first day. I said I would keep him at home the second day. And I went up then and I did say it to them so they got somebody then, they did get someone to show him around for a while until he was able to find his own way (Dixon St).

One parent suggested that some of the difficulties could be solved by providing more preparation for the transition at primary level:

More could be done. . . . There should be something before you leave primary, someone [to] come down and talk to the students about it. What it's going to be like and what subjects you are going to be doing and what is there for you. But there is nothing, none of that. It's like starting in a job for the first time, you are nervous. You don't know what way you are going to react or how other people are going to react around you (Dixon St).

Parents differed in the extent to which they were familiar with the support structures available. Some parents did not feel very well informed as to what support is available for their child in the post-primary school:

It's all new to us like because I suppose if we did have a problem . . . that's when you're going to find out whether the school has . . . the knowledge to help you out and until you kind of come across that bridge, you're not really going to know (Wattle St).

It would be nice if there was somebody there but there isn't, I don't know as far as I know there isn't anybody, the prefect sometimes helps (Barrack St).

A number of parents mentioned bullying as a concern during the transition process. The concern was heightened if the child had already been bullied in primary school. Although parents tended to mention anti-bullying policies within the school, many parents said that bullying does take place. The advice that some of the parents gave was to "stand up to the bully". According to the parents, their children did not like to involve parents or teachers if anything was happening for fear of the problem getting worse:

> I think they would rather say nothing. . . . If he goes to the teachers then he is called a squealer, so he can't win (Dixon St).

In general, parents felt that anti-bullying policies were in place in the schools:

> They have a strong policy in place and they sort it out in school (Dixon St).

One parent saw the post-primary school as having stronger anti-bullying policies than at primary level:

> They are much better now in the secondary school, they are much stricter. . . . They are just anti-bullying really and they won't accept any bullying although . . . there will always be a certain amount going on (Barrack St).

However, many of the parents seemed to see "teasing" and "messing" as a normal part of the transition process rather than serious problems:

> It's just banter that teenagers go on with. And I think that is more the rows. Just one word leads to another and then it's a push and then someone pushes them back (Dixon St).

> There is a bit of teasing and that kind of thing, pushing and shoving a bit, a bit of that goes on a bit (Park St).

8.5 CONCLUSIONS

Interviews with parents of students in the case-study schools yielded an insight into their perspective on the transition process. Parents feel their children face a number of challenges making the move to post-primary education with new subjects, teachers and different academic demands.

Most parents tend to see the adjustment period as a relatively short one. There did not seem to be any difference on the basis of disadvantaged or non-disadvantaged status or parents being "laissez-faire" or "directive". However, longer-term difficulties are apparent for some students in terms of spending less time on homework and achieving lower grades than at primary school. Furthermore, in many cases a child's difficulties in adjustment to post-primary school were linked to his/her personality and whether the child knew anybody in the school.

Bullying emerged as an important factor in the adjustment process from interviews with parents. However, it was evident that it was often seen as "slagging" and "messing" which "you get in every school". In many cases such behaviour was targeted at first-year students as "rites of passage". Parents were generally aware of the support available at school for students who get bullied. It is, however, an area that demands further attention as in some cases children are reluctant to talk about such incidences and "you have to prise it out of them".

Another general area of potential worry identified by the parents is the discontinuity between primary and post-primary sectors. This discontinuity manifests itself on the school as well as the curriculum level; often students come from much smaller and more child-orientated primary schools and find it difficult to adjust to a bigger school. Furthermore, the level at which primary schools teach different subjects can also differ, which potentially poses additional difficulty in the adjustment process. Parents are generally aware of the new requirements, rules and regulations at the post-primary level. All schools operate an open day/open evening system whereby information is provided about the post-primary school. Most parents considered the schools and teachers easily accessible should further contact be needed. However, only a few had initiated such contact themselves. In relation to school subjects, some parents reported that their children had difficulties in subjects that they had not previously taken. Different levels of subject knowledge and increased homework were reported as creating some difficulties for certain children. A number of parents commented favourably on initiatives like a "homework club". Having a teacher available to answer potential queries was seen as a good resource.

In the same vein as O'Brien's (2000) study, parents identified friends as an important factor in the adjustment process. They were seen as aiding the experience of transfer into a new school and "taking the edge off" any nervousness. Most parents reported their children making new friends within the first weeks at post-primary school. In a few cases the children had stayed with friends they had known from primary school.

Chapter Nine

CONCLUSIONS

International research has indicated that the transition from primary to post-primary education is a crucial time point for young people's educational careers. This study has set out to explore the social and academic factors which help young people settle into post-primary school in the Irish context. Within the framework of this study, the "success" of the transition into post-primary education is seen to reflect the school's approach to student integration, its approach to subject choice and the method of ability grouping used. It was expected that students would experience fewer transition difficulties and greater academic progress in schools which had a more developed student integration programme. On the other hand, being exposed to more subjects in first year in the form of a "taster" programme was expected to have negative effects on students settling into school and on their academic achievement. In keeping with previous research, it was anticipated that being in a school where students were streamed by ability would have negative consequences for student development. Over and above the effect of the school context, it was hypothesised that the nature of the transition process would differ according to individual student characteristics, such as gender, social class and prior educational success.

The study draws on data from a wide variety of sources to present the perspectives of the key stake-holders, including school management, teachers, students and parents. A national survey of school principals was supplemented by in-depth case-studies of twelve schools selected to capture key dimensions of variation in how schools manage the transition process. The study therefore draws on very rich information, both quantitative and qualitative, to explore young people's experience of the transition from primary to post-primary education. This chapter presents the main findings of the study and highlights issues for future policy development.

SETTLING INTO POST-PRIMARY EDUCATION

Post-primary schools in Ireland are found to differ in how they attempt to integrate students into the school and in how they structure the learning process for first-year students. Schools generally have an open day for students before they come to the school and, in most cases, personnel from the post-primary school visit the feeder primary schools to talk to students and/or parents. Almost all schools have an induction day for students at the start of the school year. However, the actual approach to induction varies with some schools focusing on imparting information about school rules while others have a more developed programme to ease the transition for young people. In the majority of schools, class tutors play a key role in helping first years to settle into school life. Furthermore, around half of all schools use some sort of student mentor system, with older students acting as a liaison for their first-year counterparts.

Liaison between the primary and post-primary schools may also involve the transfer of information about students. However, only a minority of school principals report receiving information on all in-coming students and a significant proportion of principals are dissatisfied with the information they receive on the students entering their school. The lowest level of satisfaction relates to information on coverage of the curriculum.

From the students' perspective, making the transition evokes many contradictory emotions with students feeling nervous but also excited. For them, the main differences between post-primary and primary school centre on having more teachers and subjects, a change in status (from being one of the older students in the school to being the youngest), having different relations with teachers, being in a "big" school and having a longer day. Among boys, stories about the "first year beating" contributed to nervousness, although overall boys reported being less nervous than girls. Such beatings did seem to occur but students tended not to see them as "serious" or as "bullying"; however, it is difficult to determine whether this reflects bravado in front of other students.

School principals, teachers, parents and students themselves felt that only a minority of students experienced serious transition difficulties in the move to post-primary education. Most students in the case-study schools reported settling into post-primary school within the first week but for a quarter of the students it takes about a month. One in six students in the case-study schools take longer than a month to settle in and a few of them still do not feel settled by the end of first year. Furthermore, the majority of students miss at least one aspect of their primary school "a lot", even at the end of first year; this usually relates to their friends or school trips but some students miss the "structural" aspects of primary schools, such as having one teacher, the kinds of subjects and the way subjects are taught. It would, therefore, appear that, while students generally feel they have settled into post-primary school, some aspects of post-primary school still require getting used to and social networks (such as friendship groups) may not be as cohesive as in primary school.

The very detailed information available on students in different school contexts allowed us to identify a number of key differences (both objective and subjective) between students who report settling into post-primary school relatively quickly and those who take longer to adjust. This allows us to highlight potentially "at risk" groups as a basis for policy intervention.

On the whole, boys tend to report settling in quicker than girls, a pattern that is consistent with that found in international research. Students who are less self-confident and have a more negative view of themselves tend to experience greater transition difficulties. Students from non-national or Traveller backgrounds report more transition difficulties than other students. Among Traveller children, older students tend to experience more difficulties settling in, although age is not a factor for students as a whole. Students themselves see social networks (having friends from primary school and taking part in extra-curricular activities) as the most important factors in helping them to settle in.

Students who have little idea what to expect from post-primary school take longer to settle in. This is partly related to the amount of contact they have with the school beforehand with greater pre-entry contact between post-primary schools and in-coming students and their parents giving students a better idea what to expect from their new school. However, students also appear to draw on more informal sources of information (such as parents and wider family) in forming their expectations of post-primary school life.

In keeping with our expectations, students tend to settle in quicker in schools with more developed student integration programmes. Induction programmes and school personnel (such as class tutors and student mentors) are seen as helpful by the majority of students. Less academic students and those from a travelling background appear to be more reliant on key people within the school in the settling-in process, indicating the potential for targeted support for these "at-risk" students. However, there is considerable variation in the "settling in" process across schools with such integration programmes. This variation is mainly related to differences in school climate. The informal climate of the school is influential with students who report negative interaction with teachers in September experiencing greater transition difficulties. Similarly, students who experience negative interaction with their peers in the form of bullying at the start of first year take longer to settle in. Those who are disaffected with school or their teachers early in the year also take longer to settle in. A school's formal structures to promote student integration appear to be successful only to the extent that they give students a better idea of what to expect and are underpinned by a positive informal climate.

The way in which learning is structured within the school influences students' social adjustment to post-primary school. Contrary to our expectations, taking a taster programme as such does not seem to impact on settling in. However, students who *feel* they are taking too many subjects report more difficulties. This is likely to be related to students feeling unable to cope with the academic demands of first year more generally (see below). The nature of organisational differences between primary and post-primary levels also influence the transition process among first-year students. Lack of curriculum continuity plays a role; students are more likely to experience transition problems if they feel their primary subjects did not prepare them for post-primary school, if they feel the subjects do not follow on from their primary subjects and if they are not enjoying first-year subjects. Students in the higher class within streamed schools report more transition difficulties than those in the lower stream classes. This appears to be related to their finding some of the subjects more difficult than in primary school.

CURRICULUM AND LEARNING IN FIRST YEAR

Previous research has highlighted the differences in subjects taught and teaching methods used in the primary and post-primary sectors. A substantial group of students in the case-study schools reported experiencing a discontinuity in learning experiences between primary and post-primary levels. A significant proportion of first-year students do not see the post-primary curriculum as following on naturally from that at primary level and the majority see the teaching methods used as quite different. A significant minority of students found a "mismatch" in the standards of Irish, English or Mathematics between primary and post-primary level. This tended to vary within school, indicating that students coming from different feeder schools may have different backgrounds in the various subjects. The issue of curriculum discontinuity between primary and post-primary level was also evident from the teacher's perspective with less than a third of the first-year teachers in the case-study schools feeling that the primary curriculum was a good foundation for their subject and only half reporting familiarity with the nature of the primary curriculum. However, there was some variation across schools in the reported patterns indicating the discontinuity may be more prevalent in certain school contexts.

In the majority of schools nationally, students take more subjects in first year than they do in their Junior Certificate year. Subject sampling is seen as a good idea by the majority of second-level principals, although a significant minority consider that first-year students take too many subjects. In general, students in the case-study schools saw the taster approach as the best approach to subject choice, although they differed on whether they should try subjects for the whole of first year or only part of it. Where students pick their subjects without trying them out, they tend to rely on less formal sources of information, such as their parents and friends.

Having the opportunity to try subjects out in first year means that many students are exposed to quite a number of different subjects. Students typically take thirteen or fourteen subjects in the first term of first year, although the number taken ranges from ten to twenty-one across all schools. The number of subjects taken tends to be fewer in schools which are designated disadvantaged and/or have a significant intake of students with literacy difficulties. Contrary to our expectations, there is no evidence that being exposed to a taster approach, and consequently taking more subjects, leads to transition difficulties or academic problems. However, where students *feel* they are taking too many subjects, such difficulties do arise, a pattern which appears to be related to a broader inability to cope with the academic demands of first year.

Moving from primary to post-primary school involves taking many new subjects. However, students are generally positive about their first-year subjects compared with their primary experience and they tend to see the subjects they take as useful. First-year students in the case-study schools are particularly positive about subjects with a more practical orientation. Students differ, however, in the extent to which they find some of the more academic subjects interesting and many students find these subjects difficult.

The administration of reading and computation tests to students at the beginning and end of first year allowed us to explore the effects of different aspects of school context, such as approach to integration and subject choice, on students' academic progress. Students in the case-study schools come to first year with different capacities in terms of reading and mathematics. In keeping with previous research, student scores on reading and computation tests in the case-study schools are strongly differentiated by social class background with those from higher professional backgrounds achieving the highest test scores. For the majority of students, test scores in reading and computation are broadly stable over the course of first year. There are more changes in reading scores than in computation with almost a fifth of students improving their reading compared with one tenth for computation. This is remarkable because one might have expected students to make greater progress over first year as they become exposed to different subject areas and a broader range of texts. It would appear that, in keeping with British research, the transition to post-primary school is associated with a hiatus in progress in the key competencies of reading and Mathematics.

Students with lower initial test scores tend to make the greatest progress over the year, indicating some "catching up". Students in mixed ability base classes make the most progress while those in middle or lower classes within streamed schools tend to make the least progress. The pattern varies across schools with progress in reading being more prevalent in schools with a strong emphasis on student integration and mixed ability base classes. The variation for computation is less marked but students are more likely to make progress in mixed ability schools.

ABILITY GROUPING

There has been a decline over time in the use of ability grouping for base classes in first year, with the majority of schools now having mixed ability base classes. One in six schools use setting in first year, generally for Mathematics, English or Irish. While most students supported the idea of some ability grouping, many students in streamed classes report that their teachers move too quickly or slowly in covering subject material. Furthermore, the practice of streaming/banding appeared to have resulted in a distinct labelling of students as "smart" or "stupid", even very early on in the school year.

Being allocated to the higher class within a streamed school appeared to result in increased academic demands on students relative to their experiences in primary school with adjustment taking longer for some of these students.

In keeping with previous research, students in streamed schools, especially those allocated to the lower stream classes, tend to make less academic progress than other students.

Within the case-study schools, over one tenth of students received learning support over the course of first year, mainly through withdrawal from regular class for small group or one-to-one tuition. In general, students found it helpful and students who had received learning support had a more positive view of their own abilities by the end of first year. However, a significant minority (one third) of students, especially those in lower classes in streamed schools, would like to have received such help but did not.

IMPLICATIONS FOR POLICY

Evidence from the case-study schools suggests a number of ways in which schools can help to ease the transition process for students from both a social and an academic perspective. Having contact with the post-primary school before transfer and, more importantly, having a good idea what to expect appear to ease student anxiety about the transition.

- Schools should be encouraged to develop links with their feeder primary schools and provide information on first year which is relevant to in-coming students' own concerns (for example, by dispelling anxiety about "first year beatings").

- Developing strong links with feeder schools may be impractical where schools draw on a large catchment area. It is, therefore, recommended that some aspects of the preparation for post-primary school should be generic across schools. A module which tells students the kinds of things to expect from post-primary school should be developed by the Department of Education and Science, in conjunction with the NCCA, and implemented in sixth class in all primary schools.

Having a strongly developed approach to student integration in the form of an induction programme, designated personnel (such as class tutors) and student mentors appears to ease the transition for young people as well as having a positive effect on how they fare academically.

- It is recommended that schools should be facilitated in developing structures to help students integrate into first year. These structures appear to be particularly important for "at risk" groups of students, such as students from Traveller or non-national backgrounds. Student mentors, in particular, can often provide a source of support and information for first-year students. Schools should be encouraged to develop such mentoring systems but it is important that the student mentors themselves be provided with training and support by the school. Models of good practice in this area internationally should be analysed with a view to developing common mentor training policies across Irish schools.

- Students themselves saw extracurricular activities as helping them to settle into post-primary school. Schools should therefore be given practical support (through additional resources, for example) to expand the range of extra-curricular activities on offer, including non-sports activities for students who are not interested in sports. At present, schools with more disadvantaged student intakes are likely to be at a disadvantage in securing additional "voluntary" funding from parents for such activities.

The success of a school's formal policy on student integration, however, would appear to be contingent on it forming a comprehensive integration "package" which is underpinned by a positive informal climate. Students who have been bullied take longer to settle into post-primary education and bullying has a highly negative effect on their self-perceptions.

- All schools should have clear policies and effective practice on bullying, addressing a wide array of bullying practices, including verbal abuse and mobile phone text messaging as well as physical violence.

- Even where schools have clear anti-bullying policies, students may be reluctant to come forward to report bullying. Student mentors provide one way of supporting students who have experienced bullying. Issues around bullying should also be addressed through personal and social development programmes such as Social, Personal and Health Education.

The school climate of the school is not just influenced by interaction among students but by the quality of interaction between teachers and students. Students also report greater transition difficulties where they have experienced negative interaction with teachers.

- The informal climate of the school should be a matter for consideration in school development planning with schools encouraged to develop structures (such as teacher involvement in decision-making and formal student involvement) which promote cohesion among the different partners within the school.

The (dis)continuity between the primary and post-primary curriculum was found to influence student experiences of first year. Many students feel that their primary schooling did not prepare them adequately for subjects at post-primary level and students appear to come to post-primary school with different levels of core competencies depending on their social class background and the primary school they attended. In addition, many teachers perceive a discontinuity between the two levels and school principals are dissatisfied with the information they receive on the curriculum covered by in-coming first years.

- There is a need to develop greater awareness among post-primary teachers of the primary curriculum and provide information to primary teachers about the curriculum and approach taken within post-primary school. It is recommended that common components should be developed in pre-service education for primary and post-primary teachers and information be incorporated on the curriculum at both levels into initial and continuing training for teachers.

- There should be greater co-operation between the primary and post-primary sectors in terms of curriculum development and transfer of good practice in relation to teaching methodologies.

- A framework for the transfer of information on the curriculum covered at primary school should be developed in order to help post-primary teachers to tailor lessons to the competency levels of the students involved.

A considerable proportion of schools now provide students with the opportunity to try out different subjects before selecting their subjects for the Junior Certificate. This approach is seen as positive by most principals and students. Contrary to our expectations, an opportunity to try out different subjects in first year does not appear to have a negative impact on adjustment to post-primary school or academic progress among students. Indeed, a taster approach has advantages in terms of allowing students to make a more informed decision about the kinds of subjects which best suit their interests and abilities.

- Schools should be encouraged to provide students with some exposure to a range of subjects before they are required to select their Junior Certificate subjects. However, such an approach may cause practical difficulties for schools in terms of teacher resources and time available to cover the Junior Certificate curriculum.

- It is recommended, therefore, that the provision of a diverse curriculum should be facilitated, and student choice maximised, through providing schools with the resources to provide a taster programme.

- Curriculum content and assessment at junior cycle should reflect the fact that some students will have spent less time on particular subjects in first year because of their participation in a taster programme.

- Where students select their subjects before entry to post-primary education, they tend to rely on family and friends as their main sources of advice. It is important, therefore, that schools attempt to involve parents in subject choice at junior cycle and provide them with appropriate information on the curriculum, especially the "newer" subjects.

Making the move to post-primary education means that students take a considerable number of new subjects. Students are generally quite positive about the first year curriculum, especially subjects with a more practical orientation. However, schools currently vary in the extent to which they provide such subjects. Subjects with a more practical orientation appear to provide a way of engaging students in the first year curriculum and of providing a route to success for less academically oriented students.

- It is recommended that schools be facilitated in providing a range of subjects with a more practical orientation in order to promote engagement, particularly among students who are less interested in the traditional academic subjects.

- The on-going expansion of IT provision to post-primary schools is to be welcomed in this respect as exposure to IT courses within first year tends to result in very positive attitudes to the subject by the end of first year.

- Providing more hands-on activities within class across a range of subjects would also appear to provide a way of promoting student engagement.

The majority of post-primary schools nationally use mixed ability base classes for first-year students. However, in keeping with previous research, where streaming (that is, grouping students by ability into their base classes) is used, it is found to have a negative effect for those allocated to the lower stream classes. Furthermore, being allocated to a higher class within a streamed school is associated with greater transition difficulties among students.

- Schools should be encouraged to develop alternative approaches to streaming. However, it is recognised that moving to mixed ability teaching poses challenges for schools and teachers. Schools should therefore be supported through in-service and other forms of professional development. The role of learning support is also particularly important in the mixed ability setting and schools should be fully supported in the provision of extra assistance to students.

A significant minority of first-year students find some of the academic subjects difficult and would like extra help with their schoolwork. However, as it is currently structured, learning support provision is aimed at those students with the most severe literacy and numeracy difficulties. This means that the "low-average" group of students do not receive the extra assistance with learning which they require.

- Greater flexibility in the provision of extra teaching resources to students, particularly in the early phase of first year, should be allowed, especially at the crucial transition period, given that students may come to post-primary school with very different standards in the core competencies. Students should also have access to extra supports such as supervised study programmes.

In sum, the transition to post-primary school is a time not only of social adjustment but also of an encounter with a range of different learning experiences. The extent to which students can cope with the demands of schoolwork in first year is likely to have long-term implications for their engagement with education. It is crucial therefore that support should be given to schools to ease the transition process for students and provide greater continuity in learning between the primary and post-primary levels.

REFERENCES

Anderson, L.W., Jacobs, J., Schramm, S., and Splittherber, F. 2000, "School Transitions: Beginning of the End or a New Beginning?", *International Journal of Educational Research*, vol. 33, pp. 325–339.

Berliner, B.A. 1993, *Adolescence, School Transitions and Prevention*, NWREL: Portland, Oregon, Western Regional Center for Drug-free Schools and Communities.

Burke, A. 1987, "From Primary to Post-primary: Bridge or Barrier", *Oideas* 30, 5–23.

Callan, J. 1997, "Active learning in the classroom: challenge to existing educational values and practices", *Issues in Education*, Vol. 2, pp.21–37.

Crockett, L. and Losoff, M. 1984, "Perceptions of the Peer Group and Friendship in Early Adolescence", *Journal of Early Adolescence*, vol. 4, no. 2, pp. 155–181.

Crockett, L.J., Petersen, A.G., Graber, J.A., Schulenberg, J.E. and Ebata, A. 1989, "School transitions and adjustment during early adolescence", *Journal of Early Adolescence*, Vol. 9, pp. 181–210.

Demetriou, H., Goalen, P., and Rudduck, J. 2000, "Academic Performance, Transfer, Transition and Friendship: Listening to the Student Voice", *International Journal of Educational Research*, vol. 33, pp. 425–441.

Desforges, C. and Abouchaar, A. 2003, "The Impact of Parental Involvement, Parental Support and Family Education on Pupil Achievements and Adjustment: A literature Review", *Department of Education and Skills*, Research Report No. 433.

Devine, D. 1993, "A study of reading ability groups: primary school children's experiences and views", *Irish Educational Studies*, Vol. 12, pp. 134–142.

Dockett, S. and Perry, B. 2001, "Starting School: Effective Transitions", *Early Childhood Research and Practice*, vol. 3,no. 2.

Drudy, S. and Lynch, K. 1993, *Schools and Society in Ireland*, Dublin, Gill and Macmillan.

Eccles, J.S., Midgley, C., Wigfield, A., Buchanan, C.M., Reuman, D.A., Flanagan, C., and MacIver, D. 1993, "Development During Adolescence. The Impact of Stage-Environment Fit on Young Adolescents' Experiences in Schools and in Families", *American Psychologist*, vol. 48,no. 2, pp. 90–101.

Ferguson, P.D. and Fraser, B.J. 1999, "Changes in Learning Environment During the Transition from Primary to Secondary School", *Learning Environments Research*, vol. 1, pp. 369–383.

Franklin, A. and Madge, N. 2001, *Paths to Progress: The Transition from Primary to Secondary Education in the London Borough of Waltham Forest*, National Children's Bureau, London.

Galton, M., Gray, J., and Rudduck, J. 1999, *The Impact of School Transitions and Transfers on Pupil Progress and Attainment*, Department of Education and Employment/ Homerton College, Cambridge, Norwich, Research Report No. 131.

Galton, M., Morrison, I., and Pell, T. 2000, "Transfer and Transition in English Schools: Reviewing the Evidence", *International Journal of Educational Research*, vol. 33, pp. 341–363.

Galton, M., Gray, J., and Rudduck, J. 2003, *Transfer and Transitions in the Middle Years of Schooling (7–14): Continuities and Discontinuities in Learning*, Queen's Printer, University of Cambridge, Research Report no. 443.

Galton, M. and Willcocks, J. (eds.) 1983, *Moving from the Primary Classroom*, London, Routledge and Kegan Paul.

Ginsburg, M.B. and Meyenn, R.J. 1980, "In the Middle: First and Upper School Teachers' Relations with Middle School Colleagues," in *Middle Schools: Origins, Ideology and Practice*, A. Hargreaves and L. Tickle, eds., Harper and Row, London, pp. 277–296.

Gleeson, J. 2000, "Sectoral interest versus the common good? Legitimation, fragmentation and contestation in Irish post-primary curriculum policy and practice", *Irish Educational Studies*, vol. 19, pp.16–33.

Gorard, S., Taylor, C., and Fitz, J. 2002, "Does School Choice Lead to 'Spirals of Decline'?", *Journal of Education Policy*, vol. 17,no. 3, pp. 367–384.

Grolnick, W.S., Kurowshi, C.O., Dunlap, K.G., and Hevey, C. 2000, "Parental Resources and the Transition to Junior High", *Journal of Research on Adolescence*, vol. 10, no. 4, pp. 465–488.

Gutman, L.M. and Midgley, C. 2000, "The Role of Protective Factors in Supporting the Academic Achievement of Poor African American Students During the Middle School Transition", *Journal of Youth and Adolescence*, vol. 29, no. 2, pp. 223–248.

Hannan, D.F. and Boyle, M. 1987, *Schooling Decisions: The Origins and Consequences of Selection and Streaming in Irish Post-Primary Schools*, General Research Series No. 136, Dublin: ESRI.

Hannan, D. F., Smyth, E., McCullagh, J., O'Leary, R., McMahon, D. 1996, *Co-education and Gender Equality: Exam Performance, Stress and Personal Development*, Dublin, Oak Tree Press/ESRI.

Hargreaves, A. and Tickle, L. (eds.) 1980, *Middle Schools: Origins, Ideology, Practice*, London, Harper and Row.

Hargreaves, L. and Galton, M. 2002, *Transfer from the Primary Classroom: Twenty Years On*, London, Routledge/Falmer.

Harland, J., Moor, H., Kinder, K., and Ashworth, M. 2002, *Is the Curriculum Working? The Key Stage 3 Phase of the Northern Ireland Curriculum Cohort Study*, The National Foundation for Educational Research (NFER).

Harlen, W. and Malcolm, H. 1997, *Setting and Streaming: A Research Review*, Edinburgh, SCRE.

Hirsch, B.J. and Rapkin, B.D. 1987, "The Transition to Junior High School: A Longitudinal Study of Self-Esteem, Psychological Symptomatology, School Life and Social Support", *Child Development*, vol. 58, pp. 1235–1243.

Ireson, J. and Hallam, S. 2001, *Ability Grouping in Education*, London, Sage.

Jackson, C. and Warin, J. 2000, "The Importance of Gender as an Aspect of Identity at Key Transition Points in Compulsory Education", *British Educational Research Journal*, vol. 26, no. 3.

Keys, W. and Fernandes, C. 1993, *What Do Students Think About School?*, Slough, NFER.

Lord, P. and Harland, J. 2000, *Pupils' Experiences and Perspectives of the National Curriculum: Research Review*, NFER, Slough, Research Review conducted for Qualifications and Curriculum Authority.

Lord, S.E., Eccles J.S. and McCarthy, K.A. 1994, "Surviving the Junior High School Transition: Family Processes and Self-Perceptions as Protective and Risk Factors", *Journal of Early Adolescence*, vol. 14,no. 2, pp. 162–199.

Lucey, H. and Reay, D. 2000, "Identities in Transition: Anxiety and Excitement in the Move to Secondary School", *Oxford Review of Education*, vol. 26, no. 2.

Lucey, H. and Reay, D. 2002, "Carrying the Beacon of Excellence: Social Class Differentiation and the Anxiety at the Time of Transition", *Journal of Education Policy*, vol. 17, no. 3, pp. 321–336.

Lynch, K. and Lodge, A. 2002, *Equality and Power in Schools*, London, Routledge/Falmer.

Lyons, M., Lynch, K., Sheerin, E., Close, S. and Boland, P. 2003, *Inside Classrooms: The Teaching and Learning of Mathematics in Social Context*, Dublin: IPA.

Ma, X., Stewin, L.L. and Mah, D.L. 2001, "Bullying in school: nature, effects and remedies", *Research Papers in Education*, Vol. 16, No. 3, pp. 247–270.

McCallum, B. 2000, "The Transfer and Use of Assessment Information Between Primary and Secondary Schools", *British Journal of Curriculum and Assessment*, vol. 6, no. 3, pp. 10–15.

McCoy, S. 2000, *Do Schools Count? Key School Structural and Process Influences on Early School Leaving*, PhD Dissertation, The Queen's University, Belfast.

Measor, L. and Woods, P. 1984, *Changing Schools*, Milton Keynes, Open University Press.

Naughton, P.A. 2000, *The Age of Possibilities — A Study of the Schooling Transition of Early Adolescents*, PhD Dissertation, University College Cork.

Naughton, P. 2003, "Primary to second-level transition programmes: rationale, principles and a framework", *Oideas*, 50, pp.40–65.

NCCA 1999, *Junior Cycle Review Progress Report: Issues and Options for Development*, Dublin, NCCA.

Oakes, J. 1985, *Keeping Track: How Schools Structure Inequality*, New Haven, Yale University Press.

O'Brien, M. 2001, *A Study of Student Transfer from Primary to Second Level Schooling: Pupils', Parents' and Teachers' Perspectives*, Report to the Department of Education and Science, Dublin.

Ó Dalaigh, S. and Aherne, D. 1990, "From Primary to Postprimary: Report of a Local Transition Committee", *Oideas*, vol. 35, pp. 86–100.

OECD 1991, *Review of National Policies for Education: Ireland*, Paris, OECD.

Pellegrini, A.D. and Long, J.D. 2002, "A Longitudinal Study of Bullying, Dominance and Victimization During the Transition from Primary School Through Secondary School", *British Journal of Developmental Psychology*, vol. 20, pp. 259–280.

Reyes, O., Gillock, K., and Kobus, K. 1994, "A Longitudinal Study of School Adjustment in Urban, Minority Adolescents: Effects of a High School Transition Program", *American Journal of Community Psychology*, vol. 22, no. 3, pp. 341–369.

Ross, C.E. and Broh, B.A. 2000, "The Roles of Self-Esteem and the Sense of Personal Control in the Academic Achievement Process", *Sociology of Education*, vol. 73, pp. 270–284.

Rudduck, J. 1996, "Going to 'the big school': the turbulence of transition", in J. Rudduck, R. Chaplain and G. Wallace (eds.), *School Improvement: What Can Pupils Tell Us?*, London, David Fulton.

Shiel, G. 1994, *Drumcondra Primary Reading Test Manual*, Dublin, Educational Research Centre.

Shiel, G. 1998, *Drumcondra Primary Mathematics Test Manual*, Dublin, Educational Research Centre.

Simmons, R.G. and Blyth, D.A. 1987, *Moving into Adolescence: The Impact of Pubertal Change and School Context*, Hawthorne, NY, Aldine De Gruyter.

Simmons, R.G., Black, A. and Zhou, Y. 1991, "African-American versus white children and the transition into junior high school", *American Journal of Education*, Vol. 99, pp. 481–520.

Slavin, R.E. 1990, "Student achievement effects of ability grouping in secondary schools: a best-evidence synthesis", *Review of Educational Research*, vol. 60, no. 3, pp. 471–499.

Smith, J.B. 1997, "Effects of Eighth-Grade Transition Programs on High School Retention and Experiences", *The Journal of Educational Research*, vol. 90, no. 3, pp. 144–152.

Smyth, E. 1999, *Do Schools Differ? Academic and Personal Development among Pupils in the Second-Level Sector*, Dublin, Oak Tree Press/ESRI.

Stables, K. 1995, "Discontinuity in transition: pupils' experience of technology in year 6 and year 7", *International Journal of Technology and Design Education*, vol. 5, pp. 157–169.

Walsh, M.E. 1995, "Rural Students' Transitions to Secondary School: Culture, Curriculum and Context", *The Curriculum Journal*, vol. 6, no. 1, pp. 115–127.

Ward, R. 2000, "Transfer from Middle to Secondary School: A New Zealand Study", *International Journal of Educational Research*, vol. 33, pp. 365–374.

Wigfield, A., Eccles, J.S., Mac Iver, D., Reuman, D.A., and Midgley, C. 1991, "Transitions During Early Adolescence: Changes in Children's Domain-Specific Self-Perceptions and General Self-Esteem Across the Transition to Junior High School", *Developmental Psychology*, vol. 27, no. 4, pp. 552–565.